ENCYCLOPEDIA OF THE
HORSE

ENCYCLOPEDIA OF THE
HORSE

CRESCENT BOOKS
NEW YORK

COVER : A gray Anglo-Arabian stallion.

PAGE 2 : The care of the stabled horse is covered in Chapter 19.

First published in 1997 by the
Promotional Reprint Company Ltd,
Kiln House, 210 New Kings Road, London SW6 4NZ

This edition produced for
Crescent Books, a division of Random House
Value Publishing, Inc,
201 East 50th Street, New York, NY 10022.

Crescent Books and colophon are trademarks of Random House Value Publishing, Inc.

Random House
New York • Toronto • London • Sydney • Auckland
http://www.randomhouse.com/

A CIP catalog record for this book is available from the Library of congress.

8 7 6 5 4 3 2 1

ISBN 0 517 18461 3

Printed and bound in China

Neither the publisher nor the Author take any responsibility for the implementation of any recommendations, ideas or techniques expressed and described in this book. Any use to which the recommendations, ideas and techniques are put is at the Reader's sole discretion and risk. Where the health of the horse is concerned, always consult a veterinary practitioner.

CONTENTS

INTRODUCTION

TOP: A spectacular moment from a Lipizzaner of the Spanish Riding School.

ABOVE: A Holstein foal.

LEFT: A rare sight today, but the only means of transport before the railways.

ABOVE RIGHT: Polo has been played for centuries.

CENTER RIGHT: Western riding the native American way — a Wild West show.

BELOW RIGHT: A Shetland pony.

Man's best friend is said to be the dog, and a case can be made for many animals as to which has been most important to man — the cow, the deer, the bison. But before the age of steam, only one animal provided speedy personal mobility on land, improving food gathering by hunting, industry, communications, agriculture, and — more detrimentally — warfare. It was the speed and strength of the horse that gave mankind a mobility he never had before.

How did man first domesticate the horse? We don't know but what is certain is that around 9,000 years ago, the hunter-gatherers of western Asia began to alter their way of life. They started keeping flocks of live animals, first sheep and goats, then cattle and pigs until they finally encompassed horses.

It happened relatively recently, in about 3000BC in southern Russia and western Asia and 2000BC in Europe and with domestication came breeding — for submissiveness as well as hardiness and ease of feeding. Man also learned to breed types of horses especially adapted to the work needed of them, a process which continues to this day.

In 1492 Columbus discovered the New World and, as he and successive waves of conquistadores claimed it for Spain and Christendom, so the horse was introduced to the Americas. It was to play a huge part in the development of the Continent. The legacy of the western horse — from Red Indian pony to the mounts of the Seventh Cavalry — has been raised to the level of myth by film and television: stagecoaches, the Pony Express, posses on horseback and, of course, at home on the range, lariat in hand, those heroes of the far frontier who kept those dogies rolling — cowboys.

For 5,000 years the horse dominated the world at the tip of an immense industry which affected every level of life. No decent-sized town could survive without stables, farrier or coaching inn; no reasonably affluent residence was built without stables; and most of the conquering hordes — Mongol, Turk and Hun — would have been little without horses.

The canals needed horses, the original railways were pulled by horses as were the first omnibuses. It was only the advent of the steam engine and the industrial revolution, that led to the bicycle and the internal combustion engine, which in turn brought cars, buses, trucks and tractors. Slowly the horse's importance in agriculture, industry and everyday life lessened, as did its importance to communications on the arrival of the

telegraph and telephone. Horses would still see huge use under extreme conditions — the German army at the end of World War II could boast more four-legged than four-wheeled beasts of burden — but fossil fuels and mass transit systems relegated the horse in the developed world to its use today: for social and recreational purposes.

Today, in the western world, horses are used for pleasure — for exercise, horseracing, polo or sports. Every little girl would like a pony — but as a pet rather than as a means of transport.

A new industry has grown up: not as all-encompassing as during the equine millennia before the 20th century, but significant nonetheless. Racing and breeding racehorses continues to hold its allure; the inclusion of equestrian sports in early Olympic Games ensured a worldwide commitment to equestrian sports; recreational use of horses — vacations, long-distance rides, trekking — is growing; and, of course, the gymkhana, point-to-point and, to a lesser extent, hunting continue to hold their interest in Britain, as do their equivalents elsewhere — rodeos and western riding competitions for example.

This book is not a detailed history of the horse and man, although the opening chapters sketch its evolution from *Eohippus* to *Equus caballus*. It is, rather, a general introduction to the world of the horse, the world of equestrianism and equine pursuits. After an examination of its history, we look at the ways that horses are used today; at the fundamentals of horse care and management — stabling, basic health, feeding, breeding and buying; we identify the world's horse and pony types and breeds; finally there's a detailed glossary of equine terminology.

Today the military use of horses is mainly ceremonial, a far cry from the days when the cavalry ruled the battlefield.

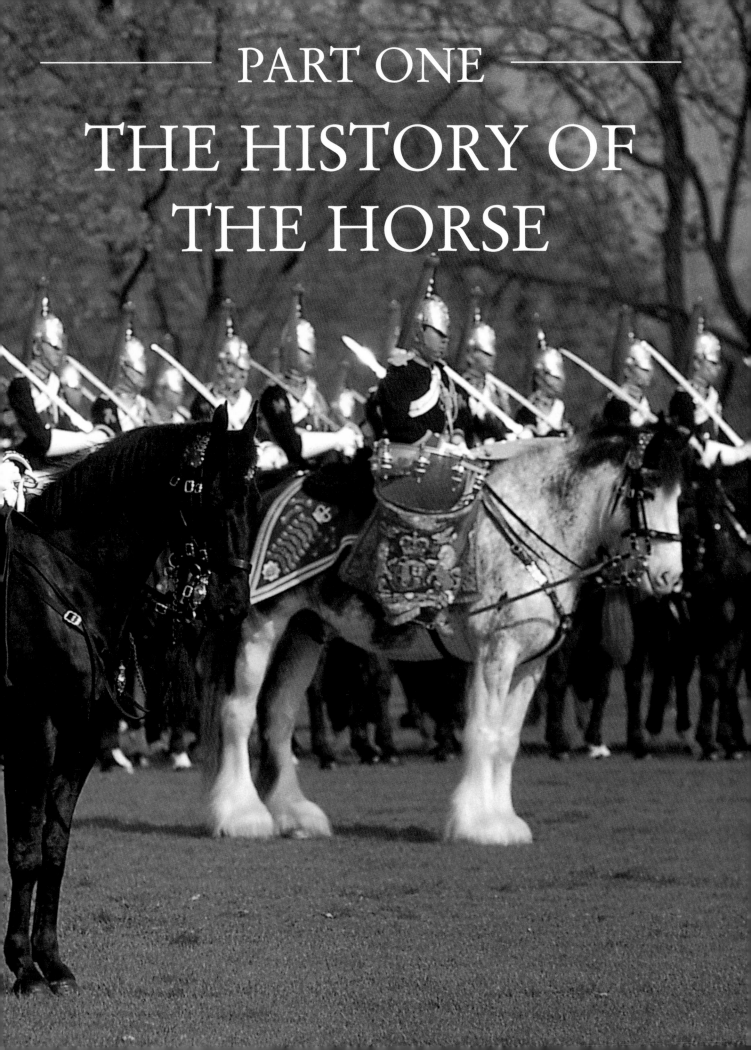

PART ONE
THE HISTORY OF THE HORSE

CHAPTER 1

EARLY MAN AND THE HORSE

Annette Sanderson

It is likely that before domestication occurred the early relationship of man and horse was simply that of a hunter and his prey. The bones of 10,000 horses at the foot of the Solutré cliffs in France must be the result of Cro-Magnon man driving herds over the edge generation after generation. The Paleolithic cave art of Western Europe is rich in accurate representations of horses. The preponderance of horses at caves such as Lascaux, Les Trois Frères and Altamira point to the fact that the horse already held an important place in everyday life, whether on a practical plane as food, on a spiritual level as a symbol of fertility or as a messenger of the gods.

From closely watching the horse in order to kill him, man acquired a detailed knowledge of his diet, social structure and habits — and probably the empathy for his prey that we can still observe in primitive people. This feeling would later prove invaluable when man started domesticating the horse and would lead to a partnership that would prove to be hugely influential to man's economic progress and history: the horse's speed and strength gave mankind a mobility he never had before.

The best cave paintings of northern Europe — like those in the Ekain cave, northern Spain — show us the horse as he was between 15,000 and 17,000 years ago: short-legged, stocky, usually bay with a lighter belly and muzzle, upright mane and dark stripes on the shoulders and sometimes across the legs. This type of horse reminds us strongly of the Przewalski and the reconstituted Tarpan; leg stripes still appear occasionally on New Forest and other native British ponies.

How did man first domesticate the horse? Did he take some orphaned foal into the tribe and rear it? The horse, being a social animal, would integrate relatively easily into human society. Or did man follow the herds until he managed to get them used to his presence and started influencing their grazing patterns, eventually herding them and using them for his own purposes in the way the Laps have done with the rein-

deer? What is certain is that around 9,000 years ago, the hunter-gatherers of western Asia began to alter their way of life. They started keeping flocks of live animals, first sheep and goats, then cattle and pigs until they finally encompassed horses.

With domestication, the horse had to adapt to its new environment and lifestyle. If the primitive horse exhibited the extreme aggressive behavior shown by Przewalski stallions in captivity, man had to breed for submissiveness as well as hardiness and ease of feeding. This happened only relatively recently: in about 3000BC in southern Russia and western Asia, from the Ukraine to Turkestan, and 2000BC in Europe. The domestication of the horse spread out from this arc; it enabled man to travel great distances over most kinds of terrain, as well as to hunt and wage war more efficiently as he developed increasingly refined means of controlling the horse by the use of bits, saddles and stirrups. Furthermore, by using the horse's strength more efficiently, with increasingly sophisticated means of harnessing him, man was able to depend on his physical stamina to help him with the agricultural workload. He also learned to breed types of horses especially adapted to the work needed of them.

By 1500BC, we can discern two different types of horse: the northern stocky ponies and the more refined southern type. Celtic ponies seldom exceeded 9.75hh (3ft 3in) at that time, while the Scythian and Russian steppe horses could reach 14.25hh (4ft 9in).

The earliest bits found in Britain date from the Bronze Age (2000BC): plain snaffles, usually jointed with wheel-shaped cheek pieces containing spikes on the inner surface. Earlier bits may have been made of wood or horn but these have not survived. Deer antler cheek pieces have been found in a cave in County Durham, England, but the bits themselves have perished. The Iron Age Celts used light, resilient chariots drawn by small local ponies until the beginning of the Roman invasion: these are immortalised by the images of Queen Buddica of the Iceni tribe who fought the Roman invaders and who killed herself in AD62 after being defeated. The Irish, in their isolation, would use the chariot until AD400.

The Iron Age saw the flourishing in Britain and Ireland of the cult of Epona, meaning the Great Mare, usually represented as a woman riding a mare and accompanied by foals. Her cult persisted up until the Christian era when the Church took stern measures to eradicate the northern European horse cults.

Among the Norsemen and Saxons the horse figured heavily in mythology. One of Odin's numerous incarnations was as a horse. Freyr, god of fertility, had horses dedicated to him and a white one was slaughtered during his rites. Partaking of the meat and liver of the sacred horses was believed to reinforce the deity as well as endowing the participant with some of the horse's qualities. In its fight against the horse the Church forbade the eating of horseflesh.

The first horseshoes and nails have been found in Celtic burial sites in barrow mounds throughout northern Europe. In Iron Age Britain (450BC), the shoes were made with a typical wavy outline caused by punching round nail holes. They were sometimes fitted with calkins (50BC–AD50). Improved plain shoes have been found on the Thames foreshore, dating from about the 1st century AD.

It is possible that the first people both to ride and harness the horse were the nomadic tribes of China: there are Chinese ceramic representations of ridden and harnessed horses dating from about 3000BC. The Chinese also had different types of horses for different uses and must have practiced selective breeding. Their famous Heavenly Horses were brought from Ferghana in 128BC by Emperor Wu Ti to provide remounts in the constant fight against the Huns. These horses were reputed to be the descendants of horses left behind by Alexander's army and are recorded in some of the finest art of the Han period. The Chinese aristocracy hunted the hare and the pheasant from horseback using trained birds of prey. Later, the Tatars

LEFT: The Przewalski was once thought to be the common breed from which all horses were descended. It comes from Mongolia and horses like this were the steeds of Genghis Khan's Mongol warriors, the scourge of Eastern Europe.

ABOVE: The Tarpan can no longer be found in the wild; it is the last surviving example of the steppe horses and ancestor to many European breeds.

BELOW: The civilizations of antiquity have left us many examples of the horse in their art.

or Mongols introduced polo and even women played.

The Chinese adopted the stirrup they saw used by the Hun raiders who harassed them for centuries. The first mention of the stirrup appears in a document written by a Chinese officer in AD477. It would not reach Europe before AD800 when it would improve the efficiency of the ordinary rider and revolutionize warfare by increasing the stability of the rider. Even though the famous "Parthian shot," fired backward over the shoulder while riding away, was performed without the benefit of stirrups, for close combat with heavy equipment stirrups were essential. They would play a large part in the style of warfare of the Middle Ages with its massively armored mounted knights.

Far from China, the Sumerians, Hittites, Assyrians and Egyptians were also mastering the horse. The earliest text we have on the care and rearing of horses was written around 1400BC by a Hittite, Kikkuli of Mittani, who wrote in detail about the care of the horse and even gave a day-by-day plan of how to get a horse fit in 75 days. The Egyptian elite hunted and went to war in light two-wheeled chariots. A stallion dating from 1650BC exhumed in Egypt had had a bit in its mouth, and was approximately 14hh (4ft 8in), with fine limbs and only five lumbar vertebrae like the Arabian and the Przewalski horses.

The Assyrians' kingdom lay around the Tigris and Euphrates basin. We know their horses mainly from their monumental art and the marvelous bas-relief of the palace of King Assurbanipal at Nineveh, dated between 9BC and 7BC. These realistically depict well-groomed, corn-fed, fit horses used for hunting and war, either ridden or harnessed to chariots according to the terrain. They set up one of the first effective cavalries in the 9th century BC. These mounted troops used riding pads, bits and martingales but no stirrups and rode horses up to 16 hh (5ft 4in) in height. Their horses came originally from Armenia and Iran and were well able to sustain the epic marches of the Assyrians across the breadth of Asia Minor.

By the 5th century BC, the nomadic Scythian horsemen of south Russia rode large Arabian-type horses. The tombs at Pazyryk in western Mongolia dating from the 7th century BC to the 1st century AD contain remarkably well-preserved horses. All the horses were either harnessed, some with wood-bar bits, others with bronze bits, leather saddles and felt saddlecloths. They ranged in size from 13hh (4ft 4in) to 14.25hh (4ft 9in), the largest being of the Turkoman type. There is also a frieze on a Ukrainian vase (400BC) representing horses being broken. The Scythians' raids took them as far as Egypt in 611BC and the upper Seine valley a few years later. Their way of life was that typical of the Mongolian herdsmen: they drank the mares' milk, ate the foals and would bleed their horses to drink the blood if food ran out. This apparently harsh treatment

of their horses has to be balanced with the fact that, unlike the Mediterranean people, they castrated their horses, and were consequently able to ensure that only the best stallions would reproduce. The Greek and Roman horses came from Scythian stock, bought or looted like the 20,000 mares Philip of Macedon seized during his campaigns.

One interesting and little known fact is that quite a large number of the uncovered Scythian and neighboring Sarmatian kurgans, or graves, dated around the 7th and 6th centuries BC, contain the skeletons of female warriors, some buried in groups with bows, arrows and battle-belts to protect their groins, or singly like the Sarmatian princess who was buried with her battle-axe beside the harness of her own horse team. The Scythian-Sarmatian world had an attitude to women and power quite unlike that of any other contemporary society. It is possible that the legendary Amazons described by Herodotus in the 5th century BC were in fact Scythian and Sarmatian women warriors. We know that Amage, wife of a Sarmatian king, seized power from her husband, led a cavalry commando into the Crimean Scythian kingdom next door and imposed a peace settlement between the Scythians and the Greeks of Sebastopol.

The height of sophistication reached by the horseman of that period can be best appreciated when reading *Hippike,* the work of the Greek statesman and horse-lover Xenophon around 400BC, who admits his indebtedness to an earlier work by Simon of Athens. We can still learn from his advice on sensitive methods of training and soft use of the rider's hands. The Greeks' love of horses is well-documented by the numerous items of painted pottery, statues and friezes which have survived. It is obvious from the writings of Homer and Aristotle that the Greeks used the horse in every conceivable fashion; for instance, chariot races were one of the most popular forms of competition of the Olympiads. There is also documentary evidence of wagers on flat races. The Greek cavalry was an important part of the army and Xenophon's treatise makes it very clear that mounted troops were well-trained and highly skilled.

We will never know whether Alexander the Great (356–323BC), son of Philip of Macedon, had read Xenophon, but he used his troops in a series of remarkable conquests extending over two million square miles and creating an empire from Egypt to India and a legend which still fascinates us today. His cavalry tactics contributed greatly to his successes: his elite "Companions" were the spearhead of his forces. For the first time heavy cavalry was used as a significant weapon in combat; hitherto their main use had been as skirmishers or mounted archers. Alexander led by example and was to be seen in the midst of battle on his famous horse Bucephalus, "ox-head." His warhorse was likely to have been of the Nisean or Thessalian breeds, slightly heavy in the head and wide between the eyes (which accounts for the name ox-head). When his beloved Bucephalus died in battle, Alexander founded a city called Bucephala after him.

According to Columella (AD40), the Romans made determined efforts to improve their stock by breeding "noble" horses for the circus and the games, good horses for mule-breeding, and ordinary horses for everyday purposes. However, they did not emulate the Greeks and use cavalry to any great extent until the end of the Empire when their infantry tactics (which had been very effective against Mediterranean and Celtic horsemen) proved inadequate against the highly mobile steppe people like the Parthians. Until then their few mounted troops were used for swift communications and scouting expeditions. By AD200 their saddles were solid leather structures, held by a surcingle, and a breastplate and a crupper, but had no trees. They used a curb bit with a port, but no stirrups, and a kind of horseshoe, the soleae, made of straw or leather. Later, the hipposandals would appear, iron plates attached with leather thongs, but it is now thought that they were only used in cases of excessive wear or injury. The Romans would learn shoeing, as we know it, from the Celts. Their chariot horses were held in high esteem and the enthusiasm they generated can be guessed from this memorandum on an Imperial edict: "No horseracing is to be encouraged outside Rome as it distracts the people"

The Roman postal service, derived from systems used by Alexander and the Persians, maintained roads and provided horses and vehicles. Goods were usually transported either on pack-animals or in ox-wagons. According to a Roman official who had laid down the maximum load for horses and wagons, a four-wheeled

The Greeks and Romans valued the horse in peace and war as shown in their art (illustrated opposite and on this page) and literature but it would be inventions of later centuries that maximized the horse's working usefulness. In the 4th century AD the Huns introduced the stirrup, which allowed a rider to brace himself for an impact and paved the way for the heavily armored medieval knight; in the 9th century the Turks invented the hames collar, allowing the use of horses for draft and agricultural work.

ABOVE: Oldenburg stallions.

RIGHT: Tarpan mares: the last herd of Tarpans lived in Poland. When it died out, the Polish authorities gathered together horses with Tarpan characteristics to restore the strain.

wagon drawn by four horses could only pull 10 hundredweight. Until the hames collar, invented by the Turks, was adopted around AD900, the use of horses for draft and agricultural work would be minimal.

When the Western Roman Empire broke up, around AD400, the roads were no longer repaired and the relay posts disappeared, lawlessness became rife and traveling a risky business — the Dark Ages would be a confused period marked by waves of invasions of Western Europe by eastern nomads.

In the 4th century AD a Hun tribe settled in Hungary; their stirrups were copied by their German neighbors and by Viking traders who took them back to northern Europe. The Byzantines were quick to adopt the stirrup and Justinian's great general, Belisarius, set up a mounted cavalry corps of heavily armored warriors called cataphracts, who carried a veritable arsenal: a lance, a broadsword, metal darts, a powerful bow and a quiver of arrows. This cataphract would be the model for the Western European knight. A new era of heavy cavalry with larger horses, different bits, saddles and tactics was dawning.

CHAPTER 2

CLASSICAL EQUITATION

Annette Sanderson

Man first trained the horse for his usefulness but, very quickly, the natural responsiveness of the animal to his human handlers prompted the more observant of them to develop a deeper relationship with their horses. This in turn caused them to refine their training methods until these methods eventually became an art in their own right. It is this art which became known as "classical equitation" during the Renaissance and which would give rise to numerous riding treatises and famous riding academies, some of which are still in existence today.

To find the sources of our contemporary riding art we have to go back to antiquity. When Simon of Athens wrote, "If a dancer was forced to dance by whip and spikes, he would be no more beautiful than a horse trained under similar conditions," he was already showing the thoughtful attitude to training which would be the hallmark of the best classical masters. His successor and disciple, the Greek Xenophon, is considered to have laid down the foundations of all classical equitation. His treatise, *Hippike*, explains in detail what to look for when purchasing a horse: how to "see to it that the colt be kind, used to the hand, and fond of men when he is put to the horse-breaker . . . for if this be done, colts must not only love men, but even long for them."

Great emphasis is placed on obedience for, "in moments of danger the master gives his own life into the keeping of his horse." The most significant part of the work, however, comes with his instructions on how to ride: "I do not approve of a seat which is as though the man were on a chair, but rather as though he were standing upright with his legs apart."

Xenophon's timing of the aids for canter, his use of the volte to supple the horse and get him to flex his jaw, his recommendations on collecting the horse and keeping him straight while doing so or on ensuring the quarters are well under the horse when leaping are as relevant today as they were then. Xenophon shows remarkable insight in his treatment of the high-met-

ABOVE: Lipizzaners — the horse most usually associated with classical equitation thanks to the fame of the Spanish Riding School in Vienna. The horses at the school are descended from the stock originally brought to Lipizza.

RIGHT: A classic Lipizzaner pose.

tled horse. Sitting quietly, avoiding any abrupt movements, coaxing the horse into going on a mild bit and yielding to the hand "with pleasure" conjure up a picture of a contemporary high-school horse.

The art of riding horses sensitively and humanely declined in the Middle Ages when war was waged by heavily armored men on cold-blooded horses fitted with incredibly severe bits and spurred with the equivalent of lethal weapons to get them to maneuver on the battlefield. Eventually, the advent of small firearms led to the development of a lighter cavalry in the 15th century which in turn revolutionized warfare. To be efficient and remain alive the cavalryman had to rediscover how to make his horse handy.

The "airs above the ground" are still practiced by the Lipizzaners, with jumps and leaps as shown here at a show in England. The Spanish Riding School is in demand the world over for its wonderful pagentry and exemplary horse control.

The needs of the army and the spirit of scientific inquiry of the Renaissance provided a favorable climate for a revival of the art of riding. A study of the ancient Greek texts furnished the new riding masters with the forgotten principles of Xenophon's equitation, while the crowned heads of Europe evinced a new interest in the art of riding and established riding academies to train horses and riders for warfare. The capriole and the piaffe became part of the repertoire of the best war horses and the discipline became so exacting and exciting that young noblemen flocked to the new academies. At the same time horses admirably suited to the new high-school discipline were spreading throughout Europe with the rise of the Spanish empire under Philip II. Spain held Naples until 1707 and when Grisone opened his riding academy in 16th century Naples he made use of the Iberian horses.

Grisone was the first riding master of the Renaissance to leave us a book on classical riding. He had studied Xenophon with great care, and faithfully followed his principles but tended to ignore the Greek's emphasis on gentleness. His *Ordini de Cavalcare*, published in 1550, extended his influence to most of Europe and was much copied by English writers — Henry VIII's riding master, Robert Alexander, had studied under Grisone. The book showed some fearsome bits and today many of the training methods seem distinctly quaint. To turn the horse, the rider would use his legs and the wand held along the outside eye. "Treading the ring" was used to school the horse and relied on the use of narrow trodden paths made in a plowed field, or between walls of gorse but if a horse were reluctant, the remedies of the time ranged from prodding it from behind with an angry cat tied to a pole, to tying a live hedgehog by the foot under the horse's tail.

Grisone's best known pupil was Pignatelli. He would also become director of the Riding Academy at Naples and teach Frenchman Antoine Pluvinel who later became riding master to Louis XIII. Pluvinel modified the teachings of Pignatelli and advocated individual treatment for the horse and humane principles. He published his riding treatise, *Le Manège du Roi*, in 1623.

Pignatelli's work also influenced M. de La Broue who lived during the reign of Henry IV (1553–1610) and was Grand Ecuyer to the duc d'Eperon. He wrote the *Traité d'Equitation* and *Cavalerie Français* which ran into several editions. The Duke of Newcastle (1592–1676), tutor to Charles II when Prince of Wales, was a disciple of his and would be the greatest English exponent of classical equitation. His methods were not unkind but his fondness for artificial gadgets such as the draw-rein, which caused many of his horses to become overbent and lack impulsion, would limit his influence. Another great high-school English rider was the Earl of Pembroke, who published *A Method of Breaking Horses and Teaching Soldiers to Ride* in 1761. He encouraged the use of athletic manège exercises to improve flexibility and maneuverability. "This lesson of reining back and piaffing is excellent . . . and puts a horse well and properly on the haunches."

The greatest riding master of France, François Robichon de La Guérinière (1688–1751), opened a riding academy in Paris in 1715. By 1730 his reputation was such that he was entrusted with the Academy of the Tuileries, where he remained director until his death. In his *École de Cavalerie*, published in 1733, he acknowledges his debt to Pignatelli, M. de La Broue and the Duke of Newcastle. He surpassed them all, however, in the depth of his insight into the art of schooling the horse. He pioneered the shoulder-in and, in the words of Alois Podhajski, produced "the most revolutionary book on riding of all times." He advocated "sparing use of the aids and chastisements as one of the most desirable traits of the rider" and gave detailed advice on how to bit a horse according to his temperament, his stage of training and the shape of his mouth. His book bears witness to his detailed knowledge of horses, their temperament, their care and the art of training them to the highest levels. His teachings would be adopted as the basis of instruction at the Spanish Riding School in Vienna and can still be seen there in daily use.

The end of the 18th century, bringing as it did the French Revolution followed by the Napoleonic Wars, meant the end of the riding academies in France and in the various courts of Europe; the Spanish Riding School alone would be the guardian of the traditions of classical equitation for an uninterrupted 400 years right up to our times.

The Imperial Riding School of Vienna had rather obscure beginnings under Archduke Charles II, Holy Roman Emperor from 1556 to 1564. In 1580 some of the best riding horses in Spain were sent to a newly formed stud on the crown lands of Lipizza. A few years earlier, in 1572, a riding school — just an open wooden structure — had been built in Vienna close to the palace. In 1735, this was replaced by a splendid building, known as the Winter Riding School. Since that time the school has survived changes in political regimes and wars, managing to preserve throughout the correctness of its classical methods. The training of horses and riders at Vienna is still concentrated on high-school riding and high-school performances. A limited number of foreigners are accepted as pupils each year, usually for one year, but the young school riders can spend up to 10 years learning their art.

The Spanish Riding School horses are descended from the stock originally brought to Lipizza. They are all gray, but used to throw an occasional bay. There are six lines of stallions and 18 lines of mares and their

Two more views of the Spanish Riding School at a show at Wembley, England — while it may be the last home in the world for this style of riding, its future seems secure.

conformation varies according to their breeding lines. They can be stocky with a Roman nose, or finer and of a more Arabian type, but they all have in common their athleticism, their medium size (around 15hh/5ft) and their action, which is higher and shorter than that of the modern dressage horse. Nowadays the Spanish Riding School continues to be regarded as the Mecca of classical equitation.

The French Riding Academy of Versailles ceased operation in 1830. Its last Ecuyer was the Comte d'Aure (1799–1863), a noted French master of equitation under Louis XVIII and Charles X. He would also be the first Ecuyer en Chef of the Cadre Noir at the academy of Saumur, a Protestant school closed by the religious wars and reopened in 1763. Eight years later it became the seat of the French Cavalry School. Closed again during the Revolution and the Empire, it reopened in 1815 when the Cadre Noir, the famous corps of riding instructors, was formed. Nowadays, the Cadre Noir upholds the classical tradition and still puts on displays of airs above the ground with sauteurs, which are Selle Français horses, and of pure dressage on Anglo-Arabs. The Cadre Noir concentrates on the training of civilian and military instructors in general riding and high-school dressage and is closely associated with the National School of Equitation. A French instructor trained at Saumur learns the classical principles before becoming proficient in cross-country riding and show jumping.

While the Comte d'Aure was turning the Versailles academy into a center for excellence, another Frenchman, François Baucher (1796–1873), was also making a name for himself as a riding master. He toured the famous European riding schools and on his return to France set up riding schools in Le Harve, Rouen and finally in Paris itself. He was a controversial figure and was much challenged by d'Aure and his followers for overbending his horses. His performances in the circus — at the time the only place to display high-school riding if one did not belong to a famous academy — heralded those of James Fillis (1834–1913). He was a Londoner who trained horses in Haute École for the circus, appearing on the Champs-Elysées from 1873 to 1866 after spending 12 years as a riding master in St Petersburg. Fillis was a great artist but the purists held against him his practice of unnatural movements, such as the canter on three legs, the canter backward and the Spanish walk. Colonel L'Hotte, Ecuyer at Saumur, blended the teachings of d'Aure and Baucher in 1860 into a method which is still followed by the Cadre Noir.

Spain and Portugal adopted the riding style of the rest of Europe in the 16th and 17th centuries: straight legs, deep seat and a highly collected horse as shown in the court paintings of the period. In Spain, two names stand out as exponents of classical dressage, Pedro

Aguilar and Vargas de Mahuca, who had studied under Grisone in Naples. In Portugal, King Duarte (1401–1438) set out principles of lightness of aids even earlier in his training treatises which were much copied until, 150 years later, the Marquis of Marialva — whose methods of softness and lightness in the manège are still followed — became highly influential. The book published by his Ecuyer, Manuel Carlos Andrade, is still the classical horseman's Bible in the Iberian Peninsula. The most famous contemporary riding master of Portugal was Mestre Nuno Oliveira whose school near Lisbon received visitors and pupils from all over the world. Anthony Crossley was so impressed by what he saw there that he wrote, "The Oliveira theme is embodied in the three principles of collection, impulsion and lightness, the first and the last being taken to a degree beyond the conception of most riders . . . such heights of artistry must raise and enrich the conception of what dressage is all about."

The tours by Nuno Oliveira, the Cadre Noir and the Spanish Riding School greatly contributed to the burgeoning revival of classical equitation which started a few years ago. They inspire with their artistry and, like our riders in the 16th and 17th centuries, contemporary riders wish to discover the principles behind this harmony and perfection of movement. If this small "renaissance" were to continue to grow into a thriving movement in the future, it could only be to the all-round benefit of both horses and their riders.

ABOVE: The control is total, the pose practiced: a Lipizzaner milks the applause at a US show.

RIGHT: A long-rein half-pass — one of the spectacular movements of a Spanish Riding School show.

CHAPTER 3

THE ARABIAN

Annette Sanderson

According to the *Koran* the Arabian horse was created by Allah out of a handful of South Wind. This poetic legend is well-suited to a charismatic breed which has inspired admiration for centuries, but what really are the origins of the Arabian?

The horses depicted in the Egyptian art of 3,000 years ago show a fine, oriental breed which could well have been the precursor of the Arabian. At the same time the Bedouin legends tell us that it was in Yemen that Ishmael caught and tamed a wild mare and her foal for the first time and bred from them, thus starting the Arabian breed. For a long time, this was deemed to have been impossible due to the prevailing desert conditions in this area but some drawings and fossil bones discovered in the Libyan mountains of the Fezzan in the late 1950s seem to support the theory that conditions suitable for wild horses developed in central and south Arabia before it became arid.

We also have the evidence of pre-Islamic poetry and of the rock inscriptions at Taima to support the belief that Bedouins were breeding fine, proud spirited horses well before Mohammed. But it was under the influence of Mohammed (AD570–632) that the Arabian horse would rise to its position of eminence among world breeds. Mohammed needed an efficient, swift body of mounted warriors to fight for Islam, and encouraged the raising of suitable horses: "As many grains of barley as thou givest thy horse, so many sins shall be forgiven thee!"

Mohammed himself bought horses from the Bedouins to found his stud making payment in slaves. We are told that he chose the best among his trained mares (the Bedouins never rode the stallions) by depriving them of water for three days then releasing them and sounding the call to battle. All but five of the mares rushed to the water: the five supremely obedient ones who came to the call of the horn became the celebrated "five mares of the Prophet" and bred the most valued Arabian stock, the "Asil" or pure-blooded strain.

The Bedouin way of life depended on the camel. It was the camel which provided fuel, meat, milk, leather,

The Arabian's influence on the horse breeds of the world is undeniable and substantial — the Wielkopolski, the Trakehner, the Akhal-Teke, the Orlov Trotter, the Anglo-Arab, the Thoroughbred, the Standardbred, the Welsh Mountain Pony: the list of breeds with Arabian blood goes on and on. The main Arabian characteristics are an eager and fiery nature, yet they are good-natured, light-boned and quick with beautiful dished faces, enormous eyes and a wide forehead.

ropes and cloth and carried all their possessions. The horse was a luxury, a source of pride and a means to conquer foreign lands and extend the influence of Islam to places the camel could not go. Bedouins became fanatical about blood lines and the pedigrees were handed down orally from father to son. The foals always had the strain of their dams and were reared in close contact with their human families so that they would be used to a variety of sights and sounds in preparation for their part in raids and battles.

During the early Middle Ages, Islam spread throughout southern Europe carried by its horses until the advance was halted by Charles Martel at the battle of Poitiers in AD732. The Arabs occupied Spain

and north Africa and their horses and their horsemanship left their mark on the breeds and the equestrian culture of these areas.

In Europe, Turkish and Barbary horses had been imported in small numbers since the Middle Ages to improve the speed of local breeds. In the 18th century three imported horses: the Byerley Turk, the Darley Arabian and the Godolphin Arabian became the founders of the Thoroughbred. In the early 19th century, European travelers started bringing back Arabian horses from Egypt and from the Nejd on the banks of the Euphrates. Wilfred Scawen Blunt and his wife, Ann, founded the Crabbet stud in England which would prove enormously important for the spread of the Arabian horse not only at home but also in the United States, Russia and Poland. Russia had regularly used Arabian horses in its studs since the 15th century and the Arabian had shared in the foundation of the Orlov Trotter, while in Poland it had been a favorite for centuries and some of the finest Arabian horses still come out of Janow Podlaski.

The popularity of the Arabian horse has been rising steadily throughout Europe, Australia and the United States since the 19th century. In 1881, a section for the Arabian was added to the *General Stud Book*. Nowadays, the Arabian and the part-bred Arabians have their own stud book and form a large proportion of our equine population. For a long time, the Arabian was regarded by the general rider as a pretty pony of limited usefulness and was in danger of spending its days being a show breed. The main use of Arabian stock was still in breeding show ponies by crossing it with native ponies. The rise of endurance sports, Arabian racing and leisure equitation have changed the image of the breed.

Poland and Russia have long had a policy of testing on the racetrack all their Arabian colts and fillies for two years; Arabian racing is expanding in England and becoming ever more professional and throughout the world endurance riding is one of the fastest growing sports. This means that it is now possible to buy an Arabian for its performance potential as well as for its looks, a welcome development which should spell a very healthy future for the breed.

Another reason for the rising popularity of the Arabian is less easy to define. It comes from its charismatic appeal for many horse lovers. In 1863, the Emir Abd-el-Kader wrote: "Do you understand the boundless affection the Arab feels for his horse? It is only equalled by the services rendered by the latter." The physical and psychological attributes of the Arabian still inspire the same devotion in his modern owners.

The anatomical facts are well known: height between 14.2hh and 15.2hh (4ft 9in–5ft 1in), coat bay, brown, chestnut or a variety of grays, often 17 pairs of ribs only, instead of 18 or 19, dished face but this

Three beautiful Arabians: Rysleem (ABOVE), Chalyska (ABOVE RIGHT) and Zircon Khalif (BELOW RIGHT). An inspiration for artists, a good Arabian showing off is a heart-stopping spectacle but shouldn't hide the Arabian's other qualities — temperament, stamina and intelligence.

description does not begin to do justice to the Arabian. A good Arabian horse showing off is a heart-stopping spectacle: the fine head with flared nostrils held high on an incredibly arched neck, thin ears often curved at the tips straining forward, the long tail curving over the back, and the energetic, floating paces used in a dazzlingly acrobatic series of impossible twists and turns carried out at speed make it indeed the stuff of legends. When the capable, sympathetic rider discovers that this fast, athletic horse, can also be gentle, intelligent and courageous and will use his desert-born stamina to the limit for him, he is lost!

CHAPTER 4

THE HORSE IN AMERICA:
WESTERN RIDING

Sarah Simmons

As dressage, which is an athletic, elegant discipline, was derived from movements that were taught to the horse for warfare, so "Western Riding" as we know it today, originated from those movements required from the working ranch horse.

For centuries, before Europeans arrived, North America's plains were roamed and hunted by native Indians but, contrary to popular belief, no horses were present until 1519. This was the year the horse arrived in the form of five mares and 11 stallions brought to Mexico by Hernando Cortes and his conquistadores. From this small band of Spanish Barb descended horses, was to come the cowboy's working horse.

Initially, because the Spanish did not believe in or practice castration and also because of the temperate climate — namely the ideal surroundings and lush grass of southern Mexico — the number of horses increased rapidly. Eventually Mexico was overstocked with horses and many were turned loose: so the mustang was created. He became a tough and wiry feral beast. Towards the end of the 18th century the Plains Indian learned to capture and break these wild animals and they became well known for their skills in horsemanship. Quickly thereafter, as America was opened up by the pioneers and settlers, the demand for transport and communications increased so the horse was needed even more.

This was typified by the short-lived Pony Express Mail Delivery, which was founded in April 1860 and ran until October 1861. It covered a distance of 1,966 miles over the plains, mountains and deserts from St. Joseph, Missouri, to Sacramento, California. The Pony Express line consisted of 25 home stations, roughly 75 miles apart, where the riders were changed, and 165 swing stations, 15 miles apart, where the horses were changed. The nearly 2,000-mile journey took about 10 days to complete. The average age of the riders was about 19 years old and there were many characters, undoubtedly the most famous being William "Buffalo Bill" Cody. During the 19 months of the Pony Express only one rider was killed by hostile Indians and only one bag of mail was lost! The introduction of the telegraph line caused the demise of the Pony Express.

ABOVE: Today's western riding is a far cry from the days of cattle driving.

With the end of the American Civil War in 1865 came the start of the cowboy era. During the 1860s and 1870s, cow towns sprang up, because of a higher demand for beef. The cow pony was now coming into its own. The Texas Longhorn was the first breed of cattle to be marketed but then the Shorthorn and the Hereford became more favored for their greater meat production, and their stronger resistance to Texas tick fever. When these heavier cattle were introduced, a stronger, faster horse was required, so imported stock from Europe, England and the East, were crossed with the mustangs. As the great demand for beef cattle increased, many more horses and men were trained in the skills necessary to cope with the tough tasks set before them. These horses became the forerunners of the Quarter Horse as we know it now and the skills are still employed today on working ranches. Like dressage, which derived its movements from the mounted knight in battle (at work!), so competition western riding has derived its movements from that of the working cow pony.

TACK

As new skills for horse and rider were developed so also came alteration of the tack. Probably the two biggest earlier inventions were the horse collar and the stirrup. Previously the lack of a proper collar was the limiting factor of horse transport in the ancient world; it was probably one of man's most important inventions, enabling the efficient use of the horse for haulage purposes. For instance, the Romans used an inefficient yoke and strap system for horse-drawn transport, whether it be chariot or cart. The introduction of the rigid horse collar designed and made to fit the horse enabled him to use his shoulders for pulling heavier loads more easily; thus one horse was able to pull loads that previously needed three horses.

Another important invention was the stirrup. Once again necessity had become the mother of invention. The stirrup, first known about 2BC was designed to hold only the big toe of the rider — this was because Hindus did not wear boots or shoes. This type of stirrup spread across from Asia to China. It appears from Turkish equine history, that the Turks got the idea of the stirrup from the Chinese during the war of AD694. This innovation allowed the rider to have both hands free to use his weapons and, equally importantly, he could use all his weight to wield his weapons, or to direct his horse, by leaning over to one side (with the added use of the reins).

For the working cowboy his tack was equally important — the very nature of his work demanded that the saddle be comfortable for horse and rider because of the long, hard hours spent at their job. The tack needed to have a strong enough framework to hold a roped steer when secured to the horn of the saddle; it needed a high cantle and swells to hold the rider in when going up or down steep hills, or prevent him from being unseated when doing fast maneuvers such as cutting cattle. Fenders helped to prevent the riders' legs being chafed from the horse's sweat and could be crossed over the seat of the saddle to keep the seat dry when not being used.

At the bottom of the fenders were the hobble straps, which were used to prevent the horse from straying too far while the cowboy was sleeping. Hobble straps are essentially two cuffs usually made of leather fitted around the horse's legs and are attached by a short chain or strong leather, similar to those used in prisons in medieval times. The stirrup, which had a wide tread, enabled the rider to stand off the horse's back to see over the herd, or to stand up out of the saddle to make it easier on the horse's back muscles when the animal was tired. The saddle blanket had to be thick enough to prevent pressure sores and may as well have been used as a pillow for the cowboy. Saddle skirts were made wide enough to allow room

ABOVE: A western saddle: note saddle blanket, high cantle and swells and fenders.

BELOW: Western bit and harness.

for a poncho, bedroll, lariat and a rifle to be attached to the saddle strings. The rear cinch, or the flank cinch, was there to prevent the saddle being tipped forward when taking the weight of a steer on the horn and possibly to prevent the saddle from slapping on the horse's back if he started bucking. The breast collar stopped the saddle from slipping backwards when riding uphill and to keep the saddle from moving around if it did not fit perfectly — for a cowboy may well have owned several horses and would not be able to have saddles for each of them.

The cowboy would have a day horse and a night horse (who had to be sure-footed in the dark). He would have a pack horse to carry his supplies, plus maybe a river horse, who was a confident leader for the others to follow across, and, of course, a good roping and cutting horse. Imagine having to pick out all their hooves first thing in the morning!

Back to the saddle. Yes, it may be more difficult to lift some western saddles compared to our classical dressage or general purpose saddles but being wider all-round the weight is distributed more evenly across the horse's back and therefore is much kinder and easier for the horse when carrying a rider all day long through a hot day.

The western bridle consists of a very simple framework and there are three main types. The simplest form is the split-ear, made from a leather strip with a large enough slit carved out to fit over one ear and simple leather ties to attach the bit and reins. The sliding-ear bridle is a more complicated version of this,

A simple western bridle: the split-ear fitted over one ear.

with a leather strip for a headpiece and a semicircular strip of leather fitted onto the main headpiece. The semicircular strip is known as the sliding earpiece and can be placed over either ear: it fits better around the ears than the split-ear bridle. These two types of bridle need no throatlatch or browband which makes them more comfortable for the horse.

The third type of bridle is similar to the English bridle pattern — with browband and throatlatch attached. It is sometimes considered safer for breaking and training colts. Nosebands were not often used in the past although today western trainers often used nosebands made from waxed rope or rawhide.

Two main types of rein are used: split reins and California reins. Split reins are not joined together and some horses can be trained to stand still when both or one of the reins are dropped on the ground; this is important because out in the open there is often no place to tether a horse: this method is called ground tying. This method of ground-tying may also be practiced by the Field Master during hunting if he should have to get off his horse and tend to his hounds, although he is usually lucky enough to be able to ask his staff to hold his horse.

California reins are joined together at the ends and finished in a single long rein called the "romal." This ends in a leaf-shaped piece of leather called a "quirt." The romal can be used as an artificial aid, like the riding whip but not during competitions.

Another type of useful bridle is the bosal, otherwise known as the hackamore. The term bosal derives from the Spanish word for noseband. It has no attached bit, so is kinder to a horse with teething problems: it is also used by some cowboys for teaching the basics to the young horse being broken or "backed." It consists of a headpiece, browband and a fiador (which acted as a throatlatch) and cheekpieces that attached to the braided rawhide bosal. The mecate (plaited horsehair) reins are attached under the chin area on the bosal and therefore do not have great direct rein pressure, so the horse has to be taught to neck-rein, as well as to understand other communications from the rider — voice, seat and legs.

The bristly horsehair reins used to be made from the tail hair of horses, but today if used in the show ring, they are usually made from the softer mane hair. Though slightly more expensive, it is easier on the rider's hands. Because of the texture of the reins, it is easier to teach the horse to neck rein. The horsehair reins, which consist of one long loop, also have another single rein coming from the heel knot under the chin. A cowboy might tuck the end of the single rein into his trouser belt so, should he be thrown from the saddle, he would still have hold of his horse. Although the bit-less bosal bridle appears harmless, in the wrong hands it is possible to damage the horse's nose and it

TOP: *Training western style.*

ABOVE: *The compact powerful lines of the American Quarter Horse.*

RIGHT: *Not all cowboys are American: Italian cowboys — butteri — on Maremmano horses.*

ABOVE: Cowboy Riding the Line of the Barbed Wire Fence. *The classic image of the cowboy as depicted by one of the Old West's greatest artists, Frederic Remington.*

must be properly fitted and sized to avoid discomfort. Bosals differ in thickness; the finer the size, the more severe the pressure on the horse's nose.

Today, if you visit a Western show, you will see that the tack has not changed its form but it is often more ornately garnished with silver; the leather, too, may well be a different color from the usual tan or dark brown working saddle. Also some show saddles have intricate tooling on the skirts, fenders and swells of the saddle. The seats are often suede or covered with a soft leather. Both the suede seat and the patterned tooling offer a little more grip for the rider but do require a touch more maintenance.

The bridles seen at shows are often gleaming with silver decoration or may have finely braided rawhide and/or horsehair embedded in the leather. Also you may see more fleece-padded cinches or washable padded cotton cinches instead of the old string cinches. The saddle blankets are often colorful and chosen to match the rider's clothes. Although the show rider still has to conform to wearing a western hat (a Stetson), a long-sleeved shirt or blouse with a collar and cowboy boots, chaps and spurs are optional.

CLOTHES

The working cowboy's attire had to be hard-wearing and practical. His hat was made of heavyweight material, thick felt or leather. It was mainly used as a sun and rain shield but could also be used for collecting water or as a fan to revive the dying embers of a camp fire. The neckerchief was useful as a dust mask when riding behind other horses or a herd of cattle, a sweat rag and an emergency first-aid dressing for horse or rider, almost the same principle as the huntsman's stock. The shirt would have been mainly long-sleeved to protect the arms from scratches when going through dense brush and protection from biting insects and the sun's burning rays.

His jacket, if he ever wore one, was suede or leather and had tassels hanging from the shoulders and arms to help drain away the water quicker when caught in a storm. These tassels had a practical use in that they could be cut away for a quick repair job on a bridle or used for tying. Gloves would have been soft enough leather to be comfortable but strong and thick enough to protect the hands and withstand the rough tasks like fence repairing and in particular roping.

The cowboy's belt was not just there to hold up his trousers but could be used for replacing broken tack; a split-ear bridle can easily be made from a thick belt. His trousers were tough material like heavy cotton, later denim. Leather chaps were worn over the trousers to give extra warmth and protection from the elements; these also gave the rider more grip and helped to prevent sore, chafed legs.

The western horse tacked up and, showing its training, waiting patiently for the photographer.

Cowboy boots were designed for riding, not for walking, and were probably made from cowhide or soft leather for comfort. Spurs were worn on the boot for an extra aid, the same reason some English riders use them. Instead of a "fixed spur," western cowboys had a rowel: although sharper than an English spur, it rotated. The reason for this is to prevent the cowboy's horse from having a nasty accidental wound from the rider's legs being squashed into his flanks by rowdy cattle. Instead, it would roll up the horse's flank rather than "dig in." Also it makes a beautiful "chinking" noise when the rider walks on the ground — a forewarning to make sure the cowboy's dinner is waiting ready and hot on the table!

These days, like the tack, the rider's show clothes are more decorative — for instance, colored felt hats or straw hats for summer, sometimes garnished with a silver band or a thin-braided horsehair band; fancy tailored shirts or blouses with sequins or different patterns in colored buttons; custom-made chaps, now often made of soft suede with tassels or scallops down the outside of the leg. The tassels on the chaps have their practical uses in the same way as the jacket, to disperse the rainwater quicker but they do have a drawback — if the rider's show horse does not move smoothly the tassels flap around a lot and it may catch

the judges' eyes. Scallops, or just a plain cut, are a better choice when riding rough striding horses. Boots today can be made in exotic leathers, such as crocodile, ostrich or snake and have also been developed to walk comfortably as well as ride. Spurs are more decorative and clip-on spurs may also be found: they are a lot quicker to put on but may not be strong enough to stay on all day. Often the competition class dictates the level of decoration — for example in the Working Cowhorse class the rider's attire and the horse's blankets may be a little flashy in their colors but are more workmanlike in their appearance than, say, the Western Pleasure class.

TACKING UP A WESTERN HORSE

First of all — tie up the horse safely. Ensure that the horse is clean, especially where the saddle and bridle fit. Place the front edge of the saddle pad and blanket a few inches forward, off the withers, then slide them back a little to lay the hair coat flat. Place the saddle gently on top, making sure the blanket has 1–2in (2–5cm) showing in front of the saddle and lift the front edge of the saddle pad up away from the withers to prevent it from making the horse sore. If you have two cinches, always fasten the front one first. The flank-cinch should be nearly snug but not tight. It is very important to make sure you have connected the two cinches by a short lace or strap, or you may have your rear cinch wandering close to your horse's stifle

31

and find yourself enjoying an involuntary flying lesson! After you have put on the bridle, go back to the cinch and tighten it again. This time, lift up his legs one at a time and gently pull them forwards to remove any wrinkles in the skin under or around the cinch.

When you are riding in cold weather, if possible warm his bit up for him by holding it in your hand for a couple of minutes, or put your bridle inside your jacket while saddling up. Remove the head collar, then put the reins over the horse's head. Hold the top of the bridle in your right hand between his ears; this will prevent him from raising his head. Then, with the thumb on your left hand, push between the bars of the mouth (a space with no teeth) and tickle his tongue. Usually he will open his mouth for you to insert the bit. If he does not, try tickling the roof of his mouth with your thumb. Pull the bridle over his ears gently and make sure the bridle is not pinching his ears and that his forelock and mane lay flat underneath.

Also, check regularly for loose stitching or cracks in the leather when cleaning or oiling the tack. Supple tack is more comfortable for the horse and rider, and is less likely to crack. Although comfort for the horse and rider is important, safety of the tack is the number one priority — no matter if you are going for an amble through the woods, or riding flat-out at the gallop on the range.

MOUNTING

Mount from the near side of the horse. Take the reins in the left hand and put this hand on the horse's withers. Facing towards the horse's head, hold the stirrup with your right hand and place your left foot into it with your toe pointing towards his elbow. This will save you from hopping all the way round and maybe accidentally digging your toe into his belly. Now place your right hand either on the horn, or on the right swell of the saddle, bounce up and quietly swing your right leg over the horse's back and lower yourself gently onto the saddle. Place the ball of your foot in the stirrup. To dismount, it is usual for the rider to step down because swinging off, as done in classical saddles, could leave you dangling, caught by the horn!

POSITION OF THE RIDER

Many people have a Hollywood image of western riding — hands held high, long straight legs and the rider comfortably "slouched" in his armchair. Although western riding style is generally more relaxed, it still calls for the rider to move harmoniously with the horse. Not unlike classical riding, the rider should sit squarely on the horse with an imaginary line passing from the ear to shoulder through to the hip and down to the back of the heel. The stirrups may be longer but

must still enable the rider to bend his knee a little to absorb movement from the horse and he should be able to keep his heels lower than his toes. If the rider were to stand up in his stirrups, his seat should be about 3in (7.6cm) clear of the saddle. Feet may be placed home in the stirrup, with the heel of the boot touching it — something particularly practiced in speed events such as barrel racing or cutting when losing a stirrup could be disastrous.

The rider should be looking ahead and not downward since this tends to tip the upper body further forward. Shoulders should be back and down yet relaxed; the back should be flat but flexible, absorbing the movement of the horse, not creating it. There should be a straight line from the elbow to the horse's mouth. The rein hand should be held immediately above or slightly in front of the saddle horn. Usually, if the rider is right-handed, he will have his reins in his left hand, so his right hand is free for roping. As long as the rider does not switch hands it does not matter. If he has romal reins, the off hand should be around the romal with at least 16in (40cm) between both hands. With split reins, only one finger between the reins is allowed, with the rest of the rein coming out of the heel of the hand and the remainder of the reins falling on the same side as his rein hand. Reins are looser and longer than English style but the rider should still have a light contact with the horse's mouth. The reins should be at a length where a slight hand movement would be effective, often with just the weight of the rein being picked up.

The rider usually sits for the trot or jog and remains seated in the canter but sometimes, when not competing, will rise (post) at the fast trot. The position of the rider is vertical at all gaits and to the untrained eye there often seems a magical communication between horse and rider. No pulling, no kicking just very subtle cues from the rider. The aim is to have the horse balance himself with his rider's weight with very little help from the rider, thus attaining the best result for the least amount of effort.

BITTING THE WESTERN HORSE

When training a western horse, a snaffle bit is often the first bit used because it is easier for the horse to understand how to move left and right, backward, forward and rating speed. It is a milder bit than the curb bit and is used with two hands in the beginning. The snaffle

RIGHT: Sarah Simmons riding Famous Mint, a Quarter Horse who won the European Championship, Western Pleasure class. Famous Mint is doing a Western Pleasure "jog."

gives the rider more of a direct, straight pull and acts by putting pressure on the corners of the mouth, the bars of the mouth (the space between his incisors and premolars) and on the tongue. This is most popularly used for training western horses, because the rider has a more consistent although soft contact or feel on the reins, without too severe a reaction. A young horse needs more contact to help balance him and to make him feel more relaxed and secure, which he will not feel if there is a very loose rein, that is suddenly grabbed and yanked to slow him down or turn him. It's almost like when you are introducing yourself to someone with a handshake: as the other person offers you his hand, you withdraw your own hand. It makes the other person feel insecure.

When the horse understands the basics, such as accepting the bit, moving in a free, relaxed and balanced rhythm at the walk and jog and lope on a loose rein, he may be ready to accept the curb bit. The curb bit, as seen in the western movies, acts very differently from a snaffle and should be treated with respect. Any bit, whether it is a fat egg-butt snaffle or a high-ported, long-shaked bit, can be a tool of torture if not used correctly. Before putting any bit in a horse's mouth, a few things should be considered. Do you have heavy hands? If so, a light bit should be used. You should use the lightest, mildest bit possible to get the desired results without too much hand action. It is a well known fact that most horses prefer a mouthpiece that is porous (such as a combination of copper and mild steel) because it breathes and is prone to rusting, which stimulates salivation. This does not mean a heavily eroded and rusty bit with sharp edges: this would be unsafe and uncomfortable for the horse.

If the horse likes the taste of the mouthpiece, he will play with it with his tongue and this, in turn, relaxes his lower jaw. When his lower jaw relaxes, providing the rider is riding correctly, the rest of the horse's body will relax. If a horse is to be athletic, he must be supple. To become more supple he must first relax. This is why it is so important to choose the right bit, fit it correctly and use it correctly: you are fiddling with the most sensitive part of the horse's body. The port of the curb bit acts by pressing on the roof (palate) of the mouth, although not all curb bits have ports. The mouthpiece presses on the tongue, and the bars of the mouth, the chin-strap, which is either leather or chain, puts pressure on the chin groove. The length of the shanks also determines the severity of the pressure on the poll as well as the other points already mentioned.

THE WESTERN GAITS

There are two styles of western riding: the Californian and the Texan. The California style has a more classical carriage, and there is usually a little more contact with the horse's mouth than in the Texas style. The latter has a less collected outline and the horse travels with a longer, lower, head carriage. His poll is about level with his withers and he travels on a looser rein. Today the Texas style is the most popular in competition work.

The gaits of the western horse are slower than their English counterparts. The main reasons for this are economy of energy, since they have to be on the move for long hours, a non-excitable gait — one which will not scatter cattle easily when working the herd — and, of course, comfort for the rider. The walk should have a free-flowing stride that covers as much ground as the horse's conformation allows. The jog — for which the rider usually sits — is a slow smooth trot that can be kept up for long periods of time. The lope is a slow collected canter and, as with all the gaits, the rider should not feel as though the horse is bouncy. Because of the horse's long low outline, the spine lengthens and produces a smoother ride. The horse's hindquarters should still be engaged and the forehand should feel light in the rider's hands. The horse's feet should caress, not pound, the ground.

There is less impulsion — the feeling that the horse's energy is as tightly controlled as a coiled spring — with a western pleasure horse than a dressage horse. Impulsion takes a lot of energy out of a horse and rider and although dressage has to be appreciated for the rigor, discipline and dedication of training, impulsion would not be appropriate for the western horse. The long, low, loose-reined style allows the western horse to do his job with little help from the rider, just as a border collie works the sheep off his leash.

WESTERN TRAINING

In the early days, most of the horses used were born and bred out on the range. They were tough and wiry to look at and to handle — unlike most western horses today: they are born in a barn and handled at birth. The methods used for breaking these wild creatures did not instill trust. Cowboys did not have the time to teach the horse patience and other qualities, such as working on the long reins or on the lunge.

The bronco-buster would tie up the horse to something solid — like a tree — and "sack him out." This meant throwing and flapping the saddle blanket all around his body until he stopped flinching. He would then throw the saddle on and cinch it up tight and wait

RIGHT: Sarah Simmons and Mr-Dial-a-Bell won the European Championship, Western Showmanship class.

until the horse exhausted himself bucking and trying to remove this burden from his back. Some horses were noosed with a rope around their neck and fought so hard that they actually fell to the ground when the noose tightened, gasping for air. Once the horse gave up, the rider would mount and sit out the bucks and leaps until submission or exhaustion.

Another method used was to mount the horse in deep water. This made it harder for the animal to dish out the huge bucks and twists made on dry ground. It would be wrong to say these horses were all broken in such a rough manner — some cowboys took the time to work with the horse and not against him — nevertheless the job still had to be done as quickly as possible. Once the horse was broken enough to ride, the cowboy would start teaching the horse the necessary skills to work the herd.

Today's methods of breaking and training have a softer approach. First of all the horse must be easily caught and led. Then he must be taught to "tie up." Many horses are taught to ground tie by tying them to something fairly heavy like a tractor tire, or a heavy log on the ground. The handler will tell the horse to "stand" and then walk a small distance from the animal keeping an eye on him. Gradually, over a period of time, the horse can be trusted to stand still for a few minutes. Eventually, just dropping his lead rope or reins should be enough to give him the cue to stand and think he is still tied to the ground.

When tying up a horse for the first time, it is advisable to wear a pair of gloves to prevent a rope burn. Thread the rope through a solid ring on the wall; do not tie it up but hold it firmly. Every time the horse steps back and pulls, tap him lightly on his rump with a stick, being careful not to be kicked. As soon as he takes a step forward, release the rope's pressure for his reward. Once he has understood that he gets a warning on his rump when he pulls back but a welcoming pat on his neck and no rope tension when he walks forward or stops fighting, try tying him up properly. This can be done initially onto a rubber inner-tube, so that, should the horse panic, there is plenty of give in the retaining rubber and rope. Many a horse has hurt his back or neck through panicking and throwing his weight against rope alone. Pick the right moment and have enough time to spend with him until he trusts you and relaxes even when you are out of sight. Always tie a quick-release knot unless the horse is clever enough to untie it when you turn your back; in which case, pass the rope through the ring on the wall (or the baler twine) and then, instead of tying to the ring or twine where he can reach the knot, tie it to his head-collar under his chin.

As with most horses, grooming will help to relax the animal and to form a bond between man and his steed. When a horse is relaxed about being touched and patted all over his body, then introduce the saddle blanket. Let him sniff it and then gently rub his shoulder with it giving him soft reassuring words, working your way up his neck then down to his back. He is likely to be a bit sensitive around his belly and flanks so move slowly and be patient. Soon you should be able to slap the blanket gently all around him and even let it fall over the other side of his back. Once he has gained confidence in you, put the saddle on as already described. Do his cinch up snugly, so if he does object and buck, his saddle will not hit the floor. Often if a horse is used to wearing blankets and surcingles, he will not make too much fuss.

When you introduce the bridle and bit for the first time, let down the cheek pieces a couple of holes to make it easier to pop the headpiece over his ears. Once bridled, hook up the bit so he has a good smile, not just a wrinkle as usual. This will stop him learning to get his tongue over the bit. Some people like to use a breaking bit so the horse can play with it and in due course relax and accept it. Most horses will take kindly to a plain rusty snaffle or one with a copper roller mouthpiece. Once he accepts the bit, tie the split-reins loosely with a quick release onto the stirrups.

Lead him with his halter under his bridle, or let him wander around his stable — under supervision of course. Then tie his head to the stirrup on one side just enough to have a slight bend in his neck. The idea of this is to teach him to yield to rein pressure. The weight of the stirrup is heavy enough to pull gently on one side of his mouth — he will probably walk quite a few circles wondering what is happening, or he may just stand quietly, looking appalled. Eventually he should work out that turning his head towards the stirrup releases the pressure on his mouth. Once you have "backed" him you will be able to pick up one rein and with a gentle feel he should willingly give his head to you without resistance. Before you "back" him though, long-reining and lunging would be beneficial. This teaches the horse to be supple, relaxed, obedient to the voice, submissive to the hand and should also help him to build the muscle and strength necessary to carry a rider.

Many people in the United States and other countries use a ring for some of their training. Rings can be various sizes from 60ft (20m) or more in diameter. The fence can be solid or with small gaps to give a feeling of more space. It is usually filled with sand but there are a variety of surfaces from which to choose. Drainage is important as is a safe gate to enter and exit the ring. The idea behind a ring is that the horse can be worked "free," with no tack or lunge line if desired and with no worries of the horse escaping. The horse can be taught to do all three gaits and also a roll-back, which is a quick stop, turn on the haunches to the outside of the ring and trot or lope off in the other direc-

ABOVE: Neck-reining is taught from an early age.

tion. This is all done with the person's body movement, voice and whip. No lunge line is needed.

Neck-reining should be taught from an early age. Use two hands on the reins to start: when turning left, for example, open your left hand to the left and pull the rein enough to see the horse's left eye. At the same time, the right rein presses up against the hair on the horse's neck. Then use your left leg on the girth to stop the horse from leaning in with his shoulders and your right leg behind the girth, a little stronger to push him to the left. The horse will learn to move away and forward from leg pressure and yield to rein pressure. Eventually you will be able to bring your hands closer until you can put both reins in one hand and mainly use the outside or opposite leg to the direction of turning. Beware of one common fault — when the horse's head turns to the outside when neck-reining. It is important that the horse's head remains in the direction of turning unless leg-yielding.

Many of the aids for western riding are similar to the classical aids but the main difference is the horse is taught self-carriage with little or no rein contact and less leg contact. Instead of "holding" the horse in its ideal frame, the western horse is corrected with hand, leg and weight control, then released until he can hold that frame himself, with little help from the rider. In this way the working western horse is allowed more freedom to use his own instincts when cutting a steer or heifer from the main herd, just as a working sheepdog would be allowed to use his own instincts, without too much interference from the shepherd.

COMPETITION CLASSES

These are some of the classes you may come across at a western show:

Showmanship at Halter The handler is judged on how he presents the horse for the judge. The horse does not have to be the best conformed but he must be groomed immaculately, well shod, led to and from the judge and stand still squarely when being judged. The handler must never be between the horse and the judge since this would not give the judge the full picture of the horse. Many young children enjoy competing in this class with a quiet horse.

Western Horsemanship The rider is judged on how he controls his horse, his position and his showmanship — for example, being able to slow and collect his horse in the lope if the horse in front of him is going slower. He should be able to overtake other riders safely and courteously if his horse has a quicker or longer stride. This class usually has a set pattern; for example it could go like this: Start. Right-lead lope. Stop. 180° turn on forehand to left. Left-lead lope. Stop. Rein-back at least five steps. The pattern is obviously executed individually.

Western Reining This is like a high-speed dressage test. Horse and rider are judged on spins (ie, turns on haunches), stops, sliding stop (when a horse gallops and then is asked to stop: the horse locks up his hind legs, which slide under him and his front legs keep moving). Speed control (a fast large circle moving swiftly to a small slow circle) at the lope, flying changes and the roll-back. All these maneuvers are those used when working cattle, but have been exaggerated a little to create a more spectacular class for even non-horse enthusiasts to watch.

Western Riding The horse is judged on its ability to negotiate a gate, lope over a pole, perform a series of flying changes, stop and roll-back.

Western Trail This is an obstacle course that is not timed but is judged on the way the horse negotiates the obstacles the actual nature of which vary from show to show. The horse must pass through a gate, standing in the gateway so as not to let through any cattle. The rider should be able to hold onto the gate at all times and the horse should move smoothly and fluently. He must negotiate a small bridge, move sideways along poles without touching them and move backwards between poles or a pattern of cones. The rider must be able to don a poncho on horseback. The horse must then trot over or lope over some poles and be able to do a 360° turn within a small square.

Working Cowhorse This is divided into two classes — the reining portion, as described previously, and the cow-work portion. In the cow-work the rider has to contain the cow in the arena at one end for a short time to demonstrate the ability of the horse to "hold" the cow in that area. After a sufficient amount of time, the rider has to take the cow down the fence, making at least one turn each way on the fence. The rider then "takes" the cow into an open space within the arena and circles it at least once in both directions.

There are many more classes but the most spectacular form of western riding is undoubtedly the rodeo. Here you may see racing around three barrels in a clover shape, pole bending, bull-wrestling, calf-roping, heading and heeling, bareback riding and saddle-bronc riding — judged on style of spurring horse in front of cinch, as well as staying on for over eight seconds. There are many rules and regulations for each of the many individual classes. Good competitors can win significant prize money, and or earn points towards qualifying for larger shows or a title.

JUST A RANCH HORSE
The following article is reproduced here in its original form by Jim Jennings, Editor-in-chief of the *Quarter Horse Journal* (May 1995) is reproduced by permission.

"All I want is just an old ranch horse." How many times have you heard that? There was a time when most people used the term "Ranch Horse" to signify a horse that was broke and that would do several things, but was a specialist in none. The theory was that, although you could put a rope on him, he wasn't a trained rope horse. He wasn't a show horse. He wasn't a trail horse. He wasn't a pleasure horse.

How wrong could they have been?

The ranch horse then, as well as today, was one of the most highly trained animals of the breed. The Texas Agricultural Extension Service, in one of its programs, lists some of the requirements of a good ranch horse;

He must be easy to catch, saddle and lead, and he must load and unload willingly. He must also stand hobbled. He must have a soft trot, because it is at that gait that the cowboy most often travels in a pasture of several thousand acres but he must also have a nice lope.

He must have a decent stop, and handle well. He must be able to cut cattle and drive particular animals from a herd, and he must be able to literally push cattle into a squeeze chute for doctoring.

The rider must be able to rope cattle in a pen or a pasture and then drag whatever was roped to a branding crew or into a trailer. The rider must also be able to open and close gates while mounted.

The ranch horse must be able to run fast, and do so when called upon. Then he must settle down immediately to perform slower work.

The ranch horse must be able and willing to cross creeks and rivers where necessary, even if it means swimming, and he must endure obstacles such as brush so thick that light barely permeates it. He must also be able to maneuver in rocky ground without losing his footing.

He must ground-tie, and he must be willing to carry a calf across the saddle if necessary. He must also stand quietly while the rider dons a rain poncho.

The ranch horse must be sound and able to be ridden every day if necessary but he also must be able to be used sparingly (once a week or less), then not have

TOP LEFT: Just an old ranch horse — Quarter Horse parade.

ABOVE LEFT and ABOVE: Training a Quarter Horse.

to be retrained the next time he is called upon.

Finally, the ranch horse must agreeably be corralled with a number of other horses and not cause any problems.

When you look back at this list, it sounds as if the ranch horse meets all the requirements of a good show horse, regardless of the event. That makes it easy to understand why the ranch was where it all started, why Bob Denhardt went to the ranchers when he was trying to organize the American Quarter Horse Association.

"All I want is just an old ranch horse."

Don't we all.

Having read of what is required by "Just a ranch horse," how many times have you heard someone say; "All I want is just a horse to hack out on" What they are really asking by this statement is:

A horse that is easy to catch, to tack up, box and lead, that stands tied up quietly. Is comfortable to ride, forward going but stops easily. A horse good at negotiating gates and other obstacles, such as ditches or water and is sure-footed, sound in wind and limb, a sensible animal of good nature and well behaved in traffic.

So, whether we ride Western or English, we all expect quite a lot more from our horse than either of the two statements, "Just a Ranch Horse" and "Just a Horse to hack out on."

To sum up: Whatever our chosen disciplines there is another quality many of us look for in our horse . . . and that's . . . a friend.

CHAPTER 5

THE HISTORY OF THE HORSE IN AUSTRALIA

Sarah Trangmar

The horse is not indigenous to Australia; however, his remarkable powers of adaptation and resilience and his relationship to humankind have made him an integral part of Australian life since the early days of European settlement. These attributes have also allowed the horse to become established in the wild and now Australia is one of the few countries where wild horses run.

It is thought that the first horses probably arrived with the Spanish and Portuguese explorers in the 16th century, or maybe later with the traders from the Cape of Good Hope landing on the north and northwest shores. Over on the east coast there are signs of horses descended from the Indonesian pony. The first recorded landing of horses in Australia was at 10am on January 20, 1788 with the First Fleet at Botany Bay. On board were one stallion, three mares, one colt and two fillies for the Governor and his family to use.

By 1800 the colony's vital need for harness horses had increased the number to 203. About this time it began to make commercial sense to begin breeding horses rather than importing them and the first stallion for breeding purposes arrived from England in 1802. As settlement extended further, communication and transport — vital to new communities — made the horse an even more necessary part of life. The first stagecoach service began between Sydney, Windsor and Richmond in 1814.

By 1830 Australia's economy was wool-based and in rural areas vast properties were being turned into pasture to sustain the new wool industry. The aboriginal people, with their natural affinity for animals, combined so well with horses that they became renowned as stock men. Stock horses being used to round up sheep are even today synonymous with images of rural Australia. Thus breeding became centered around creating the perfect stock horse.

The Waler, the first Australian breed of horse, created by the need for a strong, agile, stock horse — is famous for its stamina and also for its jumping ability. (In 1940 a Waler claimed the world high-jump record of 8ft 4in — just over 3m.) The Walers' abilities soon were recognized worldwide and breeding reached its peak as they became replacements for the cavalry horses lost in combat.

With the spread of pastoral development, inevitably horses escaped; many of them adapted well to their new environment and became wild. As early as 1830 "bush horses" — Brumbies — could be seen in the hills around Sydney. Furthermore, when gold was discovered and the 'rush' began in 1851, many horse breeders and their clients succumbed to the lure of gold. They abandoned their horses, who soon became feral forming the herds of wild Brumbies. Another influx of domestic horses to the ranks of the Brumbies came when mechanization replaced the need for army remounts and the horses bred for that purpose were simply left to roam free.

Brumbies tend to be smaller, with bigger heads and shorter necks than domestic horses, although many still look very similar thanks to the fairly recent genetic boost from the abandoned army remounts. However, they are considered virtually impossible to break. They can graze up to 31 miles (about 50km) from water and so have quite a marked environmental impact. The Northern Territory alone supports approximately four times the number of wild horses than the USA does. Australia-wide their numbers may be as high as 600,000 head and with a natural increase in population in a good year of 25 percent some controls need to be implemented.

Wrangling Brumbies is a difficult task at the best of times and where the terrain and the remoteness of the region makes horseback wrangling impossible, helicopters are used.

RIGHT: The horse is not indigenous to Australia and was brought to the Antipodes by European explorers. It quickly became indispensable and widespread. It is estimated that there are four times the number of wild horses in Australia than in the USA — 600,000 in total.

THE HORSE TODAY

Horse races have been held sporadically since the early days of European settlement but its development was dogged by failure because of lack of financial resources and quality stock. However, when the Australian Jockey Club was formed, it succeeded at last and horse racing has been one of Australia's best loved sports ever since. Where else would you get a public holiday for a horserace? Each state has its Melbourne Cup equivalent and several states have public holidays for them. Run since the 1870s, the Melbourne Cup is still considered Australia's most prestigious race and is internationally acclaimed.

Steeplechasing is rare because of the concerns over animal welfare but there are a few notable exceptions. Oakbank in South Australia is one of them, held over the Easter weekend; it is a great tradition and thousands flock to the small town in the Adelaide hills to enjoy the annual meet. There are several unusual meetings: one is held on a beach on South Australia's far west coast, but probably the best known are the Birdsville races. Held once a year in midwinter, Birdsville is so remote that there are more planes in the parking lot than cars.

Ever since World War II racehorse breeding has become dynamic and Australian horses are gaining an impressive international reputation. Their speed and stamina is complemented by the resilience and adaptability needed to cope with travelling of thousands of miles between meetings and the range of climatic conditions.

Although racing is the best known, all horse sports are practiced and enjoyed by many Australians: everything from rodeo riding to show jumping and endurance eventing. Trekking the Outback on horse or "Equiteking" is a wonderful way of enjoying this stunning and vast country while getting some feeling of how the first European explorers felt discovering the diversity of this vast land.

LEGENDS OF THE HORSE WORLD

Australians take their love of horses very seriously and some have reached superhero status! Perhaps the most notable of these is Phar Lap. He was a great racehorse and between1928 and 1932 he won 37 of the 51 races he entered. His spirit captured the hearts and imaginations of a public suffering through the throes of the Great Depression. He died in America after winning the Agua Caliente Handicap in Mexico. Although his death was officially registered as acute enteritis, many suspected that he had been poisoned. Phar Lap was preserved and presented to the Museum of Victoria by his owners; he can still be seen there and is the museum's most popular single exhibit.

Today racehorses are still given hero status; Super Impose and Octagonal are two great favorites.

Many of Australia's early poets were famous horsemen and horses are featured strongly in many ballads such as *The Man from Snowy River* by Banjo Paterson. Two of these horseman-poets are Adam Lindsey Gordon and Harry "Breaker" Morant. "Breaker" Morant was nicknamed after his skill and daring as a horse breaker. Adam Lindsey Gordon was known for many exploits on horseback, the crowning glory being his feat of jumping a four-rail fence onto a small ledge of rock 197ft (60m) above Mt. Gambier's Blue Lake.

Horses are still used on the sheep stations, although mechanization has taken over to a large extent. Mounted police are a common and popular sight on their traditional grays and the army still has horses who are a highly applauded part of any parade. Harness horses are still pulling carts for some brewery and dairy companies and their popular appeal keeps this fine tradition going.

BELOW: Trekking through Australia's subtropical forests allows a glimpse of nature one would miss traveling by car.

ABOVE RIGHT: The Australian Outback has strong similarities to the Wild West! Here the everyday job of breaking in a new horse.

BELOW RIGHT: Horses are still used for working cattle, although mechanization is continuing apace.

PART TWO

THE SPORTING HORSE

Today a wide variety of sports and outdoor activities involve horses — from traditional games such as polo through to endurance riding and long-distance trekking.

CHAPTER 6

RACING AND RACEHORSES

Leisa Crook

In March 1996, at Dubai's state-of-the-art Nad al Sheba racetrack, the American-bred horse Cigar claimed victory in the racing world's ultimate challenge — the Dubai World Cup. At stake was the title of World Champion Racehorse and substantial prize money. Cigar and all modern Thoroughbreds throughout the world trace their ancestry in the male line to just three famous Eastern stallions — the Byerley Turk, the Darley Arabian and the Godolphin Arabian, all of which were sent to Britain at the end of the 17th century. Over the next 300 years, through a program of skillful breeding with native stock, a new breed of horse evolved into the masterpiece of strength, beauty, speed and stamina of today's English Thoroughbred.

As the breed was refined, so too the sport of horseracing developed from informal, rule-free races, to sophisticated and complex meetings. The early races at Newmarket, in Suffolk, were run on long courses of about four miles and the horses participating were usually four or five year olds — mature by today's standards. The late 18th century was a time of great change in the pattern of racing in England: two-year-old races were instituted late in the century; the introduction of handicaps, aiming to even the chances of the field, made horse racing a more entertaining betting medium; and most significantly, what became the Classic races were first staged — the St. Leger in 1776, the Oaks in 1779, the Derby in 1780 and the Two Thousand and One Thousand Guineas following in 1809 and 1814, respectively. For many people, these five races, although founded individually, collectively remain the ultimate test of the Thoroughbred.

Early races were practically without rules and corruption was widespread. In an attempt to regularize and control the sport, a Jockey Club was formed in Newmarket in 1750. A self-elected body, with executive powers invested in stewards, the club's influence gradually extended to all racetracks. The early history of the club is dominated by three figures: Sir Charles Bunbury, a founding member and steward, was influential in promoting the authority of the club and improving the speed of the early Thoroughbred by introducing shorter races for younger horses. It was during his regime that the Classics were founded. Lord George Bentinck followed Bunbury as head of the club and it was during his term as its head that numbering of horses, racecards and flag-starting were introduced. The third member of this illustrious trio, Admiral John Henry Rous, was responsible for the introduction of handicapping and his basic scales and calculations remain in use today.

The club remained racing's governing authority until 1993, when the British Horseracing Board was set up, leaving the club to administer such matters as discipline and the Rules of Racing. Financial control now rests in the hands of the Horserace Betting Levy Board and the day-to-day administration is carried out by the family firm of Wetherby which was founded in 1773.

The important functions of control, administration and finance provide racing with a structure which enables the competitive side of the sport to be carefully designed and controlled. In flat racing the key element is the Pattern, which includes the Classics.

The introduction of the Pattern has been one of modern racing's most important progressions. Set up in 1960 in response to concern about lack of balance in French and British racing, the Pattern of Racing Committee aimed to provide a complete system of tests for the best horses of all ages over all distances. Thus, the Pattern races or group races have become the elite contests of flat racing — together they give the season its carefully constructed form, ensuring top-class and competitive racing on a Europe-wide scale.

The refined system was implemented in 1971 with the Pattern races divided into three groups: Group One comprises the Classics and other races of major international importance; Group Two is comprised of races of international importance but at a level just below championship standard; Group Three covers domestic races regarded as preparatory contests for the higher groups.

The development of horse racing has followed a similar pattern around the world. In North America, the fledgling sport began as Quarter Horse racing, so named because it took place on rough, quarter-mile strips cleared in forest. This sport enjoyed a short popularity — but left a direct legacy: Quarter Horses today are still the fastest over a two-furlong (400m) gallop. Thoroughbred racing did not gain many adherents until after the Revolutionary War , when many influential stud horses were imported from Britain. The Civil War had a catastrophic effect on racing and breeding in the southern states but development continued in the north. New York became a major racing center, as did the mid and far west, and the border states of Maryland and Kentucky.

Just as England has its Classics, so too does the US and they all came into being in the years after the Civil War. First, in 1867, came the Belmont Stakes named after leading owner and breeder of the day, August Belmont. Since 1905, the stakes has been raced at Belmont Park, New York, over 1½ miles (2.4km). Six years later, in 1873, the Preakness Stakes was established on the Pimlico course near Baltimore, Maryland. It is run over 1 mile 1½ furlongs (1.9km). In 1875 the first Kentucky Derby was held, over 1¼ miles (2km), at Churchill Downs, Louisville, Kentucky. These three races, run by three-year olds on dirt in the early part of the season, constitute the American "Triple Crown" and remain the backbone of the American racing year.

In America, as in Britain, the sport suffered early setbacks due to unscrupulous participants and fell

ABOVE: No longer just the sport of kings, horse racing has broadened its appeal and today thousands of fans enjoy ownership through syndicates, clubs and commercial companies. It supports a huge industry — breeding, stabling, training, racing and betting — and is practiced the world over, as here in Buenos Aires.

BELOW: All the Thoroughbreds of today — in other words the racehorses which run day in, day out worldwide — descend from just three stallions: the Byerley Turk, the Darley Arabian and the Godolphin Arabian (pictured here).

from public favor for a time. Measures such as the establishment of the American version of the Jockey Club did little to raise the standards in the eyes of the public and racing declined to the point where bookmakers were prohibited, as legislators bowed to the pressure from "reform" groups. However, when the French system of totalisator wagering (in the US "pari-mutuel betting") was introduced, whereby the odds or dividends are decided in direct relation to the amounts staked on each horse, legislators saw in it an easy form of tax gathering and so the future of racing was ensured. With the Jockey Club exercising overall control and guidance, interest slowly resurged to the point where it is now the US's biggest spectator sport.

The main breeding area is concentrated around the Lexington area of Kentucky. The nearby Keeneland sales annually offer the highest quality bloodstock in the world. The inauguration of the Breeder's Cup program in 1984 changed the face of world flat racing by staging one of the richest day's racing in the world. Breeder's Cup Day in late October or early November (the timing and venue change from year to year) now offers an extremely valuable end-of-season target to the world's best horses. The brainchild of one of Kentucky's most famous breeders, John Gaines, its principal aim was to prevent the decline of racing in America by establishing an event of prime importance on the international racing calendar.

In Europe and the US, flat racing takes place year-round, on oval dirt or grass tracks, and the season runs from January 1 to December 31. During the winter in Britain and Ireland, National Hunt racing, staged over fences and hurdles, also operates, attracting almost as large a following as flat racing in these countries. However, jump racing does not support as large a breeding industry as that of flat racing and, although some horses are bred with jump racing in mind, the majority are those that have proved unsuitable for flat racing or are past their prime.

Jump races take place over fences of birch or gorse (steeplechase) or hurdles, are longer (minimum two miles or 3,200m) and contested by older animals. Hunting is the direct ancestor of steeplechasing and the first half of the 19th century saw a gradual division of the sport, one half retaining the essentially amateur hunting-based element which was to become the foundation of point-to-pointing and the other more professional, with jumping races on regular public courses over hurdles and fences. The year 1839 saw the first running of the world's greatest steeplechase, the Grand National at Aintree, near Liverpool.

In flat racing, jockeys and trainers are licensed professionals and amateurs cannot compete in the same race. But the amateur rider is strongly represented in the jumping game and in National Hunt races professional and amateur jockeys may compete side-by-side.

In point-to-pointing, the professional rider is prohibited. Originally started by hunting people as an end-of-season gathering where sportsmen raced their hunters against one another across natural countryside, point-to-pointing gradually became a focal point in the Hunt calendar and the social aspect gained prominence. The point-to-point aspect gave way to a start and finish located at the same spot and courses gradually evolved into the round, oval or triangular shapes that they are today.

In Britain today there are 59 racetracks staging over 1,000 events annually. Some courses, such as Newmarket, offer flat races exclusivel; others, such as Cheltenham, stage jump races only, while many promote both. Today, Thoroughbred racing takes place in about 50 countries; some of the more important racing and breeding centers outside Britain and the United States include France, Italy, Australia, New Zealand and Japan. Prize money remains the incentive in all countries other than those where racing is totally state-run. The money directly affects the quality of the horses, the level of entertainment offered to the public and the prosperity of the supporting breeding industry. Betting, through the percentage deducted from pari-mutuels (totalisators), provides a large assured income where machine betting has a monopoly. Racetracks receive fixed amounts according to their grading and also put up money. Owners contribute their own prizes by way of entry fees and stakes and over a quarter of the total is provided by sponsors.

The development of modern air transport has enabled the increase in international competition and,

ABOVE and RIGHT: Each April Newmarket hosts two of England's five Classic races, both over a one-mile course named after King Charles II's favorite horse — the Rowley Mile. While not the oldest of the Classics (that honor falls to Doncaster's St. Leger which was established in 1778; the Derby and Oaks date from 1779) the 2,000 Guineas, for colts, was established in 1809 and the 1,000 Guineas, for fillies, in 1814.

more recently, international breeding has seen further progress made in the world of horse racing. Early racing was known as the "sport of kings" due, in part, to the high cost of keeping and training horses.

Today, modern rules and regulations have made the sport more accessible to a much wider variety of people and income brackets. Regulations have enabled many thousands of racing fans to enjoy ownership through syndicates, clubs and commercial companies, although ownership of the very best racehorses is still exclusively dominated by a handful of extremely wealthy people, who own large strings of horses around the world. However, with the basic training fees per horse set at about $300 (£150) per week, a fee which excludes charges to the farrier, transportation costs, vet bills, jockey fees, insurance premiums and registration fees, the chances of making a profit are remote. In very round numbers, it can cost about $20,000 (£10,000) per year to keep a horse in training, so it still seems that any person considering ownership or part ownership of a Thoroughbred would do so out of genuine love for racehorses or the sport of racing.

LEFT: There are classic races all over the world today: the Prix de l'Arc at Longchamps in Paris, the Kentucky Derby in Louisville but it is oil-rich Dubai that now holds the racing world's highest prize money race — the Dubai World Cup.

BELOW: To many, however, the most important race meet in the calendar will always be the four days in June when a small English town hosts a glittering pageant of costume and color at a course established at the start of the 18th century by Queen Anne: Royal Ascot.

RIGHT: For most of the world, horse racing is run on the flat; in Europe there's a winter season when steeplechasing takes place. A direct relation of hunting, racing "over the sticks" is not as well patronized as the flat: it doesn't have the same breeding program, for example. But it does have some exceptional races like the Maryland Hunt Cup and the Aintree-based Grand National.

CHAPTER 7

HUNTING

Frances Nunn

Man has hunted using horse and hounds since antiquity. Although the ancient civilizations of Greece, China and Egypt hunted mainly on foot when using hounds, we know they also used horses for the chase from classical authors like Xenophon and Oppian, who described the attributes that a hunt horse should possess: namely, obedience, stamina and substance. Hunters still need these but the hunting horse of today is a far cry from those of yesteryear.

Hounds, horses and the hunt itself have evolved together over the years as their purpose has changed. Initially, the primary purpose for the hunt was either a search for an aggressive local predator — bear, lion or leopard depending on the locality — or a search for food, albeit often a pleasurable and sporting one. Whole tracts of land were given over to hunting with hounds or hawks, and it was very much the occupation of the ruling classes: prince and baron. Carried out in forests — from the latin *foris* meaning not necessarily a heavily wooded area but an uncultivated tract of land, including heathland, set aside for hunting — the main game was the deer, although wild boar and other woodland animals figured too. It was a dangerous sport: William the Conquerer's son William Rufus was killed by an arrow in a hunting accident, as were brother Rufus's uncle and nephew in separate, almost identical circumstances.

In Britain, from the 17th century onward, reduction in wooded areas, the enclosure of fields and the introduction of accurate firearms reduced forest-based hunting. British landowners took to foxhunting — again, primarily for sport but also because it rid the countryside of a nuisance to their flocks. This sport would set the pattern for hunting in other continents, in particular in Australia, India and the US.

The foxhunting horses and hounds had to have physical attributes and abilities very different from the hunting horses of the past to match the speed and ability of the quarry, as well as to meet the challenge of new landscapes punctuated with a proliferation of fences and hedges. They had to have good speed — particularly over the vast tracts of grazing land in the English shires — coupled with the stamina and agility needed to cope with a range of obstacles — everything from open ditches to stone walls and wooden fences. Soon it became apparent that the existing horse stock was not sufficiently fit or strong to survive the rigors of a day's hunting. While this could be bypassed by using more than one mount, it was obvious that breeding and fitness were the keys — as they were in horse racing which was also developing at the same time. As in racing, Thoroughbreds were used to inject quality into the bloodlines and, even in a world where personal transport had been dominated by the horse for millenia, top-class hunters began to command huge sums of money.

In 1885 the Hunters' Improvement and National Light Horse Breeding Society — HIS — was founded to encourage breeding in Britain: it still provides an indispensable service, distributing each year premiums to stallions selected at the annual show, held in Newmarket in the spring. Today Britain and Ireland have well-established hunter-breeding industries. Foxhunting — like fur coats — may have gained a level of modern urban-dwellers' opprobrium but the hunt is still here and the hunter is still sought after all over the world for his enduring qualities.

From the end of the 19th century, as organized sports began to develop, a range of equine sports based on hunting were instituted. They were picked up worldwide, something emphasized by the inclusion of show jumping in the 1900 Olympic Games at Paris. Endurance racing, National Hunt racing, point-to-pointing, three-day eventing and, of course, show jumping — owe their existence to the hunt. British hunters, helped by the HIS, have produced fine winners in all disciplines.

In England, the great county shows and events such as the Royal International and Horse of the Year, are venues for the show hunter classes. Despite prize money being much lower than for show jumping, these events are highly competitive.

ABOVE RIGHT: Hunting in England's New Forest.

BELOW RIGHT: There are a number of hunts in North America: this is the London Hunt in Canada.

GOING HUNTING

Riding with the hunt — like back-country skiing — is an invigorating and satisfying experience, and not overly dangerous as long as the practicalities are understood. It is an immensely popular sport for this reason, because of the unexpected terrain, the riding technique required and the thrill of the chase. Most horses, too, enjoy hunting and the proximity of other horses, the pleasure of open country instead of the usual field, the excitement of the gallop — but not all of them. Some, particularly those that are too young or not in good enough condition, can be ruined by hunting. Added to this, you will definitely not enjoy yourself if your horse doesn't behave, if it pulls too much, kicks or is badly behaved. You may tolerate bad manners in your horse when you are by yourself (although it is definitely not a good idea to do so), but you will spoil your day — and other people's — if you are not courteous while hunting; indeed, if you are a nuisance you may be sent home. Most horses, if they have been worked in the summer, will be fairly fit — and this is good preparation for the hunting season. It may not, however, be enough and it's sensible to increase his workload to get his fitness and breathing right.

Until you gain experience, it's best to be cautious; ride economically, take the easiest route, don't jump unless you have to — there will be plenty of opportu- nities and excitements in the course of a day without pushing too early and blowing your mount. Look for a reliable person to follow, but be careful that you don't get into trouble by doing so: your model and their horse may well be accomplished jumpers and your horse may try to emulate his leader. Whatever you do, watch the hounds: they rarely run in a straight line, often split and get in your path.

Clothing is important, as is tack. The hunt staff usu- ally wear red, carry whips and the huntsman will carry a horn. You should wear sturdy boots, good gloves, warm underclothing (tights for both sexes are sensi- ble!), a black coat or tweed jacket and a black hunt cap. Your clothes, like the horse's tack, must be well fitting to avoid chafing. It is sensible to clip your horse, who could otherwise overheat — but be careful he doesn't get cold after the day's sport.

To gain experience, or simply if you don't fancy hunting, join the cub hunters or go drag hunting. This sport is very popular in Europe; it involves the hounds chasing a pre-set trail, usually aniseed, over a two- hour course and is often heavy on the jumping. It can certainly reduce problems with crops and local landowners and has much to recommend it.

BELOW and RIGHT: Oscar Wilde's famous quip ("The English country gentleman galloping after a fox — the unspeakable in full pursuit of the uneatable") may have found more favor in recent times, but the sight and sound of the hunt is still quite a spectacle: Belvoir, England, 1992.

CHAPTER 8

SHOW JUMPING

Sandra Forty

In the show jumping arena all the excitement and color of the horse world is compressed into one intensive, highly charged occasion. The biggest competitions, such as the Olympics and the Horse of the Year show, are televised around the world for a viewing audience of many millions. As each competition reaches its climax the audience plays a bigger and bigger part — the excitement mounts, until in the very final stages you could hear a pin drop as the audience holds its collective breath as rider and horse risk all to complete a clear round.

Both rider and horse have to be supreme athletes, and, of course, they have to have a special rapport to achieve honors at the highest level. Show jumping is a highly stylized competition where the best horses and riders compete against each other and the clock to produce a perfect round. Huge amounts of money are awarded as prizes as well as unbeatable equestrian prestige. Yet its origins are far away from all this.

Show jumping developed out of hunting when horses had to be able to jump over a variety of obstacles in the course of a day's riding. As with so much to do with horses, it seems that the Irish were the first to develop a form of show jumping which appeared as a leaping competition at the Royal Dublin Society's annual show in 1865. More-or-less simultaneously in Russia and France other jumping-type competitions were started. Eleven years later jumping came officially to London for the first time at the Agricultural Hall in Islington, although leaping competitions were by then regularly held at local agricultural shows. Interestingly, right from the start style was an important element decided by judges.

By 1900 horse jumping was truly international; in the Olympic Games in Paris that year three jumping events were held — Long Jump, High Jump and Prize Jumping. However the first known official international "show jumping" took place in Turin the following year between German and Italian army officers. The first International Horse Show was held in London at Olympia in 1907 with not inconsiderable prize money for the time. Competitors from all over Europe and the United States took part in the high and wide jumping, but the Belgians and Dutch between them divided up the main spoils.

Despite all this at the turn of the century, equestrian sports were not an established part of the Olympic games. However, the founder of the modern games, Baron Pierre de Coubertin, gave them his tacit blessing and events were included in the 1908 London games only to be dropped at the last minute because there were too many entrants — 88 competitors from eight countries! The next Olympic games, held in Stockholm in 1912, were organized better and produced three equestrian events — dressage, the Military (three-day event) and show jumping.

In November 1921 the Federation Equestre Internationale (FEI) was founded in Paris, primarily by Sweden and France, but with the participation of Belgium, Italy, Denmark, Japan, Norway and the United States. Germany became affiliated the following year but Britain didn't join until 1926. The FEI set about regulating all matters equestrian, particularly in relation to competitive sports. Their first real showcase was the Paris Olympics of 1924 where they delineated the rules under which equestrian events were held. Seventeen countries contested the games by sending 99 riders on 110 horses. A year before the Olympics, in 1923, under the presidency of Lord Lonsdale, the British Show Jumping Association was founded with the intention of getting a grip on the enthusiastic but chaotic show jumping situation in Britain, which badly needed regulation of courses, riders and judges.

Until after World War II show jumping was not a timed event; riders were allowed to go at their own pace to assess and balance themselves and their horses before actually committing themselves to each jump. Consequently rounds could take a considerable length of time and were only of interest to the cognoscenti. To compound matters, show jumping courses were uninteresting, with just a row of upright jumps along each side of the ring and either a large spread or water jump in the center. It took some years to sort out the scoring system which initially was so complicated that at some shows every fence had its own judge!

Col. Sir Michael Ansell, chairman of the British Show Jumping Association, was only too well aware of the problems and determined to change all this. With the support of the association he developed a grading system which allocated prize money, with the idea that horses of roughly equal ability could compete fairly against each other. Then, after some searching, White City in London was chosen as the venue; it was an inspired choice, proving so successful that it became the spiritual home of British show jumping.

As show jumping developed as a competitive sport it became more regulated; in 1948 the FEI held the first official championships for Juniors — riders between the ages of 14 and 18. Then, in Paris in 1953, the first World Championship was won by a Spaniard.

LEFT: Jus de Pommes ridden by Ulrich Kirchhoff at Atlanta. Tragically, the horse died shortly after the Olympics.

TOP: Sarah Bowen and Yorkshire Gent at the Hickstead Derby.

ABOVE: Trevor Coyle and Cruising at Dublin in 1995.

BELOW: John Whittaker on Granansoth.

Initially held annually, by 1955, it was decided to hold it every four years. At this time both professionals and amateurs were allowed to enter all FEI events, but women were excluded. The Men's European Championships were initiated to be held every two years. In 1957 a European Championship for women was introduced. These two events were amalgamated in 1975; since then men and women have competed together equally when under FEI jurisdiction.

However, women were not admitted to Olympic show jumping until the Stockholm Olympics in 1956 but they were still unable to compete with the men until 1975. Also in 1956, the FEI started the European Amateur Championship and then to encourage team spirit in an essentially individual sport, they started the President's Cup in 1965. This has proved a success despite the vast distances some teams have to travel.

COMPETITIONS

The object in a show jumping competition is for a horse and rider to jump successfully without dislodging or disturbing any part of a series of jumps and obstacles, refusing a jump or taking the fences in the wrong order, all of which incurs penalties and sometimes disqualification. The winner is the pairing which successfully completes a clear round — ie, without faults. Should more than one pair do this successfully, the obstacles are changed and the jump-off has to take place within a given time. The ultimate winner is the one who completes the course within the quickest time with the least number of faults.

All this is helped if the horse is an exhibitionist who responds to the noisy crowd, rather than a timid animal who needs coaxing. The horses tend to be between 15.3hh and 16.3hh (5ft 3in–5ft 7in), although slightly larger or smaller horses compete successfully. A small horse can have difficulty negotiating the larger spreads and higher jumps, while the bigger horse might not be maneuverable enough to make tight turns.

The show jumping arena varies somewhat in size with a course designed to test both horse and rider. But the fences are always designed around the standard measurement of an average horse's stride with fences are at least 60ft (18m) apart. The horse sometimes has to turn within its own length, stop dead, collect itself and then take off again. The most basic jumps are just upright poles such as parallels and the wall. Other obstacles, such as the water jump, test the stride and attention of the horse. Then there are fences designed to intimidate with their spread and complexity. The double and treble combinations are one or two paces apart and call for determined skill from both horse and rider. They are always major features in any show jumping event.

LEFT: *Olympic pairing Korskinsky and Eros jump for the USA.*

TOP and ABOVE: *More views from Atlanta — the arena with the show jumping competition in full swing; and Nick Skelton jumping a replica of Mt. Rushmore on Showtime.*

BELOW: *Kilbaha at Hickstead, 1996.*

CHAPTER 9

DRESSAGE

Annette Sanderson

Dressage as a competitive sport was only developed in Europe in the early years of this century. First included in the Olympic Games in Stockholm in 1912, it is now a fast growing sport in most countries as more and more riders discover the fascination of mastering the techniques that enable them to train their horses and be in harmony with them.

The horse is naturally a well-balanced quadruped, who can spring into a headlong run, turn quickly or stop within his own length without outside assistance. Why do we need to write books on the subject or to expend a lot of time and effort teaching him how to do these simple maneuvers? It all stems from the fact that horse riding is the invention of man and that the horse was not specifically designed to carry a rider. When the young horse first accepts the weight of a man on his back, he has to brace himself to counteract the enormous and unexpected shift in his own center of gravity. If he is unlucky, he will have to find his own way of coping; if he is lucky, his trainer skillfully will help him to adjust by teaching him how to use himself so that he can carry his burden painlessly and gracefully — he will school him and give him back his natural balance.

The schooling of the horse intended for dressage follows a systematic progression from the early stages of working in a relaxed outline to the extreme collection of the Grand Prix horse. The training is the most important factor in the success of any dressage horse and rider. The other factors are the choice of horse and the rider's ability and dedication.

Choosing a horse for dressage is as easy or as difficult as one's ambition. For the lower levels, an honest riding club horse should do very well and some small faults may even be overlooked — for example, a horse that has a slight breathing defect could be perfectly suitable for dressage, as he will not have to perform at speed for any length of time. If the rider is inexperienced, he has to decide whether he wants to buy a "schoolmaster," which can give him the feel of what he is aiming for, or whether he wants to progress more slowly and carefully by sharing the learning process with a relatively green horse.

The horse's conformation is important because it is easier for a well-proportioned horse to be supple and balanced. He should not be too heavy in front; his head should be set at such an angle that he will not it find uncomfortable to work in a correct outline. The neck should be reasonably long and come out of the shoulders neither too low nor too high. The shoulders should be sloping, the back strong and well-muscled, particularly over the loins, and the croup should be neither short nor flat. The hind legs should not be too straight nor the front legs show any obvious weaknesses such as being back at the knee.

The paces of the horse will markedly influence his value. The way a horse moves can be improved to a certain extent with training, but there is no substitute for natural athleticism. A good ground-covering walk is the first quality to look for as it normally reflects the other paces. An elastic trot with a clear moment of suspension and a light and rhythmic canter will complete a promising picture.

The temperament of the dressage horse is equally important. If he is nervous he will find it very difficult to settle enough to give of his best in the dressage arena. A lazy horse will be forever in danger of "dying" on his rider. On the other hand, a placid horse can be a great comfort to a rider who is a bundle of nerves!

It is really the combination of the horse's and the rider's temperaments which must be looked at carefully. The nervous horse may become a superlative performer with a calm rider who gives him confidence. The "lunatic" can display tremendous impulsion when his excess energy has been channeled successfully. The attitude of the dressage horse to his work can also depend on many factors — from his conformation to his willingness to please humans, which could be a direct consequence of his earliest experiences.

The breeds favored for dressage have changed with the riding styles of various periods. The Renaissance riders who wanted their horses to show tremendous collection, favoured Andalusians, whose paces are more rounded and lighter, while nowadays we sometimes see big horses capable of impressive extensions but whose riders look as if they are carrying them. The

RIGHT: The French rider Margit Otto-Crepin on Lucky Lord at the 1996 Olympic Games in Atlanta.

Warmblood, particularly Dutch and German, commands big prices and does very well in competitions. The Thoroughbred, with his longish frame and volatile temperament, needs a skillful rider to show at his best. The present trend is towards a Warmblood with enough Thoroughbred in his make-up to lighten his heavy frame and give him more quality.

The rider who wants to practice dressage needs first to become proficient by having regular lessons and so develop an independent and effective seat and learn how to apply the aids accurately and lightly. The best way to acquire a deep correct seat is to be lunged on a dependable horse by a good instructor. The rider can concentrate on his position without having to worry about the horse. This is the way the Spanish Riding School riders are taught. The aim is to be able to keep the legs under the center of gravity while balancing on the seat bones. The upper body absorbs the movements of the horse and the rider remains relaxed and in balance throughout. Constant practice will be necessary to achieve the required awareness and control of the muscles. Various techniques of inner visualization — as used by a number of top sportsmen and women — can help with this process. Impartial watching of a video of yourself on the horse will also help you to spot your weak points.

The rider needs to learn how to apply the aids — the means he uses to communicate with his horse. These aids should be clearly understood by the horse but nearly invisible to the onlooker. The natural aids are seat, legs, hands and voice — but note that use of the voice is not permitted during a dressage test. The artificial aids are the dressage whip and the spurs, which should only be worn when the rider is able to use leg aids without touching the horse with them.

A suitable area must be found to train the horse. Competitions are held in arenas 65.5x131ft (20x40m) or 131x197ft (40x60m) — the International Equestrian Federation size. The surface can be grass or a variety of specially chosen materials such as sand or chopped rubber. If no arena is available, it is important to choose a schooling area which is as level as possible and where the surface will not be poached, hard or very deep. When the site has been selected, around the perimeter are placed markers bearing the conventional letters used as points of reference for the various school movements. Their origin is obscure and their sequence without apparent logic, causing many a headache to aspiring dressage riders!

The horse's equipment consists of a saddle with fairly straight-cut panels to enable the rider to sit with a long, relatively straight leg. A general-purpose saddle can be used at the beginning, but a dressage saddle will help develop and maintain a good position. The bits allowed in competition are the snaffle and, for more collected work, the double bridle, which consists

of a snaffle, bridoon and "weymouth" — an unjointed bit with cheeks and a curb-chain. It is inadvisable to train in a bit with a markedly different action from that of the bits allowed. The bit must be the right size, suit the conformation of the horse's mouth and be carefully adjusted.

A drop-noseband or a flash-noseband are often used in conjunction with the snaffle, and a plain cavesson noseband is mandatory with a double bridle. In training it is advisable to put leg protection on the horse as he may knock himself, particularly if he becomes unbalanced or is learning lateral work. Various gadgets such as the Chambon are sometimes used to try and overcome a training problem, but they have to be used with discrimination and skill.

The rider's equipment is basically the same as that used for general riding: a hat up to current safety standards, breeches or jodhpurs, and a pair of long riding boots. Because gloves are compulsory in competition, it is a good idea to get used to wearing them even if they are not necessary. A schooling whip should not be too flexible since it will flap and may flick the horse unintentionally. It should be long enough for the tip to

touch the horse without having to alter the position of your hand beyond a slight turn of the wrist.

The training of the horse needs to be planned carefully but the timing has to be flexible. Neither the rider nor the horse will always be fit and keen to work and problems may arise which will necessitate rethinking and sometimes a return to basics. Each schooling session will consist of three sections. First is the warm-up period, to increase the bloodflow to the muscles and loosen them. This is the time when the rider will become aware of how the horse feels: is he very fresh or stiff from a previous training session? The horse will also react to his rider's mood. The rider needs to be relaxed, to correct his position and to decide how to conduct the rest of the session.

When the horse is moving freely and calmly, the second section, that of actual work, can be started by reminding the horse of what he has done in previous lessons then building on it by introducing new exercises. The session should end on a good note even if it means going back to a less advanced movement the horse can do really well. Finally, he will need to be cooled off by letting him relax until he is walking on a loose rein. It is important to end on a good note for two reasons — the horse will remember the lesson with pleasure and so will be more willing to work next

ABOVE LEFT and ABOVE: Isabell Werth and Gigolo represented Germany at the 1996 Olympic Games and took the gold medal.

BELOW: Another German rider, Nicole Uphoff-Becker on Rembrant at Atlanta.

time. Stopping work is a reward and the horse should not feel he is being rewarded for an inadequate performance. As well as stopping on a good note, it is also a good idea to give the horse a change of routine once in a while to avoid becoming stale. Hacking, going out in the field, being led in hand or going over some jumps will refresh the horse. It is possible to school during a hack and the increased impulsion that usually comes with the greater freedom can be helpful in achieving some movements.

To be able to teach the horse well, it is necessary to understand how he moves and, eventually, to be aware of what each leg is doing at any given moment in order to time the aids accurately. The gaits are the walk, the trot and the canter (a horse doing dressage does not gallop, at least not with his rider's consent).

The walk is a four-time pace which means that the four feet can be heard hitting the ground separately. The trot is a two-time pace: the horse moves one front foot and the diagonally opposite hind foot together, then the other front foot and hind foot. As he jumps from one diagonal to the other he leaves a moment of suspension between each hoofbeat. The rider can remain seated or can rise on alternate beats so that he rises every time the right shoulder moves forward, for instance. To build up his horse's muscles evenly he must regularly change the diagonal he rises and sits with. The canter is a three-time pace where one diagonal pair of legs moves together and the other two legs move separately. There is a moment of suspension between each stride. The horse is said to be in "right canter" when the right foreleg is leading and in "left canter" when the left foreleg is leading. The transition into canter is called the "strike-off."

For dressage, the rider must work on the quality of the paces and gradually improve the balance of the horse so that he becomes capable of carrying more and more of his weight on his hindquarters. This is called collection and it takes several years of training to achieve this to a high degree.

In the first stages of training after the breaking-in period, the horse will be asked to move in a natural "free" walk, a "working" trot and a "working" canter. The paces will not be hurried, yet will show a good activity. The outline will be round with a slight, but steady, rein contact. As the horse becomes more balanced and supple and develops greater engagement of his hind legs, he will become able to cover more ground without altering his rhythm and to develop "medium" paces. A still greater engagement of the hind legs will lead to "collection." The "extended" paces will result from a lengthening of the whole horse's frame without loss of balance. In extended trot, the moment of suspension is prolonged and some horses appear to hardly touch the ground at all.

The outline of the horse's body is very important in dressage. The horse must be "round" and "on the bit." When seen in profile, the top line from poll to croup must give an impression of convexity: the hind legs step well under the body, rounding and lowering the croup, the back muscles support the rider easily (not sagging under his weight), and the neck rises in a more or less pronounced curve to the poll, with the head held near the vertical. The whole horse looks as if he is going "uphill." In this position, the bit is held lightly and softly by the horse's relaxed jaw.

The gradual training of the horse is going to be achieved by practicing transitions and school movements of increasing difficulty. Each supples the horse further and leads to increased collection.

Transitions are changes from one gait to another or between working, medium, collected and extended paces. The transitions can be greatly improved by making sure the horse is balanced before asking for them. This is achieved by the use of the "half-halt" which is a brief check that lasts only one stride and can be practiced at any pace. It also prepares the horse before any school movement. From the simple transitions between walk, trot and canter, the horse will gradually learn to go from trot to halt, halt to trot, walk to canter and canter to walk. Work at the canter will include changes of rein, at first by going back to trot for a few steps, then later by executing a flying change of leg. When the halt is balanced, the horse can be taught the rein-back which, like the trot, involves the legs moving diagonally.

As the training progresses, the horse's rhythm, balance and impulsion should improve until a feeling of softness and elasticity combined with power and athleticism can be felt and seen. When the horse can remain balanced throughout all his work, he is said to be in "self-carriage." The school movements will aim at bringing this about, and also at making the horse supple and straight in his body.

The basic school movements are circles, half circles and serpentines. They can be ridden at all paces and their severity is directly related to how small they are. A young horse should start with gentle turns and very large circles to avoid damage to the limbs. The serpentine can be taught from shallow loops. When riding loops or serpentines in canter, the horse will find himself on the "wrong" leg on half the bends. This is called "counter-canter" and is a movement required in the more advanced tests; it prepares the horse for the flying change of leg at the canter.

Collection and suppleness are also increased by "lateral work." So far, the horse has been moving his hind legs directly behind his forelegs. In lateral work,

RIGHT: Another 1996 Olympic Games view — Robert Dover on Metallic. American riders and horses consistently do well at this difficult discipline.

he moves sideways as well as forward, and the prints left by his hind legs are more or less to the side of those left by his front legs.

The turn on the forelegs is accomplished by making the horse move his hindquarters in a semicircle around his forehand. This teaches him to move sideways away from the rider's leg. The next stage is called leg-yielding, where the horse moves sideways and forward but does not need to be bent or collected. Shoulder-in is similar but requires more bend and is one of the most important exercises in dressage training. Travers, half-pass and renvers are lateral movements in which the horse is bent in the direction in which he is travelling.

The half-pirouette is a 180° turn where the horse moves his forehand in a half-circle around his hindquarters. If performed at the walk, it is called a "turn on the haunches."

When the horse has completed his elementary training, he can be taught the more advanced movements. The zigzag in canter, flying changes in sequence up to changes of leg at every stride, the piaffe and passage. The piaffe is a springy cadenced trot performed on the spot and the passage could be described as a forward piaffe, where the horse moves in very short strides with a pronounced moment of suspension. The passage and piaffe, and the transitions from one to the other, are the ultimate in collection, submission and obedience.

The dressage competitions or tests are divided into several categories to suit the level of training of the horses taking part. The six standards are Preliminary, Novice, Elementary, Medium, Advanced Medium and Advanced. The competitions can be Unaffiliated or Affiliated. In Great Britain, the British Horse Society Dressage Group's Affiliated competitions make up a graduated system. A horse placed in a test earns points and progresses up to more advanced levels. For instance, when a horse has earned 50 points, he stops being a Novice and is graded Elementary.

International competitions are organized by the FEI (International Equestrian Federation) and are the Prix St. George, the Intermediaire I and II, and the Grand Prix and Grand Prix Special. A relatively new development is performing dressage to music and there are now freestyle tests to music from Novice standard to Grand Prix level. A given number of appropriate movements have to be incorporated into a program of music chosen by the rider. This has proved extremely popular with spectators and has contributed to the increased interest in dressage shown by the general public.

Finally, before actually going to a competition, make absolutely sure you have read the rules and that your horse's equipment and your own conform to them. If you are going to compete in a grass arena, which may be slippery, it would be worth asking the

ABOVE: Gira Capelman on Cyprys.

farrier to fit stud holes in the shoes. When you enter a class, you will receive a copy of the test. Learn it, but do not practice it on the horse from start to finish more than a few times or he will start anticipating your aids. Practice the various movements during the course of your schooling sessions and learn the correct sequence by doing the test on foot or "thinking" yourself through it when you have a few spare moments to concentrate during the day.

For the test, both you and your horse need to be turned out neatly and correctly. Arrive in plenty of time (at least one hour before the test) so that you do not have to rush your preparations and can remain relaxed. Report to the secretary and get your number if necessary, check that the time of your test has not been changed and in which arena your test is. Find out where you can warm up and, if you have time, go and watch one or two other competitors to remind yourself of the test and see how the arena rides before tacking up your horse and warming him up.

With experience, you will work out what warm-up routine is best for your particular horse. You need to relax him then to get him to concentrate on you and on the aids, practicing the movements of the test. Do

ABOVE: David O'Connor and Lightfoot in the Dressage event at Badminton in 1996.

BELOW: A dressage saddle has a straight flap and a more pronounced dip in the middle than the usual saddle. This allows the rider to sit deeply and show a long leg. It's interesting to note the differences between this specialised saddle and the western one on page 27.

not try anything new which might confuse the horse. Keep an eye on your class and give yourself a few minutes to remove boots or bandages before you start. You are allowed a short preparation time between the end of the previous test and the start of your own, when you can ride around the arena. Show your number or give your name to the "writer" who sits by the side of the judge and only enter the arena after you have heard the signal to start. If you are worried that you may forget your test you can get somebody to "read" it for you at most competitions. When you have finished, praise your horse and leave quietly: you are still under the judge's eye!

After the competition, cool your horse, make him comfortable and get him ready for the return journey. By then your mark will probably be on the score board and, if you wait until the class is over, you will be able to collect your sheet with the judge's marks and comments. Treat this constructively to learn how you can improve your performance. A test is never perfect but enjoy the good parts: with time and application, they will become more and more frequent.

CHAPTER 10

EVENTING

Frances Nunn

The equine sport known as "Eventing" is a complete test of all-round ability and the "Three-Day Event" is the supreme test of a horse and rider, testing obedience and physique through dressage, stamina and speed through the cross-country course and precision jumping through the show jumping course.

Many ridden sports stem from hunting or from the army, and eventing is no exception. Its origins are in the training of hunters, in the military equitation of the classical school as practiced all over Europe and in the trials of cavalry horses, which tested the character, fitness and ability of chargers and their riders. On campaign they had to be able to cover long distances at a good speed; they had to be able to tackle many obstacles and hazards. The horse and rider had to act as a team in battle: and the next day they had to be able to get up and do it all over again.

It was the advent of the modern Olympic Games which gave birth to international competition. As might be expected, the first competitors for the equestrian events were military men, but over the years civilians and women began to take part. The Three-Day Event was known as the *Concors Complet* (complete competition) and as the army mechanized so military competitors have dwindled. Between the wars the Concors Complet took on the form in which we know it today:

DAY 1: DRESSAGE

A set program of some 20 different movements of a medium difficulty, it is performed in walk, trot and canter, in an arena. Marks are allotted by a panel of judges who assess fluency, accuracy, obedience to the rider's aids, balance, rhythm and impulsion, as well as the rider's seat and riding ability.

DAY 2: CROSS-COUNTRY

A four-phase test consisting of two phases held over roads and tracks totaling 6–12 miles (10–20km) to be ridden at trot or slow canter; a steeplechase course 1–2½ miles (2–4km) long with 10–12 fences, to be ridden at a gallop; and the speed and endurance phase, a cross-country course between 3–5 miles (5–8km) with 20–32 fixed obstacles to be ridden at the gallop. Time penalties are incurred for falls and refusals and for exceeding the minimum time allotted for each phase.

DAY 3: SHOW JUMPING

A course of 10–12 obstacles. Penalties are incurred for falls or refusals and for exceeding the time allowed.

The whole competition is interspersed with veterinary inspections and the same horse and rider must take part in each test. Obviously, no two events are the same and the rider must undertake a great deal of preparation for each competition, apart from the obvious day-to-day fitness programs necessary to keep their horses in peak condition!

If you decide to start eventing yourself, you'll start with one-day novice events. These will quickly show whether you and the horse have the aptitude and interest in this sport. Don't try to go too quickly: transition from one-day to three-day events is a big step — not only in the level of competition but also in both the time involved and the expense. Some key points to remember:

• This may sound self-evident, but choose the right type of horse. The range of disciplines involved in eventing taxes horses to the extreme and you'll want a stayer. The minimum accepted height for an eventer is 15hh (5ft). In reality one of 16hh (5ft 4in) is ideally sized; he should be calm, move well for the dressage and have good conformation. Ideally a Thoroughbred or near-Thoroughbred five or six years of age is the horse you want, although many riders prefer a horse with a hardier mix than this.
• Don't train too hard too soon. Confidence is everything when jumping is involved: if you or the horse lose it, you won't be able to compete. Ensure that you train on banks and taking fences at an angle — difficult tasks for the horse but both things will be necessary at an event. At some stage you will have to

RIGHT: Badminton 1996 and it's Day Two. Here David O'Connor and Custom Made are going full tilt around the course. This is a real endurance test of both rider and horse, but also one of trust, for the horse must have complete faith that his rider will guide him around safely.

carry weights: practice with them if they are going to be necessary.

- Make sure you consult a farrier to get the right shoes for your horse — with correction as necessary — and shoe him regularly. An eventer will be heavy on shoes because of the wear and tear of the event and it's important that his feet are just right.
- Get your gear right: make sure that your hat is well fitting, that the horse has a breastplate and girth to keep the saddle tight; protect his legs for the jumping but, above all, make sure that you are both immaculately turned out for the dressage. The judges are not expecting an eventer to perform at the same level as a dressage horse, but your turnout will be noted. Calmness is the key to dressage: see which warm-up routines work best for you and your horse before entering the ring; you both want to be ready, but not too tense.
- Walk the courses well — not just the cross-country but also the jumps. It's not just the fences that need careful study but the way of going all along the course, undulations in the ground, where shadows will fall and so on. Experienced competitors will know the course so well beforehand that they will be able to change their plans should the horse or weather conditions on the day require it; this is especially important on timed courses where slopes can get very heavy and a lot of time lost easily. Many jumps offer alternatives, which although less large or less scary, take slightly longer. However, for less experienced horses, the longer, easier route is more desirable than maybe overtaxing them and making them lose confidence. Assess the show jumping course carefully and use the arena to give as long a run up to the next fence as is practical.
- Ask questions if you don't understand anything — and make sure that you know where everything is, especially compulsory flags in the cross-country: you'll be disqualified if you miss one.
- Make sure you have an accurate stopwatch for the cross-country; remember to start the watch when you set off; check the time regularly.
- Look after yourself and your horse well during the event, particularly once you have started the three-day events. Don't let him eat too much before a gallop; keep him cool if it's hot and warm if it's cold. If you're using studs think carefully about when and where to put them on so that they won't hurt him. Keep an eye out for any leg damage.

There are now three-day events in most major countries of the world. Great Britain holds Badminton, Burghley and Gatcombe, but interest has spread worldwide through the US, South America, Australia and New Zealand. Indeed, many of the world's greatest riders come from Australasia as the recent results at the Atlanta Olympics show, with Australia taking the team gold and New Zealand taking individual gold and silver.

Equestrian events such as show jumping and eventing are among the very few in which women can compete on equal footing alongside men, with at least as much success. Indeed, in recent times eventing has been dominated by women such as Princess Anne, Ginny Leng, Lucinda Green and Mary King.

The standards of preparation, fitness and training have improved dramatically along with the large-scale development of three-day events as a whole. Years of research have gone into how equine athletes recover after tough competitions, especially in adverse weather conditions, such as extreme humidity as was encountered in Atlanta. There huge fans were placed at the end of the course and in large hangar-like tents to help the horses cool down; in addition the horses were closely watched throughout the competition.

RIGHT and BELOW: Kerry Milliken and Out and About competing in the cross-country section (right) and in the show jumping arena (below) of the Three-Day Event at the Atlanta Olympics, 1996. They won the bronze medal following New Zealanders Sally Clark and Blyth Tait who won gold and silver.

CHAPTER 11

ENDURANCE RIDING

Annette Sanderson

History abounds in tales of epic marches by armies or of heroic rides by individual riders but the first organized long-distance riding competitions did not take place until the beginning of the 20th century. The first long-distance rides in Britain were run by the Arab Horse Society in the 1920s, when each horse had to carry 182lb (83kg) over 300 miles (483km) in five days and was subjected to stringent veterinary checks during and after the ride. In the United States, the Tevis Cup Ride was born when five riders led by Wendell Robie and Nick Mansfield set out in August 1955 to prove that modern riders and horses could still emulate the achievements of the Pony Express riders. They rode 100 miles (161km) over the Sierras in just over 22 hours; their route is still followed every year by the Tevis Cup riders.

In the US, there are numerous Trail Ride Associations. At present Great Britain has two endurance riding organizations — the BHS Long Distance Riding Group (LDRG) and the Endurance Horse and Pony Society (EHPS). Their rules and competitions differ slightly. The LDRG concentrates on events where a certain distance has to be covered at a set average speed, starting with Bronze Buckle Qualifiers ridden over 20 miles (32km) at 6.5mph (10.5kph), up to the Golden Horseshoe, 100 miles (161km) to be ridden over two days at 8mph (13kph). The EHPS also holds short rides to be ridden at a given speed called competitive trail rides, but the riders can go on to endurance rides where the fastest horse to finish sound is the winner. Both organizations place great emphasis on the horse's welfare and no horse is allowed to go on if he fails one of the veterinary examinations. One of the most important of these endurance races is the Summer Solstice run over 100 miles (161km) in one day. Both societies also hold shorter non-competitive pleasure or training rides.

The two most famous endurance rides in the world are America's Tevis Cup Ride in California and Australia's Tom Quilty Endurance Ride first held in 1966. In Europe, the European Long Distance Rides Conference (ELDRIC) organizes international rides and the European championships. The best riders can take part in the World Championships which Great Britain won in its first year in 1986.

To start competing in endurance rides, you need a sound, willing horse, a set of well-fitting tack and a certain amount of personal stamina. If you already have a horse, take an honest look at him and decide whether his conformation is good enough to enable him to cover 25 miles (40km) at a set speed without injuring himself. If the horse has had leg, feet or lung problems in the past, it might be a good idea to ask veterinary advice before putting him through a fitness program. If you decide to buy a horse, you need to be clear in your mind about the level you may eventually want to reach. There is a world of difference between a 100-miler and other horses. The horse's conformation, stamina and temperament must be as outstanding as possible to avoid disappointments in the future. Many aspiring long-distance riders buy an Arabian, a breed famous for its stamina. But even the best Arabian must be schooled and trained properly to succeed. He and his rider must also see eye to eye, not always easy with an often highly individualistic and very determined mount!

Once you have decided on the horse, look at your tack. It must be completely safe and it must not hurt the horse anywhere. There are now a number of endurance saddles and bridles on the market and they are very good but not necessary when you start. The saddle should have a large bearing surface to spread the load and the bit you use should enable you to keep control without bruising the horse's mouth, which loses you veterinary points as well as damaging the

RIGHT: American riders and horses are particularly strong in long-distance and endurance riding which is enjoyed all over the world, particularly at home in the US, where the Tevis Cup takes place. The competition was first run in 1955 and is named after a president of Wells Fargo, a company renowned for its Pony Express mail service. The cup is run over a 100-mile course, which takes in the Sierra Nevada mountain range. Here the USA team at the World Equestrian Games in 1994 are out on the trail.

horse. It is often kinder to use a stronger bit gently than to haul for all your might on a mild bit. If you want to use leg or foot protection or any unusual items of tack, consult the rule books to make sure they are allowed.

To condition your horse, you need to pay attention to several areas. Stable management must be good: clean bed, clean water, a dust-free atmosphere, daily check of the horse's health, particularly of tendons and feet, are the minimum requirements. Feeding does not need to be specialized at this stage but it must be balanced and of good quality and keep pace with the amount of exercise the horse receives. Protein is necessary, but it is carbohydrates which provide energy. Salt and minerals must be replenished because a horse who sweats can lose a great deal. The horse's shoeing must not be neglected either. If you wait until the shoes are loose or the feet overgrown to call the blacksmith, you are risking injury and the horse's feet will have been unbalanced for some time with consequent stress on the structures of the leg and foot.

It is also vital that the horse be made fit slowly. If you want to learn how to monitor your horse's fitness using heart and breathing rates, it is best to consult a specialist publication.

Start with walking for two or three weeks if you are starting from scratch. Ideally your horse should reach a walking speed of around 4mph (6.5kph) or more. When you start trotting, keep the horse balanced and do not go pounding on the roads. Endurance riding can be hard on the horse's legs: save them for when it matters! Do not forget to keep schooling your horse as your training progresses; it helps build muscle, increases balance and co-ordination and it will go a long way toward giving you brakes. There are some sorry tales in long-distance riding of brake failure, with sometimes bad injuries to the horses and riders involved, to say nothing of the nuisance value of a rider out of control on a ride upsetting other competitors and their horses.

The rider also needs to be fit and wear the right gear. If you do all your horse's training and look after him yourself, you probably do not need to do extra exercise (it is also unlikely you will have the time or the energy to go to the gym as well). Eat a balanced diet, get enough sleep and enjoy yourself and you should be all right. Hard hats up to high standards are compulsory in most countries, and your footwear must have a heel. If it does not, you will need to purchase some kind of stirrup cage. Riders tend to wear what

they find most comfortable by way of trousers and tops and you will have to decide what is best for you. Even if you do not use them normally, take a pair of gloves with you. The wear and tear on your hands may well exceed what you expect and wet hands can get very cold and numb. Spurs are not allowed and you should not need them.

Before you go to your first competition, make a list of what you will need to take. Spare reins, leathers and girth should be taken along besides the tack you will be using. Take a first-aid kit (human and animal), plenty of water, a grooming kit and a sweat blanket, ideally the type which allows the horse to dry without getting chilled. Essential, too, are a feedbag and feed to give after the competition when the horse is cool and calm. Most riders carry a small emergency bag on the ride with hoofpick, compass, string, pocket knife, candy, analgesicss, bandage, money for phone, a good map and your route instructions.

On arrival, collect your number and check for possible changes of route. Then take your horse along for his tack and veterinary inspections, if appropriate. It may be advisable to lead your horse in a bridle if he seems excited by the proceedings. When you start, try not to set off at top speed: you want to teach your horse to conserve his energy. During the ride, be prepared for markers to be missing; learn to read a map. The ride organizers do all they can to mark the course but it is not unusual for the route markers to have disappeared.

With experience you will learn to judge your horse's pace, and to anticipate which sections will ride faster or slower. Make sure you do not miss the check points and that the steward has seen you. At veterinary inspections, either during the competition or at the finish, cool your horse sufficiently without chilling him and check that your horse's heartbeat is down to the required rate. When you have completed the ride, however exhausted you feel, remember the horse has carried you and, even if you feel he has been less than angelic, look after him: he did not ask to go long-distance riding!

LEFT: The American endurance team tending to their mounts. Each horse needs to be fit and strong with plenty of stamina and a determined temperament suited to long distance riding.

ABOVE RIGHT: The American team sets out fresh and enthusiastic with a hard day in prospect in the early morning light

RIGHT: It is not just the horse that needs to be fit and tough – prepare well if you decide to give it a try!

CHAPTER 12

MOUNTED GAMES

Peter Wroe, Philip Broomfield, Ray Cooper and Lynda Springate

Do you give the horse his strength?
Have you clothed his neck with a mane?
Do you make him quiver like a locust's wings, when
his shrill neigh strikes terror?
He shows his mettle as he paws and prances;
in his might he charges the armored line.
He scorns alarms and knows no dismay;
he does not shy away before the sword.
The quiver rattles at his side, the spear and saber flash.
Trembling with eagerness, he devours the ground
and when the trumpet sounds there is no holding him;
at the trumpet call he cries "Aha!"
and from afar he scents the battle,
the shouting of the captains, and the war cries.

This quotation from the *Book of Job* shows that, from earliest times, the horse was no stranger to war. Research shows that man began harnessing the horse to chariots at around 1700BC. By 600BC the Persians were breeding successful heavyweight battle horses, used to great effect by the conquerors of classical antiquity. In the 8th century AD another innovation helped change the face of warfare: the stirrup. Providing a stable platform for a mounted warrior produced the armoured knight, who would dominate western warfare until the invention of gunpowder.

The European heavy horse of the Middle Ages had to be able to carry a rider in full armor plus its own armor, a combined weight which could amount to more than 450lb (200kg). One of the most famous examples was the German Great Horse, a strong and heavy breed. In Great Britain during the reign of Richard I (the Lionheart), examples of native stock were crossed with the Belgian/Flemish heavy horses. Parliament encouraged breeders to breed bigger and better quality horses. A 1535 act required farmers or landowners to keep two mares capable of breeding foals of at least 13hh (4ft 4in).

By the end of the 16th century, the reliability of artillery and guns led to the decline of the armored knight and his great horse — but not to the use of the horse on the battlefield. It was the age of the cavalry, the dragoon, cuirassier and hussar, whose deployment in battle was essential to the success of such all-conquering armies as those of Frederick the Great and Napoleon. The dominance of the cavalry would last until the advent of the repeating rifle and machine gun, and would die in the mud and trenches of World War I: although the use of horses in military service would be significant well into World War II.

To train all these cavalrymen and improve the skills of horse and rider to keep them practiced for war, military games evolved. The successful playing of these mounted games depend on the complete harmony of horse and rider, a harmony that would certainly have its place on the battlefield. Xenophon wrote about training horse and rider to perform skilled movements that were a pleasure to look at and would also be of use in war. The Karabair and Lokai horses of the mountainous areas of Mongolia — which bred the most feared horsemen in history, Gengis Khan's Mongol hordes — to this day are ridden in the game of "goat-snatching." A rider carries a goat at full gallop while others try to snatch it away from him. Other skillful displays dating from early civilization are circus acts which make use of trained horses and skillful acrobatics. These movements require sound horsemanship if they are to be performed accurately. Polo was originally played to keep warhorses fit, and then adopted at a later date by cavalry officers.

One of the most romantic — with our 20th century perspective — examples of mounted games was the medieval tournament, where knights and their horses took part in jousting and other sports such as tilting the ring. Jousting was a brutal, but highly organized affair, with groups of referees to oversee play. Jousting associations were formed throughout Europe, with strict admission rules. As the sport got more bruising, so the rules changed to ensure that it remained a test of arms, particularly so that no horse was allowed to be wounded. Later competition rules also insisted that only the motions of fighting were to be gone through, and no one was to fight in earnest.

From the Renaissance onwards the great European

RIGHT: The armored knight and his successor, the cavalryman, were the most important weapon on the battlefield until the arrival of mechanization and machine guns. To maintain the skill levels required to be able to fight — and survive — in battle, from earliest times mounted troops have devised games of skill and courage: from jousting to polo.

Courts developed riding schools, where horses were trained in classical movements, to obey barely visible commands from the rider — skills which were essential for cavalrymen in the noise and smoke of war. The most famous of these schools — the Spanish Riding School of Vienna, mentioned in Chapter 2 — was established in the latter half of the 16th century to train young noblemen to control their horses in battle, and to develop the necessary skills for leadership. The famous French Cadre Noir also taught horse and rider dressage. But whereas the Spanish Riding School taught classical riding only, the Cadre Noir also included cross-country and jumping in their classes. A versatility test was introduced, which included, dressage, cross-country and jumping. The three-day event evolved from this test.

We can still see military training exemplified in shows of skill-at-arms today. No one who has visited the British Royal Tournament can forget the musical drives given by artillery teams. Mounted police forces worldwide display every day the skills needed by horse and rider for a variety of jobs including crowd control, where the horse has to learn to live with loud noises, traffic and crowds of shouting people.

POLO

Perhaps the most lasting of all the mounted games handed down from the past is polo. The modern game is a thrilling, spectacular, spectator sport, requiring courage, athletic ability and great toughness from both pony and rider. Over the centuries, from 600BC to the present day, the game has gradually transformed itself from a crude, fierce and dangerous tribal free-for-all into a more controlled team game played to strictly applied rules. The rules offer protection for ponies and players and the competitive format for the modern game. Even so the same original risks remain — fast brave ponies ridden by highly competitive full-blooded riders inevitably create dangerous incidents: injuries are unavoidable.

At the highest level, polo is a game for fearless acrobatic riders and fast courageous ponies, but a less taxing form of the game can be enjoyed at family, club and pony club level. Young players can start playing with one cheap pony, alternating with other players in matches. Compared to the vast stock of expensive ponies required by the best players — six to eight ponies for matches — this highlights the difference between the bottom and the top of the polo world.

The origins of the game of polo are obscure. The word "polo" comes from the Tibetan word for ball — *pulu* — but the earliest records dating from c600BC, are of Iranian tribesmen playing a form of mounted game with stick and ball.

Over the centuries, invading armies discovered and, in turn, spread the game throughout Asia, from the Turkey to Mongolia. One can see the natural aptitude of people — for whom the horse was the only means of transport for ordinary living and for waging war over vast distances — for the game as a recreational expression of personal courage and equine prowess.

The British discovered the game being played in India in the 19th century. A Lt. Joseph Sherer spotted polo being played by Manipur tribesmen. He managed to persuade them to teach him and his colleagues and within a short time the game was being played by the officer class of the British Army throughout the Empire. The mounted troops were ideally placed to embrace the game as an extension of their standard horse activities, as a social and leisure expression of the prowess and courage of horse and rider, just as the founding tribesmen did.

For the non-military, only the wealthy were in a position to afford the high costs involved in acquiring the ponies and creating the facilities for the game to be played. From its first introduction to the West the game became the sporting and social activity of the military, civilian and professional upper classes.

In the last decade of the 20th century, with changing social patterns, polo is played by a much broader cross-section of people. At the highest level the game is supported by wealthy businessmen known as patrons, who finance their own teams in competitions sponsored by other business interests. The sport is used as a medium for advertising and company promotional purposes on an international scale.

Military polo is still played by the officer class but on a much reduced scale. Mounted sections have largely disappeared because of mechanization — the cavalry now fights in tanks rather than on horseback — and the private wealth of the officer class is not what it was. Needless to say the costs of playing the game have risen inexorably since its early beginnings.

At the lower level, because of the increased affluence of the working and professional classes and the relaxing of social groupings, it is possible for club polo to be played by adults and children on self-taught-ponies. The Pony Club competitions for children up to the age of 18 years are very popular. Polo for children offers an additional discipline to show jumping, hunting and eventing. It is entirely possible for one pony to participate in all these different activities.

For many riders looking to progress into the high-

RIGHT: Because of its royal connections and the obvious wealth of many of its practitioners, polo has gained a reputation for being an exclusive sport. Its origins belie this: polo — or rather horseback games with stick and ball — has been played for over 2,000 years, wherever men have ridden horses. Polo as we know it today was codified by the British Army in India — the Silchar Club is the oldest polo club in the world — and has flourished especially in India, Argentina and the US.

Scenes from polo matches, including (BOTTOM) Prince Charles receiving a winners' medal from his mother, Queen Elizabeth II. Royal interest, and talent, in the sport has done much to keep it alive in Britain where horse ownership is more difficult than in the wide open spaces of Australia, Argentina or the US, and therefore more restricted to the wealthy.

er grades of polo the financial requirements represent an insurmountable barrier; they have to acquire more and a better class of pony, plus increased transportation with all the consequent costs.

THE GAME

Polo has a simple handicapping system, in principle not unlike golf. Handicaps range from minus 2 to 10 goals, the latter being the better player. Handicaps are awarded on a player's shot-making ability, tactical and game sense, horsemanship and sportsmanship. More than two-thirds of the world's players are rated at two goals and below.

Polo is a right-handed game. The length of the stick (48–54in /1.22–137m) varies to suit the height of the pony and size of the rider; 52in (1.32m) isaverage for a medium height rider mounted on a 15hh (5ft) pony.

A team consists of four players. The team positions are indicated by the number of the shirt worn:

No. 1 is at the front in line of attack, or direction of play. He is the main goal scorer — though anyone can score. He should be an accurate hitter on fast, handy ponies, able quickly to turn defense into attack.

No. 2 player marks the opposing team's No. 3 and supports his No. 1.

No. 3 is the team's playmaker, its best player. He controls the speed and tactics of the game.

No. 4, known as a "back," is the main defensive player and needs to have a strong backhand shot. He should always be prepared to gallop up from behind, turning defence into attack.

The polo ground is 900ft (274m) long and 600ft (183m) wide. The goalposts are placed 24ft (7.3m) apart at each end. The posts are designed to collapse on impact to avoid injury. A goal is scored when the ball is hit between the posts at any height without an infringement arising in the process. After a goal is scored the teams change the direction of play in order to equalize the ground and wind conditions.

A match is composed of a number of chukkas. Each chukka lasts seven minutes, with up to 30 seconds of overtime. If no foul occurs during the overtime the chukka ends and an interval of three minutes allows players to change to a fresh pony and take a breather. Matches are of four or six chukkas, which may be extended if the teams are tied.

PLAYING POLO

The classification of polo in rising standard of play is Low Goal, Medium Goal and High Goal. The handicap of the team is the sum of the four players' handicaps. Matches are sometimes described as 4-, 8-, 12- or 20-goal polo denoting the combined handicap limit of the players. The side with the lowest total receives the difference between the team handicaps as a score at the beginning of the match.

A game is controlled by two mounted umpires and a referee, positioned usually in an elevated position on the sidelines. The umpires only refer to the referee if they fail to agree. Infringement of the rules results in penalties being awarded. Depending on the severity of the foul the penalty can be a goal, shot at goal or a free hit from the spot where the foul occurred.

A main principle of the game is that, having hit the ball, a player is entitled to follow the line in order to take a further shot. The player having hit the ball might be considered to be on the main road and anyone coming in to challenge from a side road must do so safely or incur a penalty.

POLO PONIES

Polo ponies are a type, not a breed. Crossbred or Thoroughbred animals are used and the ability to play the game is the only thing that counts in the end. The best ponies have a high proportion of Thoroughbred blood for speed and native pony for toughness.

The earliest polo was played on true ponies, thickset, quick and maneuverable, of around 12hh (4ft). Modern polo ponies can range up to 16hh (5ft 4in) or more, to suit the rider, with the ideal type for the average player, being a short-legged deep-girthed 15hh (5ft) animal.

The requirements of a polo pony fall into a number of categories: a good natured animal — one which can be tied up close in line with other animals at the ground and whilst travelling for many hours in a horse trailer — is essential. A bad tempered kicker can damage other team animals. Speed is essential, along with an ability to gallop and accelerate when asked. The ability to stop and turn quickly is critical. The ponies must be courageous, bold and agile — spirited yet completely responsive to the rider's aids. It must be robust, healthy and a comfortable ride.

A pony must not play more than one chukka without a break and is unlikely to play more than two chukkas in a game. The rules require that the game stops immediately if a pony needs attention. Routine veterinary inspection of ponies is carried out after play to check excessive use of whip, spur and general condition. Fines for misuse are levied.

The thrill of polo for spectator and player is undeniable; some would say that it cannot be equaled. Late 20th century tendencies to impose protection on players of physical contact sports has so far not affected polo, an example being the polo hat not giving way to riding hats or helmets. Polo involves greater kinetic forces than any other game: an out-of-control pony and rider traveling in opposite directions represent potential disaster. Perhaps, the attitude that all is worth risking is what makes for the breathtaking excitement and ultimate pleasure of the bravest sportsmen and most avid spectators.

81

OTHER MOUNTED GAMES

Skill-at-arms and training for military purposes account for many of today's mounted games, but there is another major strand to the story, originating mainly in the US — the sport enjoyed by working horsemen: the rodeo.

The massive expansion of cattle ranching in the American West from the 1860s led to a huge increase in the number of working horsemen — the cowboys. Unsurprisingly for people working so closely with horses (each needed a string of horses to perform his job), their games were trials of the abilities needed to perform their work successfully: breaking the horses they needed to transport them; roping, tying and branding the cattle they were herding.

Today's rodeo — the word is Spanish for round-up

BELOW and RIGHT: Like polo, the "Gymkhana" — as practiced and enjoyed today by young people all over the world — originated in India to train cavalry.

While many of today's rodeos are wrapped in pagentry and glitz, the skills required to perform successfully are the same as those practiced daily on the range: strength, skill with a rope but, above all, horsemanship.

— is part carnival, part contest. If you go to one of the many thousand rodeos held annually in the US you'll see such entertainments as bareback riding, calf-roping, bronc and bull riding, steer wrestling, barrel and wagon racing, trick riding, fancy lasso work and Wild West pageantry on a scale commensurate with the size of the show.

But the rodeo is not the exclusive preserve of the western rider: South America, Canada — home of the famous and much-loved Royal Canadian Mounted Police; in their red jackets the "Mounties" are always a crowd pleaser — Australia and New Zealand all have their equivalents. In Australia, the Rough Riders Association controls the sport which includes bronc riding — saddled and bareback — calf-roping, steer wrestling and camp-drafting, which requires the rider to cut a cow from a herd and drive it to a pen.

Finally, although distasteful to many, there is another sport in which the horse is essential: bull fighting. Picador and toreador, on horseback, weaken the bull before the matador arrives in the ring to fight on foot.

ABOVE and BELOW LEFT:Two more views of western rodeo riding including(BELOW) a Calgary Rodeo on the ice in Canada.

ABOVE: There are many other equestrian sports and pursuits — too many to record all of them in this book. Trotting is big in the US, France and Australia and has been for years, with its own specialized breeding programmes.

RIGHT and BELOW: Driving is also highly competitive.

CHAPTER 13

SHOWING

Mayanne McCorn

Of all the disciplines in the equine world, it could be argued that none displays as much variety as the show ring. In a season normally running from April until September, from local shows to national events, from the tiniest riders in the lead reins to the giants of the horse world in Heavy Horse classes, there is truly something to interest everyone. No matter whether your chosen discipline is showing a youngster in hand or a more mature animal under saddle, a "hairy" native pony or an elegant hack, there are some common denominators.

Let us first consider showing in-hand. Generally speaking, in-hand classes are divided into youngstock (one-, two- and three-year olds) and mature animals (four years or older); the former may be split into separate classes for yearlings and the latter by gender (eg, stallions have their own class). Broodmares with foals also have special classes. As the name "in-hand" implies, the horse/pony is led around the ring at the walk, so that the judge can make an initial assessment; the animals are then trotted past the judge individually, after which the initial selection (line-up) is made. After standing the horse/pony up in front of the judge, for closer inspection, each competitor is then expected to do a short "individual" show; this usually involves walking the animal away from the judge in a straight line, turning and trotting straight back. The purpose of this is to check the horse/pony's movement.

For any event correct conformation and freedom of movement play an important part in determining whether or not the animal will do well in front of a judge but these are perhaps more important when showing in-hand when it is more difficult to disguise any imperfections. However, it must be said that a competent handler can do a lot to help a not-quite-so-perfect pony!

Teaching a pony to lead correctly alongside the handler at home can save so much heartache when it gets into the show ring. There is nothing worse from a judge's point of view than to see a quality pony misbehaving or being dragged along unwillingly behind its leader, ears laid back and showing a reluctance to do anything. How much better to see an animal walk into the ring with confidence, ears pricked, alert to his surroundings and ready to do as the handler bids. It is

also essential that the handler is aware of what is going on, by keeping a watchful eye on the steward/judge and other competitors, thus ensuring that things run smoothly and successfully.

Appearance also has a part to play in attracting the judge's eye — a clean well-presented animal will invariably do better than one who looks scruffy. Tack for in-hand classes is usually a simple halter or bridle (with or without a bit) with lead rein attached. For most classes, it is necessary to plait the mane; tails may be pulled or plaited. As with everything, there are exceptions — Arabians and the nine native British breeds (also known as Mountain and Moorland ponies) are shown with manes and tails free.

It is important for the handler to be neat and tidy too; there is no point in spending a lot of time and trouble on the animal's appearance and then being untidy oneself. Trousers, shirt, tie and jacket or waistcoat work well for both ladies and gentlemen, along with sensible shoes or boots and appropriate headgear — the ensemble determined to some extent by the type of class in which you are competing.

This brings us to ridden showing, or showing "under saddle" where there are many different classes:

Lead Rein classes are restricted to the height of the pony (maximum 12hh/4ft), and the age of the rider — usually a minimum of three years old and maximum seven years for show ponies; eight years maximum for show hunter ponies and some mountain and moorland classes. These tiny jockeys then progress through First Ridden (shown off the lead rein and restricted to age ten and under) and then beyond.

There are classes for Riding Ponies and Hunter Ponies (both usually divided by the height of the pony), Cobs, Hacks, Riding Horses, Hunters (usually divided by their weight-carrying capabilities), Working Hunters and Working Hunter Ponies (in the latter two cases, competitors are expected to display their abilities over fences as well as on the flat). Not to be forgotten are Arabians and their part-breds and the nine native British breeds. Riding horses and hunters may also be shown under side-saddle as well as the more conventional astride.

With the exception of Lead Rein and First Ridden classes, all ridden animals are shown collectively at the walk, trot and canter. At the judge's discretion, they may be galloped collectively, individually or in smaller groups. Lead rein classes are an extension of in hand showing, in that initially the ponies are walked around together and trotted out individually. In first ridden classes, generally speaking, riders are not expected to canter collectively, although the canter may be included in the individual show.

As in the in-hand ring, after the judge has made an initial line up, competitors are required to show their mount's paces individually. In this case, it is expected to see walk, trot and canter with a change of rein and short gallop. In some classes, most usually Hunters, the judge may ride the animals forward instead of the individual show. At this point the judge is assessing not only the horse or pony's paces but also its manners and way of going. (Good manners are important for both horse and rider!) Although ride and manners constitute a large proportion of the overall mark, conformation plays an important part too. To this end animals may be unsaddled (or stripped off) and run out in hand before the final decision is made.

As before, the turn-out of the horse and rider is of paramount importance, again horses and ponies have their manes plaited, with a few exceptions — Cobs, for example, usually have their manes hogged and mountain and moorland ponies are shown as naturally as possible — the level of trimming in these cases being determined by the relevant breed societies. Arabians have their manes and tails free.

In Lead Rein and novice classes it is usual to use a plain snaffle bit, while in other classes, double bridles or Pelhams are the choice. Native ponies, Hunters, Hunter Ponies and Cobs are usually shown in plain leather bridles, whereas the fashion for riding horses and ponies these days is colored browbands with "rosettes" on each side. Working Hunters and Ponies are allowed martingales.

All riders should be suitably dressed: navy or tweed jacket as appropriate for the event, jodhpurs/breeches, short boots (children) and long boots (adults), plus protective headgear (velvet cap, bowler or helmet with a plain navy or black cover). It is important, too, for grooms/attendants to be neatly dressed if they have to enter the ring.

ABOVE RIGHT: A Warmblood reserve champion.

BELOW RIGHT: Beautifully turned out Shire from the Bass Brewery Museum, England.

ABOVE: Champion Shire at the Royal Show.

LEFT: Saddlebred display, Celebration of the Horse, 1995.

RIGHT: Connemaras Silver Grey Sparrow and Grey Sparrow.

CHAPTER 14

VACATIONS WITH HORSES

Leisa Crook

The popularity of vacations involving horse riding of one form or another has grown hugely in recent years. Almost every country, large or small, offers the vacationer a chance to explore the local countryside on horseback, often using native breeds of pony or horse. From beach-front pony rides, through hacking, trekking, hunting and trail rides, a diverse range of vacations of varying lengths and duration are offered and many, fortunately, are reasonable.

The key to finding a well-maintained establishment offering good quality horses is to check its membership with local riding associations and clubs — a little research beforehand can make the difference between a great vacation on a suitable horse and disaster. Although many countries offer a wide range of riding activities, most tend to specialize in one or two types depending on the suitability of the terrain and the country's attitude toward riding in general. Thus, France offers the usual hacking, trail riding and trekking, depending on the local landscape, but is well known for vacations featuring horse-drawn caravans. It is also worth remembering that the definition of each type of riding (trekking, trail riding, hacking, etc.) varies considerably from country to country. The trail riding you experience in the Argentinean Andes will be almost completely different from that which you find in the British Isles — with an accompanying difference in the level of fitness and skill that may be required.

Often you will have to make your own riding arrangements on arrival in a country but, increasingly, travel firms offer special equestrian packages, organizing everything from flights to accommodation. Some people prefer to plan their own vacations and, if the countryside (and local language) are not too unfamiliar to you, this may be a good option, especially for those wishing to remain unrestrained by group timetables and activities. At the opposite end of the scale is the all-inclusive vacation, such as those offered in the United States, where the vacationer can spend time at an authentic western-style ranch. Here, everything is planned, from flights to daytime (and evening!) sports, which often include rodeos, cattle drives and non-riding activities such as golf, tennis and swimming.

There are two key factors which must be considered when planning a vacation on horseback — the likely weather and your riding experience. Nothing is worse than extremes of heat or cold when you're spending long hours in the saddle, especially if all you're used to is weekend riding in more favorable conditions. On the other hand, if you're an experienced rider, you may be expected to fall in line with a large group and keep to the pace of the slowest or novice rider. This often happens on trekking vacations, so it pays to find a program which caters specifically to your level of ability.

Choosing the correct clothing and equipment for the conditions in which you will be riding is also important. Of primary concern is, of course, a hard hat and full-length leather or rubber boots or, in very hot climates, short jodhpur boots, especially if there is a lot of walking as well as riding involved. Lightweight jodhpurs are easily packed and far more comfortable than jeans or trousers. Don't forget thermal long johns — essential for long, cold days in the saddle. Longer sleeves are preferable, even in warmer climates, to protect arms from sun- and wind-burn. A scarf or bandanna provides invaluable neck protection. Waterproof overclothes can also be useful and, at the very least, pack a waterproof jacket but avoid light plastic coats and ponchos. For personal comfort, sunblock, talcum powder, insect repellent and bandaids are essential!

Finally, it is rarely advisable to ride alone (three is

RIGHT: The popularity of trekking vacations grows each year as people venture away from their home countries to sample foreign climes. As with any vacation it pays to be careful booking the holiday but, additionally, pay particular attention to your clothing and riding experience. You certainly do not want to end up ill-equipped for extreme temperatures or incapable of completing a vacation that has proved too tough. Be careful to look closely at travel insurance documentation to make sure that you are covered in full.

ABOVE: While you may find a group unwieldy, it is rarely sensible to ride alone: three is considered the safe minimum.

BELOW: The US is a popular destination with plenty of trails for the novice or experienced horseperson.

RANCH AMERICA'S SOUTH TEXAS RANCHES
and
South Padre Island Resort

TEXAS

It's Like A Whole Other Country.

FULL RIDING PROGRAMME
(Subject to availability)
November 95 - November 96

usually a safe minimum number) and it is always sensible to take your own compact first-aid kit. Don't neglect important medical provisions such as vaccination requirements for the places you may be visiting, and it is always worth considering a vacation insurance policy, specific to the conditions you will be riding in. In general, with careful planning and preparation, your vacation can be as exciting or as relaxing as you choose it to be, whether it be trekking or hacking; for single person or family, there is an enjoyable vacation on horseback waiting for you.

Films and television have fostered the image of the cowboy and his faithful horse — and there are many vacations available in the US and Canada which enable you to relive the days of the Wild West from the back of a pony. Recently, with the increase of interest in native Americans, speciality vacation packages allow you not only to go horse riding but to learn Indian ways, including how to survive on berries, plants and roots. In Canada, Jasper and Banff national parks provide fascinating rides of up to six days at a time. The main trail rides are organized through the Trail Riders of the Canadian Rockies based in Calgary. There is similar riding in British Columbia.

In Yellowstone National Park, you can ride stagecoaches, with four-in-hand, or enjoy traditional trail-riding activities. In other Western states, such as Arizona and Wyoming, ranch-style vacations promise authentic Western riding, cattle drives and shows. Not all of these holidays promise as much excitement as in *City Slickers*! Texas offers ranches, Quarter Horse riding, trail riding and a chance to experience life on the range. Texas state laws restrict the type of riding which is offered, however, limiting most riding to one or two hours per day, so if a more comprehensive riding program is what you require, choose another state. Ranch America offers ranch vacations and pack trips throughout Texas, Arizona, Wyoming, Colorado, Montana, Idaho and California. In addition, cattle drives are also offered in Montana, Texas and Wyoming.

Most vacations are flexible and offer a variety of alternatives involving horses, from scenic cross-country expeditions to riding with ranch hands tending herds of cattle. Evenings, too, are full of western pleasures — barbecues, hayrides, square dances and rodeos. Pack tripping may involve a weekend or week-long excursion on horseback, usually in more remote and unspoiled areas, ensuring breathtaking scenery. You'll stay at campsites or farmhouses along the way where meals will be served and the horses looked after. Optional stops may be included for hunting, fishing, general sightseeing or for a day or two's rest at a resort. Many of the places you'll visit on a "Western" vacation hold rodeos, which are always fun for visitors and locals alike.

Elsewhere in the United States there are tours, riding centers and excellent riding country everywhere, with an infrastructure that starts even in the big cities: many of which have riding academies.

In South America, Argentina offers trail riding in the magnificent Andes for up to a week. Starting at the Rio Grande, south of Mendoza, the riders are accompanied by baquianos, local gaucho farmers, whose horsemanship is impressive and expert. The route takes the rider northwest through the mountains up to the Chilean border and returns along a different route. Travel is at high altitudes and the terrain varies from lush pasture to thorny scrub. Camp is set up each night, with all members of the group dining on campfire-cooked food and sleeping under the stars. Because of the high altitude and the possibility of the trail being made impassable by snowdrifts, this trail can only be ridden between December and March. However, year-round riding tours in a similar vein can be found in Ecuador, Chile (including Easter Island), Brazil, Paraguay and Mexico.

The United Kingdom has some of the finest riding country in the world — and enjoyed by riders from around the world. In the north, the Yorkshire Moors and Dales offer wonderful scenery, as does the Lake District with its longer trekking as well as hacking. The Peak District contains the national park and rides offered include overnight stops in small guesthouses and hotels. In the East Anglian regions of Suffolk and Norfolk, organized vacation riding on local bridle tracks is available.

The small Suffolk town of Newmarket, famous as the home of horseracing, is also the home of the National Horseracing Museum. Some of the finest Thoroughbred horses in the world may be found in training in this small, picturesque town. Traveling down into the south of England, the Cotswolds are home to one of the top training schools in Britain. Specializing in dressage, cross-country, show jumping and general horsemanship, the Talland School of Equitation runs courses throughout the year. The Home Counties regions of Sussex and Surrey provide comfortable hacking in country parks, as well as beach riding at historic Sidlesham, near Chichester. The West Country — Cornwall, Devon and Somerset — is a haven for the horse rider. Here, the varied scenery includes moorlands and magnificent hills and valleys. Foxhunting on horseback is offered throughout the area, the season extending from November to April.

In Wales, the Welsh Mountain Pony and its close cousin, the Welsh Pony, are available for pony-trekking in the mountains and valleys. Welsh Cob or cob-crosses are used extensively for trail rides in south and mid-Wales: the landscape is diverse, ranging from waterfalls and forests to heather-clad moors. Family accommodation is available at local farmhouses.

Scotland, too, offers fine horse country, with its

ABOVE: Riding vacations are excellent for children who want to learn how to look after a horse: they can, of course, have a negative effect because of the workload!

often difficult terrain and extensive trail rides. As in England, there is the chance to join one of the fohunts, and family-oriented vacations taking in woodlands, lochs, highlands and moorlands are heavily emphasized. Trekking holidays around Loch Ness are also available, with accommodation in local bed-and-breakfasts or campsites.

Jersey, in the Channel Islands, provides wonderfully long beach rides at Ville Au Neveu and St. Ouen's Bay. Both the Isle of Man and the Scilly Isles offer beach rides on ponies, for adults and children.

Ireland has long been considered one of the most suitable countries for raising horses and the Irish love of horses is evident the length and breadth of the land. There is a wide range of equestrian vacations, from half-day rides on gentle ponies to pony trekking. Residential vacations, which offer instruction with hacking and trekking, are to be found in the south and east, while the west coast offers trail riding set against stunning scenery. Riding centers may be found close to Shannon, Cork, Galway and Dublin. Counties Wicklow and Wexford in the east and Connemara in the west offer picturesque possibilities for many riding vacations, while County Cork offers horse-drawn caravans, often based on traditional Romany lines. In Northern Ireland there are numerous hunts, as well as trekking, riding and instructional vacations. Some of the best riding is to found around Rostrevor in the

Mountains of Mourne, County Down, with its stunning sea, forest and mountain views.

Italy is a land of contrasts where horse riding as a pastime is polarized — at one extreme are the often run-down, bedraggled "holiday hacks" found at some of the tourist resorts and at the other extreme are the fine and experienced riders and animals. Late spring in the Tuscany region is the perfect time to enjoy the beautiful landscape and riding tours of varying lengths crisscross the region between Sienna and Montevarchi, south of Florence. The Abruzzo and Rome region features Italy's highest mountains and also contains the National Park, which organizes a number of treks. Veneto and Venice offer various weekend packages, some of which include lessons, hacking, tours and other entertainment, such as local fishing. Campania and Naples are far less commercial, because of their remoteness; however, for those who choose to explore, it is wonderful riding country with an abundance of lakes, mountains and forests.

Spain is like Italy, particularly in the tourist areas. There are exceptions to be found, with some good establishments in the major resorts. The best riding is to be found inland, in Andalucia and, in the west, Extremadura. One of the more rugged and adventurous routes uses the well-trained Andalusian horses, traveling through the Sierra Nevada (Snowy Mountains). Tours last 7–15 days — the longer involv-

ing fairly tough riding above the snowline in places — definitely a vacation for the true horse person.

Portugal's Algarve region, with its Atlantic beaches and villas, provides excellent riding, much of it sport-oriented, and beach riding at its best. Riding schools are to be found in Quinto do Lago, recognized as the Algarve's coastal showpiece, Estrada das Sesmarias and Almansil. Also in the Almansil area, at Vilamoura, is the indoor riding school Cento Hipico Riding Centre. Trail riding on pure and crossbred Lusitanos in the Alentejo region is available as an eight-day package. Riders need to be fairly fit and reasonably confident at riding outdoors at all paces as the terrain takes in river valleys, sandy plains and forest trails.

Of all the European countries Hungary has the most highly organized equestrian vacations, offering riding tours, carriage driving and classes at studs and riding clubs. Here riding is much more than a hobby and strict controls ensure a safer vacation, but tours are definitely for the experienced rider, as the terrain is sometime treacherous. The tours are split between the hilly region of west Hungary and east Hungary — that is Pustza and the Great Hungarian Plain, with others around Lake Balaton, the Danube and to the north of Budapest.

Slovenia is the location of the Lipica Stud Farm in Sezenz, close to Trieste. It is here that the famous Lipizzaners were bred between 1580 and 1918, exclusively for the Spanish Riding School in Vienna.

LEFT and ABOVE: Britain has some of the finest riding country in the world, with a variety of terrains and trails — as exemplified in these views of Dartmoor, in Devon. Other splendid places to visit include the Lake District, North Yorkshire Moors, Peak District and Loch Ness. Ireland, too, is a wonderful country for a riding vacation offering stunning scenery and even the possibility of horse-drawn caravans!

Visitors can stay at one of the stud's two hotels, and enjoy its golf course, swimming pool and, of course, riding with hacking, dressage or advanced instruction. Situated in the Karst area, the terrain around Lipica features rocky outcrops and sparsely wooded hills which contrast markedly with the coastal resort of Porec on the Istrian peninsula.

France offers the equestrian enthusiast over hundreds of thousands of square miles of diverse terrain, landscape suited to trekking, hacking or trail riding. Much of France's superb rural riding remains a well-kept "secret," as it is patronized more by the locals than by the tourist. The handbook provided by the Association Nationale Pour le Tourisme Equestre (ANTE) at l'Equitation de Loisirs is a comprehensive guide to the diverse range of riding activities offered in the country. Emphasis is often placed on dressage, and instructional holidays are numerous. In northern France, the Nord and Pas-de-Calais region, weekend breaks with full board are available, taking in old towns, lush pastures and valleys. The Picardy region offers similar riding weekends and also longer camping-type vacations; horse-drawn caravans are a feature of the area. The Île de France is the green belt around Paris and the scenery includes chateaux, palaces, parks and forests. An eight-day tour taking in the fortified farms and villages is available, with overnight stops in tents. A horsedrawn, five-day tour around the same region is also available.

Normandy, with its famous Deauville and Trouville resorts, features weekend and hourly riding, while at Etrepagny longer and horse-drawn caravan rides are available. The coastline of Brittany stretches for almost 620 miles (1,000km) and offers every form of accommodation from camp sites and gîtes to hotels and chateaux. In this area, six-day, horse-drawn carriage tours are well organized, as are longer rides, lasting 4–28 days. In Central France, the Loire valley, Poitou-Charentes and Limousin regions weekend to week-long packages are generally offered, with accommodation in places ranging from haylofts to chateaux. Horse-drawn carriages are featured, although dressage and instructional centers are plentiful. The vast Aquitaine area, which includes the Bordeaux region, offers extensive trail-riding tours, lasting up to 14 days.

The Dordogne is a natural home to the horse-drawn caravan or *roulotte*, and a number of tours, taking in vineyards, castles and old oak forests, are featured. The Club Med village at Pompadour specializes in riding and offers 90 horses and three schools, two of which are of Olympic size. To the south, the Midi-Pyrénées, Auvergne and Languedoc-Roussillon regions are well-developed for the tourist, with a strong emphasis on outdoor activities. In Provence, the famous Camargue horses can be seen thriving on their diet of tough grass and salt water. Eastern France offers the Rhône-Alps, Burgundy, Franche-Comté, Alsace, Lorraine and the Champagne-Ardennes region, each well supplied with riding centers offering weekend and longer tours of their locallandscapes.

The Belgian Association Nationale de Tourisme Equestre (ANTE) produces an excellent guide to what is offered in the way of riding, whether instructional, competitive, hacking or trail rides for the experienced. Belgium has some of Europe's finest beaches and also boasts fertile plains and forested hillsides. Belsud, a division of the tourist office, provides information on a number of one- to eight-day routes in the Belgian Ardennes, an area of wild country containing forest and heath, steep valleys and marshy plateaux. Shorter excursions are also available in other regions such as Brabant, the capital of which is Brussels. Particularly attractive is the Forest of Soignes with its beech trees and numerous old castles. Flanders has miles of sandy beaches, including the resorts of De Oanne and Knokke-le-Zoute, both with riding centers; at Oostduinkerke they go shrimping on horseback!

For its size, Luxembourg has more horses per capita than anywhere else in Europe. One-third of the country is covered in forest and the best riding takes place around the two main sections of the Grand Duchy: the uplands of the Ardennes in the north and, in the south, the Goodland — mainly rolling farmlands and woods bordered on the east by the grape-growing valley of Moselle. The Luxembourg Federation of Equestrian Sports provides detailed information on the riding tours offered by the 14 riding centers in the Duchy.

Holland offers the dedicated rider a few surprises, not least of which is a marvellous beach ride from the Hague to the Hook of Holland. In addition, the De Hoge Veluwe national park, with over 12,850 acres (5,200ha) of woodland, sand, heath, dunes and fens is rated by some as being perhaps the best riding country in Europe. In the north of Holland, the Friesland area is home to the native Friesian horse, while the Drenthe, Overijissel and Gelderland regions offer a good selection of stables; it is in the latter region that the Veluwe National Park is located. In central Holland the regions of Utrecht, Flevoland and North and South Holland offer typically Dutch scenery: windmills, flower fields, canals and rivers, while the Flevoland area, recently reclaimed from the sea, is a coastal region acclaimed for its riding, windsurfing, yachting, cycling, hiking and camping. In the south, Zeeland, North Brabant and Limburg offer suitable terrain for vacation riding.

The Scandinavian countries of Denmark, Sweden, Norway and Finland can be summed up in three words: space, solitude and scenery. With an area of 16,600 square miles (43,000 square km), Denmark is nowhere near flat and featureless, and includes a diverse rural landscape of fields, woods, lakes, streams and rivers. A feature of the country's horse-riding vacations are the pony camps run specifically for children. Farmhouse-style accommodation is available at Rabjerg near Skagen, and Fjerritslev near Alborg. Funen, with its orchards, meadows and strong agricultural traditions, offers family vacations and Zealand, largest of the main Danish islands (whose capital is Copenhagen) offers two riding schools and the opportunity to see restored Viking ships.

Norway has fantastic scenery with breathtaking fjords where mountains plunge thousands of feet to the sea: riding tours on Norwegian Fjord ponies are held in Sogne Fjord, the Hemsedal Valley and Nordfjord. The latter area offers the Fjord Horse Centre, an indoor riding school that also holds riding camps for children as well as family vacations.

Sweden has a number of highly regarded riding centers, especially in the Dalsland and Varmland regions. Rich in lakes, forests, hills and river valleys, the Norwegian/Swedish Alps offer seven-day tours for the experienced rider. Finland offers wonderful riding possibilities, with scarce population, plentiful pine forests and abundant lakes. In the capital, Helsinki, there is excellent riding to be enjoyed, and one of the best lakeland settings is the hotel Aulanko, the stables of which offer a 40-minute ride around the huge Karlberg Estate.

The Icelandic pony is essentially identical to that relied upon by the Vikings. We can be sure of this because there have been no horses imported into Iceland for over 800 years. The Icelandic pony is tough, covers the ground well at a running walk (one of its five gaits) and is sure-footed — a major advantage in a country consisting largely of rocks, stones and desert wastes. The choice of riding is wide and the length of riding can vary from one to four hours close to the capital, Reykjavik, to eight-day highland tours for the experienced rider. One such eight-day trek from the Brekkulaekur to the magnificent Arnarvatnshedi heath includes trout fishing, with overnight stays in mountain cabins. Clothing should consist of rainwear, rubber boots, jogging suits, sneakers, hats and gloves plus a change of clothing, because you will probably be crossing many rivers!

Germany's main riding organization, Deutsche Reiterliche Vereinigung EV produces an annual guide to vacation riding, listing some 150 centers which offer vacation riding. Some organize riding tours as well, although these are few and far between. Horse riding is a very popular pastime in Germany and capabilities are expert at both a competitive and casual level. The standard, therefore, is generally high whether you ride in a town or in the rural regions, which range from the vast Luneburg Heath in the north to the Bavarian villages in the south. Bavaria contains over 100 riding establishments, and in upper Bavaria you can take in the Alps, the Munich Oktoberfest, the lake district and Berchtesgadenerland. Eastern Bavaria offers quiet river valleys, forests and lakes and also includes the area along the Danube.

The 26 towns and cities in the tourist areas of the Black Forest, Neckarland-Swabia and Lake Constance-Upper Swabia, occupy terrain that blends rivers and lakes, mountains and forests. The Rhineland, long famous for its castles and vineyards, offers equally fine riding, as does the camping area of Saarland. At Warendorf, in the north Rhine area, the West German Riding Academy not only turns out many show jumping and dressage champions but is also the administrative center for riding in West Germany.

Switzerland's dramatic landscape of mountains, lakes and flower-covered meadows lends itself to riding, although organized vacations on horseback have tended to have a low profile as many are still arranged locally. However, a diverse range of activities is avail-

Two views of the spectacular Bright Angel Trail, one of the awesome vacation possibilities in north America — both Canada and the USA are well prepared for riders and, as City Slickers *showed, on one of the cattle-driving holidays you really can be a cowboy at home on the range.*

able, the most notable being winter polo on the frozen lake at St. Moritz. In the central region — the hub of which is Lake Lucerne — there is dressage, jumping, riding tours and an indoor school at Buchrain. The Bernese-Oberland, is one of Europe's most popular tourist areas, offering riding tours set against picture-postcard valleys, snow-capped mountains and lakes. The northwest has a proliferation of riding stables and the northeast has a wide selection of riding activities, offering hacking, dressage and riding tours.

The Bernese Jura region is mostly low mountains with gorges, green valleys and forests and features horse-drawn carriage tours. In the Fribourg area there is riding at Ependes, Kerzers and Muntelier. In Jura, riding tours, hacking, dressage, jumping and an indoor school are all available.

In the Vaid, Valais, Ticino and Bernese Mitteland regions, various riding activities are available in a number of differing climates and landscapes, each varying quite markedly from the next. In the Geneva region, which is dominated by the vast, crescent-shaped lake, the region enjoys a mild climate, with part of the northern lakeland shore almost sub-tropical. Geneva is an international city and offers a number of activities as an alternative to riding, including water sports, theatres, bars and cabarets.

A riding vacation in Austria would not be complete without a visit to the capital, Vienna, and its famous Spanish Riding School. Tickets for the shows with the famous Lipizzaner horses and their displays of classical equitation must be booked well in advance — often months beforehand — so booking is best made from your home base. As far as other riding activities are concerned, Austria seems to have these in abundance, all set against an appealing alpine backdrop. The province of Tyrol encapsulates the Austrian ideal, bounded by Germany in the north and Switzerland and Italy in the south, it boasts high mountains, splendid slopes, glaciers, lush meadows and wooded valleys. The province also has its own native pony, the Haflinger, used for pulling sleighs in the winter sports' season; the area offers riding and coach-driving schools using these hardy, sure-footed ponies.

In Australia, as everywhere, interest in riding as a sport is growing, and the success of Australian and New Zealand riders at the Atlanta Olympics is bound to have a positive effect. Trail riding has intensified, in attractive areas like the Blue Mountains, the mountainous parts of the Gold Coast and the Lamington National Park. Even the heart of the Red Centre of the Great Outback, the Ross River resort, has riding. Sheep stations often take paying guests.

Since this survey has concentrated mainly on Europe and the Americas, vast areas have not been covered. For example, horse riding vacations can be enjoyed in such diverse places as Africa, Israel, Jamaica, Malaysia and the Himalayas. In fact, the growing popularity of vacations involving horses means that if you can think of a destination anywhere in the world, chances are, you will be able to enjoy that vacation riding horses!

BELOW and RIGHT: The Camargue isn't the only French destination for the rider — there are many hundreds of possibilities from the Pas-de-Calais to the Pyrénées — but there's something very distinctive about the Provençal countryside that makes it special.

Shagya Arabian mare and foal.

PART THREE

LIVING WITH HORSES

CHAPTER 15

THE ANATOMY OF THE HORSE

Simon Forty, Leisa Crook, Michael Hurley

The first horse, *Eohippus*, probably developed from a five-fingered/toed prototype mammal. Fifty million years later, *Eohippus* has evolved into *Equus caballus*: from a primitive, reclusive early mammal into today's horse.

What a transformation! Today's horse is an excellent example of form following function. Evolution meant that as *Eohippus* developed it lost the prehensile five fingers and toes on limbs which enabled dexterity and precision movements. What it got in return was the ability to move a large weight very quickly: the horse's long legs, musculature and respiratory system are designed to do just that. There is no lateral movement to the horse's limbs: the muscles, bones and digits have been reduced down to the minimum necessary for form to follow function. The horse today stands on limbs which end in a single finger (or toe), surrounded by a hard wearing nail. The result of evolution is an animal designed (primarily) for speed.

Current theory says that there are four ancestors of today's horses. Two were from hot, dry, desert conditions — one closest to today's Akhal-Teke, the other the ancestor of the Arabian and hot-blooded horses — the other two were better equipped for extreme climatic conditions and demanding terrain — one was like the Icelandic or Highland pony and the other like the Exmoor. From these ancestors came the variety of breeds shown in Part 4 of this book. Interestingly, despite the differing breeds, all horses' internal parts are basically very similar: all have 64 chromosomes and the only actual physical difference between the breeds is that Arabians have one fewer vertebrae.

BASIC DESCRIPTION

The quadruped horse is a herbivore which, like many grazing animals, has long jaws and a long head. This and the placement of the eyes set in the side of the head mean that a horse can see almost all round himself with a small blind spot immediately behind him; but it also means there's a blind spot immediately in front of his nose. His hairy muzzle enables him — unlike a cow — to break ice and eat through snow.

ABOVE: The Tarpan is the main ancestor of the small horses of Europe.

ABOVE and BELOW RIGHT: From the tiniest of ponies (here a New Forest) to the heaviest draft horse (Ardennes illustrated), they are all just different breeds of the domestic horse.

The horse's sense of smell is good: it has two olfactory organs — the ordinary nasal organ and Jacobson's organ which is thought to determine the flavor of food by aroma alone, rather than with taste.

The horse's body has a long neck, which is used as a counterbalance when moving, and long spine. A rider sits just behind the shoulder on saddles placed on the muscles to the side of the spine. It is important that saddles do not rub against the bony spines on the top of the vertebrae because this would cause sores.

This examination of the horse's body starts at the outermost layer — the epithelial layer of the skin.

THE SKIN

The horse's skin is an impermeable outer layer, a defense against infection, the elements and, in the case of the hooves, the terrain. It's composed of many layers of cells, with two main ones — the epidermis and the dermis. The epidermis is an outer epithelial layer and has two main layers itself — the *stratum corneum* and *stratum germinativum*. The inner layer is living, contains no blood vessels but does have nerve endings

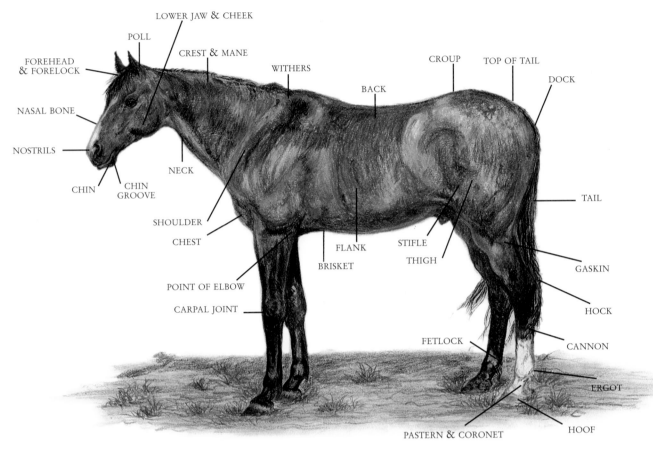

POLL

LOWER JAW & CHEEK

FOREHEAD
& FORELOCK

CREST & MANE

WITHERS

CROUP

TOP OF TAIL

BACK

DOCK

NASAL BONE

NOSTRILS

CHIN

CHIN
GROOVE

NECK

SHOULDER

CHEST

TAIL

FLANK

STIFLE

BRISKET

THIGH

GASKIN

POINT OF ELBOW

HOCK

CARPAL JOINT

CANNON

FETLOCK

ERGOT

PASTERN & CORONET

HOOF

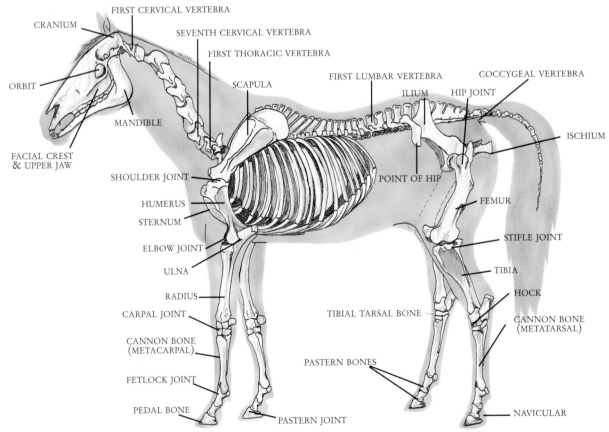

FIRST CERVICAL VERTEBRA

CRANIUM

SEVENTH CERVICAL VERTEBRA

FIRST THORACIC VERTEBRA

FIRST LUMBAR VERTEBRA

COCCYGEAL VERTEBRA

ORBIT

SCAPULA

ILIUM

HIP JOINT

ISCHIUM

MANDIBLE

POINT OF HIP

FACIAL CREST
& UPPER JAW

SHOULDER JOINT

FEMUR

HUMERUS

STERNUM

STIFLE JOINT

ELBOW JOINT

TIBIA

ULNA

HOCK

RADIUS

CARPAL JOINT

TIBIAL TARSAL BONE

CANNON BONE
(METATARSAL)

CANNON BONE
(METACARPAL)

FETLOCK JOINT

PASTERN BONES

PEDAL BONE

PASTERN JOINT

NAVICULAR

and is extremely sensitive. The dermis is the innermost layer, in which the hair follicles occur and in which blood vessels nourish the epidermal layers. The skin varies in thickness around the body — it's thinnest behind the elbow and between the back legs.

The skin, as a defense against infection, ceases to perform its function if breached by bacteria or parasite and so it is essential that all areas of concern — from serious wounds like overreach injuries to small grazes — are examined carefully and dealt with clinically. However, it's not just a penetrating wound that can cause a breach in the skin: moisture can soften the skin and allow in an infection like mud fever.

Horses sweat directly from their skin: the main concentration of sweat glands being around the neck, shoulders and flanks. Man — through clipping, rugging and exercising — affects the horse's body temperature and so needs to be very careful of his actions. The horse generates considerable levels of heat through exercise and needs to vent this to survive: he needs not only to be able to sweat, but for that sweat to evaporate. A clipped horse loses its sweat more quickly — it runs off more easily — but then it runs the risk of catching cold.

The hoof is a form of keratin — a modified type of skin, much like fingernails, which protects the foot from wear and tear. It grows quickly enough to require regular attention in the form of trimming.

THE RESPIRATORY SYSTEM

Mammals depend on oxygen for life, breathing it into the lungs, where it is transferred into the red blood cells, which, in turn, give up their carbon dioxide to the air. The horse is no exception to this, breathing between eight and 15 times a minute at rest. As soon as more energy is required, the breathing rate increases. As the demand for oxygen becomes greater, certain physiological changes can be spotted: the nostrils begin to flare, the head and neck extend, giving a straighter line passage between nostrils and lungs.

The air passes over the turbinate bones to help warm it before it reaches more sensitive tissue. At the back of the mouth the air reaches the pharynx from which it passes through the vocal chords, larynx, trachea, and the left and right bronchi tubes into the lungs before reaching the small bronchioles where it is transferred to air sacs (alveoli) where the oxygen/carbon dioxide transfer takes place. These bronchioles are very delicate and can become hypersensitive to fungal spores breathed in from the likes of hay or straw. This is chronic obstructive pulmonary disease — what used to be called broken wind. The lungs take up most of the thoracic cavity. The right hand one is bigger than the left which has to make room for the heart.

Because of the drying effects of so much air, the lining of the alveoli secretes a mucus which helps to lubricate the system: it drains up the trachea to the mouth thanks to the activity of billions of cilia.

THE CIRCULATORY SYSTEM

As with all mammals, the engine of the horse is the four-chambered heart which pumps blood through the arteries to the body; it returns via the veins. The arteries carry the oxygenated blood at high pressure, helped by muscles in their walls. If an artery is severed, the blood can jet many feet: the only answer is a pressure bandage to keep the wound closed long enough for the bleeding to stop.

The heart, larger and heavier than a man's to power the bulkier horse, is a double pump which pumps at about 40 beats a minute at rest. It takes oxygenated blood, which comes into the left atrium via the pulmonary veins from the lungs and is pumped into the left ventricle, and pumps it through the aorta to the rest of the body. The veins bring the carbon dioxide-

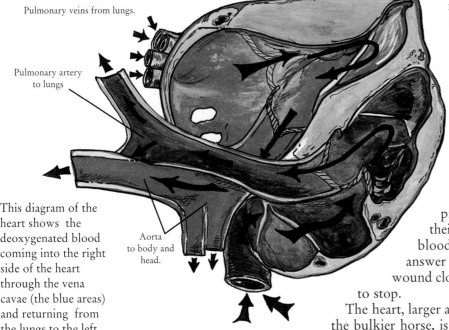

Pulmonary veins from lungs.

Pulmonary artery to lungs

Aorta to body and head.

This diagram of the heart shows the deoxygenated blood coming into the right side of the heart through the vena cavae (the blue areas) and returning from the lungs to the left side of the heart by way of the pulmonary veins exiting to the body through the aorta (the red areas).

The vena cavae: posterior from body; anterior from head.

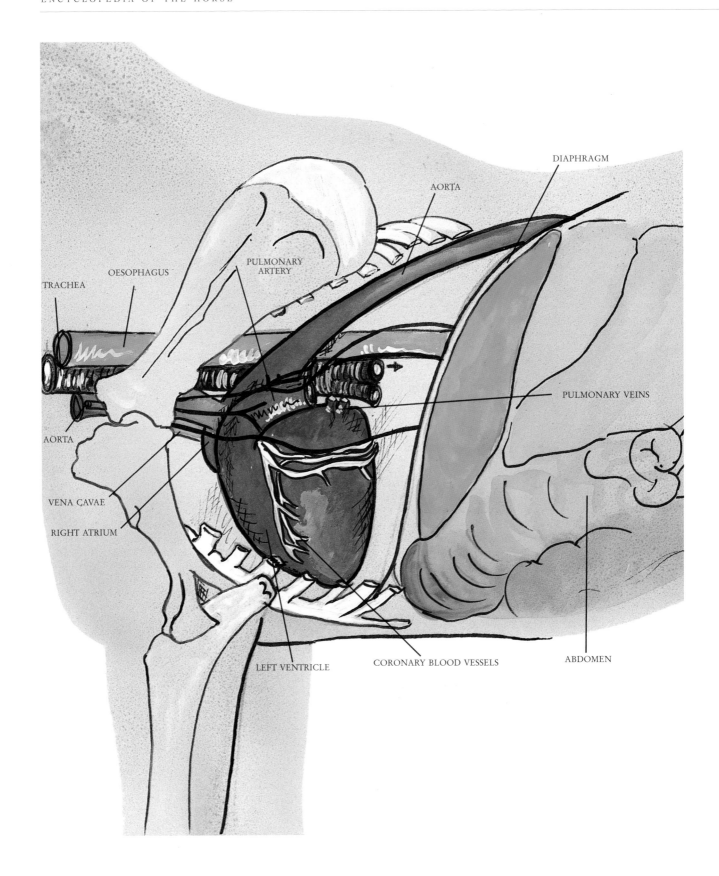

TRACHEA

OESOPHAGUS

PULMONARY
ARTERY

AORTA

DIAPHRAGM

AORTA

PULMONARY VEINS

VENA CAVAE

RIGHT ATRIUM

LEFT VENTRICLE

CORONARY BLOOD VESSELS

ABDOMEN

*The position of the heart in relation to stomach, trachea and
oesophagus.*

laden blood back to the right atrium of the heart through the vena cava — the anterior vena cava from the head and the posterior vena cava from the body.

From the right atrium blood is pumped into the right ventricle where the pulmonary artery takes it to be oxygenated in the lungs. This takes place in the alveoli, where the air in the lungs is separated from the bloodstream by no more than a cell's width. The red blood cells in the bloodstream take the oxygen from the lungs to the tissues and swap it for carbon dioxide, returning to do their job again. The rest of the blood is made up of white blood cells, fewer in number than the red and responsible primarily for fighting infection, and plasma, which carries food around the body and waste to be excreted.

To take a horse's pulse, feel for the artery which curves over the horse's lower jaw. While 40 beats a minute is the usual rate at rest, the horse in motion will experience a substantial increase in pulse rate — over 200 at times. A racehorse in top condition, like a human athlete, will have a lower heartbeat at rest, say 25–30 beats a minute; at speed that will increase to a phenomenol 240–250. The animal will also have a much bigger and heavier heart.

The horse's circulation system can have problems circulating through its lower legs if the horse cannot exercise and is kept cooped up for long periods. If this happens the legs get puffy, filled with liquid, which is carried away when the animal receives proper exercise.

An important part of the cleansing of the blood is its filtration by the liver, a large glandular organ which lies across the diaphragm, in contact with stomach, duodenum and right kidney. The liver has a multitude of functions: it stores glycogen and iron, excretes bile, breaks down old red blood cells and toxic substances, helps assimilate protein, carbohydrates and fats from the bloodstream; from the liver urea and uric acid enter the bloodstream to be excreted as urine by the kidneys. Part of the posterior vena cava passes through the liver.

THE NERVOUS SYSTEM

The brain and the spinal cord make up the central nervous system. This can be divided into two systems to explain purpose — the somatic and the autonomic. The former controls the voluntary muscles and is concerned with nerve impulses from skin, eyes etc. The autonomic system controls those functions of the body necessary to maintain basic life — regulating breathing, heart rate, the activities of liver, digestive tract, bladder, for example. The autonomic system contains sympathetic and parasympathetic nerves. Sympathetic nerves prepare the body for significant action — increasing heart rate etc; the parasympathetic nerves level everything off after the action.

The brain is divided into the cerebrum, which contains the thalamus which relays sensory nerve impulses to the cortex, the brain stem and the cerebellum. The cerebrum is concerned with memory, intelligence, volition, and is the receiving station for the senses and the voluntary control of the skeletal muscles. The cerebellum is particularly well developed in the horse, where it controls balance and complex muscular movements. Nerves are either sensory or motor — ie carrying messages to the brain and central nervous system or carrying messages from the brain.

THE LOCOMOTOR SYSTEM

The musculo-skeletal system of the horse consists of muscles, bones, tendons and ligaments.

MUSCLES
Those under the conscious control of the horse are called voluntary muscles; there are over 700 of them

BELOW: Muscles and ligaments of the horse's leg. The body weight is held upright by a series of muscles, tendons and ligaments which work to hold the joints unflexed.

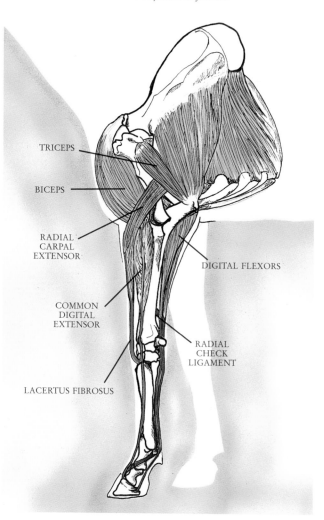

TRICEPS

BICEPS

RADIAL CARPAL EXTENSOR

DIGITAL FLEXORS

COMMON DIGITAL EXTENSOR

RADIAL CHECK LIGAMENT

LACERTUS FIBROSUS

and they are very active. These muscles are arranged over the body, most of them being attached to the skeleton by tendons. There are two main muscle types: flexors, which cause a joint to bend, and extensors, which cause a joint to straighten.

Movement is accomplished by balancing the pull between these two different types of muscle. Muscles are well nourished by a good blood supply — this helps particularly when a muscle is damaged. Muscle tone is the state of partial contraction of a muscle when it is ready for activity. The horse has the ability to build upon muscle and thereby to achieve a very high state of muscle tone and condition — which is why it can be trained to run quickly over distance.

BONES

The skeleton of the horse has over 200 bones — long bones (the major limbs), short bones (like those of the knee or hock), flat bones (those of the shoulderblade or scull), irregular bones (the vertebrae) and spongy bones (feet of horses). A young horse's bones will be composed of 60 percent tough fibrous tissue; an old one's 60 percent brittle lime salts. Most of the growth in height of a horse occurs in its first two or three years. The horse's knee equates to our wrist, the cannon bone to our middle hand bone. The first and fifth hand bones have disappeared during evolution, and the second and fourth bones are small, starting at the knee and tapering away halfway down the cannon bone. These bones fuse to the cannon bone at about four years of age — the ailment called splints is caused by the ends rubbing on the cannon bone and causing a bony growth: a splint.

The fingers have all gone except the middle — the pastern bone. At the end of the finger is the equivalent of our fingernail — the hoof. In the back leg, the stifle joint is our knee, the hock our ankle. The back and front legs are similar although the reduced bones don't form splints.

TENDONS

These attach muscles to bones or whatever the muscle operates. They are very tough, composed of dense bundles of white fibrous tissues which consist mainly of collagen.

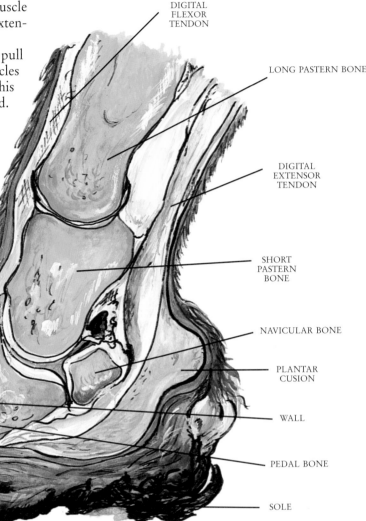

The horse's foot.

DIGITAL FLEXOR TENDON

LONG PASTERN BONE

DIGITAL EXTENSOR TENDON

SHORT PASTERN BONE

NAVICULAR BONE

PLANTAR CUSION

WALL

PEDAL BONE

SOLE

LIGAMENTS

These hold bones together at joints allowing bones to move only in those directions that they should. They are made of fibrous tissue, like tendons, but are more elastic. The surfaces of the bones in a joint are coated with articular cartilage to provide a smooth contact. In some joints the cartilage is in disk form — eg, the stifle joint between femur and tibia and fibula. The whole joint is lubricated by synovial fluid.

The horse uses its locomotor system to move in one of four main forward paces (although he can also move in various other ways — fast walk, rack, pacing or indeterminate ways).

WALK

With four beats there are at least two feet on the ground. The feet fall in the sequence right hind, right fore, left hind, left fore. Beats are slightly uneven.

The sole of the unshod foot.

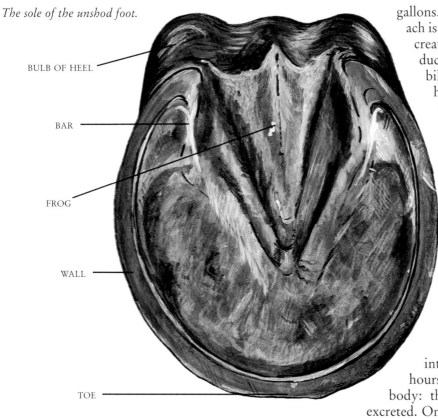

BULB OF HEEL

BAR

FROG

WALL

TOE

TROT

Two even beats to the trot, left fore and right hind hitting the floor together, followed by the right fore and left hind. Between beats the horse is in the air.

CANTER

An asymmetrical pace, the sequence is right hind, right fore and left hind together, left fore, suspension.

GALLOP

Also asymmetric — the sequence is left hind, right hind, left fore, right fore, suspension.

THE DIGESTIVE SYSTEM

The digestive system starts with eating — grazing for the horse. Its lips are quite mobile, sensitive and manipulative and it grasps the food it wants, severing it by using its incisors. The action of chewing by the molars initiates the creation of saliva and digestion.

Digestion, absorption and assimilation are the three processes by which food is taken into the body and its nutrients leeched. From the moment food enters the mouth, digestion begins through the action of saliva on starch. Digestion proper, however, begins in the stomach — not a particularly large organ in the horse — through gastric juices. The food stays in the stomach until it's about two-thirds full and then is passed to the small intestine — all 70ft of it, holding about 12

gallons. Here it is neutralized — the stomach is very acidic — and attacked by pancreatic juices and bile, which is produced in the liver. In many mammals, bile is stored in the gall bladder. The horse doesn't have one. The small intestine also sees the lymph vessels collecting fat: it is eventually passed to the bloodstream. The next step in the digestive system is the large intestine, 25ft long with a capacity of about 26 gallons, and composed of the caecum, large and small colon and rectum. The large intestine is where bacteria carries out the digestive process, breaking down cellulose. Finally waste is excreted from the body. Movement through the intestines is by peristalsis.

Water passes through to the intestines quickly and after some hours the nutrients are absorbed into the body: that which cannot be absorbed is excreted. Once the food has been absorbed it is taken around the body by the bloodstream or lymph system and each cell assimilates what it requires; eg, the muscles taking protein. Anything unassimilated is stored as fat.

THE URINARY AND REPRODUCTIVE SYSTEM

In both sexes both systems share a common outlet. The urinary system starts with the kidneys — a pair of organs high up against the roof of the abdomen and differing from each other in shape and position. Urine is produced by filtering water and other substances out of the bloodstream. These pass to the bladder by the ureter. The bladder is emptied via the urethra which empties via the penis in the male; in the female the urethra empties just above the vulva.

The mare's reproductive system starts at the ovaries, which lie near the kidneys. The eggs travel from the ovaries to the uterus. At the head of the uterus is the cervix, a sphincter which opens only to allow sperm in and the foal out. If the cervix opens during pregnancy, abortion is likely; at any time other than in heat, opening of the cervix can allow the entry of bacteria.

In the stallion sperm is generated in the testes which hang down between the back legs. The penis is safely encased in a sheath, held firmly there by the crewmaster muscle. It will engorge with blood and leave the sheath during sexual arousal or urination.

111

THE PSYCHOLOGY OF THE HORSE

Sandra Forty, Leisa Crook, Michael Hurley

While training horses a great deal of attention is given to their physical development, that is to the suppleness and build-up of muscles and to improving the stamina and speed of the animal. However, it is just as important to consider the psychological processes at work in the horse. If the mind of the animal is disturbed, then the body will not react as desired by the rider and trainer. All of a horse's experience build up to become the sum of his personality; bad habits once they become established can be difficult if not impossible to remove. The horse is not an animal of high intelligence, but it does respond well to repetitive training for it has a good memory.

Physically, the brain of the horse is very small in relation to the animal's size; also a horse is totally prompted by instinct, rather than by reason, which motivates humans. In fact, the overall mentality of the horse is based upon primitive instincts developed in the wild as a means of survival against the natural hazards of the environment and the activities of predatory carnivores — foremost of which has been man himself. If a horse's behavior can sometimes seem a puzzle, try to think like the animal, put yourself in his position and his reactions can become completely understandable.

Horses are herbivorous and, as such, have developed defensive rather than attacking mechanisms in order to survive. They don't stalk and kill prey, because they were the prey and anyway have no defensive armor such as horns. This is the reason for their highly charged senses and their physical ability to move swiftly away from danger at the slightest sign of trouble. This in turn explains why horses are very excitable and nervous and liable to start and flee from anything unexpected or out of the ordinary. Furthermore highly-strung warmbloods like Arabians react quicker than the cold blood breeds and will be more difficult to control because of their highly strung natures. It is important to realize that the horse retains these defensive mechanisms even in the domestic state and after centuries of manhandling, despite this the resultant effects on the horse's personality should be taken into account when handling and training.

ABOVE: While the physical development of a horse is, of course, important in its training, it is just as important to consider the psychological processes at work. It is not an animal of high intelligence, reacts mainly on instinct but with careful handling can be trained to perform complex movements alien to its natural inclinations. Here a Saddlebred racking — an impressive gait in which each foot is grounded in succession and at a fast pace.

The horse is a herd animal and so requires the reassurance of others of his kind around him. In the wild, horses herd together as a matter of necessity to ensure their survival, if startled they instinctively bunch together for protection and flee en masse. He is a naturally friendly animal who enjoys living in groups, consequently a horse when kept alone can become prone to neuroses which do not occur when horses live together. So in captivity, a horse does much better if kept with other horses.

A horse's stable and usual pastures become his home, the place where he feels most secure and relaxed. This is especially true when he is surrounded by other horses, left alone he can feel insecure and continuously look for other horses to mingle with. This herd instinct is used to the trainer's and rider's advantage in a number of ways, the most obvious being in the sport of racing which, in a sense, is a simulation of the herd in flight. The horse will usually try to remain with other members of his "herd" — this is frequently seen in jump racing when a horse, having

TOP: The horse is herbivorous, more likely to run away from problems than to act aggressively. But kept on his own, fed with high energy foods, he can become neurotic and defiant. These are Lipizzaner mares, capable of being precision-trained.

RIGHT and BELOW RIGHT: The herd brings companionship, protection and a leader. It is important that you take the place of the leader, firmly and consistently.

lost its rider, continues over every fence and completes the race, albeit riderless.

Leadership is an important part of horse life — even in the domestic state. All herd animals develop a strict pecking order dependant on their sex, size, strength and age. Most horses look for a dominant stallion to follow and obey. When domesticated this situation rarely develops, but the animals still follow their instinct as much as they can — in this way geldings will choose a few mares to protect. As a substitute a horse will usually accept and trust his master as his herd leader if he proves himself firm, fair and a reliable provider of food and security. It is natural, however, for the horse to test this dominance out by being uncooperative and temperamental; but the animal will back down when he realizes the human is the master. If the horse is allowed to have his own way he will take over as leader and become uncontrollable.

Boredom and loneliness in the box can lead to nervous conditions such as crib-biting. It is important to keep in mind that in order to produce a calm and receptive horse, the animal must feel secure in its immediate surroundings. Horses often form strong, bonding friendships and an animal who is unable to do this, even with a cat or dog, will feel lonely and isolated. Another important factor is food, a high protein diet is liable to increase a horse's excitability and notably alter his behavior, perhaps enough to make him defiant and difficult to handle. To counteract this the animal must be given plenty of exercise to burn off his excess energy.

Normally in the wild much of the horse's time is taken up with searching for and eating food. A domesticated horse doesn't have this problem, but he is still always on the lookout for food. He is easily distracted by the thought of food and will be particularly difficult to train if this takes place anywhere near a place he normally associates with eating — such as his stable.

Other problems of nervousness and excitement continually confront the horse trainer. The animal will champ at the bit and shy away at the slightest noise or at something unexpected that catches his eye — a fluttering piece of litter or sudden noises — even unusual smells. All this goes back to the primitive flight instinct, so deeply ingrained in the horse that some animals never actually get over it.

Although shying can never be totally eradicated, it can nonetheless be reduced to a minimum by commonsense treatment from the rider. Remember that to a horse its safety depends almost entirely on its ability to run away and everything is seen in relation to this. Actions such as continually persuading the horse to smell or touch the offending article, the use of a soothing and encouraging voice and the rider's firm seat and grip will all help the horse to overcome its fear of the unknown or unusual.

Punishment in any form only serves to increase the animal's nervousness and in some cases can cause a more extreme reaction, such as bucking. Horses have a very low pain tolerance and pain threshold. This again goes back to the wild when they were prey animals not aggressors — they didn't have to fight their food to eat it. So a horse will do everything he can to escape pain, which in turn makes him a tractable animal to domesticate and train. The mere threat of the use of the whip or spurs will move him in the desired direction.

The senses of the horse are highly developed, especially those important in ensuring their survival in the wild. They are very inquisitive and easily excited by new things. Thus, the sense of taste acts in much the same way in the horse as it does in similar animals, but sight and hearing are specifically developed to enable the horse a better chance of survival.

Horses have extremely well developed hearing because the head resembles a sound box. In addition, the horse has very mobile ears, which can be turned in the direction of any sound. This acute sense of hearing allows him to detect subtle tones, particularly those of the human voice. Similarly the horse's sense of smell has also evolved to the degree where it can detect the smell of fear around a human, to which it reacts. Horses are also able to identify the smell of blood and fear, which has been observed to cause them to become agitated and distressed.

Horses have good all-round lateral vision because their eyes are on either side of their head. This means that they cannot focus on anything directly in front of them. This is another sign of a prey animal which needs as much all-round vision as possible to spot anything with evil intent sneaking up. However, it is not so useful when it comes to jumping fences. When approaching an obstacle the horse needs to tilt its head before jumping to make sure it sees the fence from only one eye: both eyes are able to see a fence at a distance of about 45ft (13.5m) but at 4ft (1.2m) from the fence the lower part of the horse's head makes it impossible for both eyes to view it and unless the horse is able to tilt his head, he must jump blind.

The horse also appears to have a "sixth sense," as is seen in many other animals. For example, horses have been noted behaving nervously just before a thunderstorm and seem to be particularly sensitive to earthquakes. This "sixth sense" also enables them to identify people who are timid or hesitant as well as those who are confident and relaxed. Thus, the horse is able to perceive the mood of the rider or trainer and mirror it, allowing in the right circumstances a close rapport to be developed.

Horses have extremely retentive memories and their memory for both good and bad experiences and ability to associate cause and effect is used in training. If the horse performs a task well and is rewarded immediately, he connects this action with a pleasurable experience and will recall this when asked to repeat the task at a later stage. On the other hand, if the horse kicks and is immediately punished, it associates the kicking action with a painful and unpleasant experience and is not likely to repeat it. However, the horse does not comprehend delayed punishment and reward. If he is punished five minutes after being disobedient he cannot relate the punishment to the crime and will only become resentful at what seems to be unjust treatment he cannot understand.

RIGHT: The horse may seem a natural jumper, but the position of its eyes means that it rarely focuses on things in front and has to turn its head to the side to see past its nose when close to the obstacle. It's hard to believe the difficulties when you see a show jumper in full flight — as here Nick Skelton on Showtime.

CHAPTER 17

THE HEALTH OF THE HORSE

Simon Forty, Leisa Crook, Michael Hurley

A "healthy" or sound horse is generally regarded as an animal which is able to sustain its normal function — that is the ability to perform the purpose for which it is kept. On the other hand, a horse will be regarded as unhealthy or simply unsound if its normal function is in any way impaired or diminished, either temporarily or permanently, by some disease or unhealthy condition.

Disease is defined as any condition that sees the body structure altered abnormally. Diseases have a cause (etiology), a life span (pathogenesis), a likely outcome (prognosis) and a means of treatment or at least control.

All diseases found in horses can be classified into one of seven categories, based on their cause. These categories are:

- **Developmental disease and conditions** — eg, bowed legs
- **Infectious disease and conditions** — eg, strangles
- **Disease caused by cancer** — eg, lymphosarcoma
- **Disease caused by parasites** — eg, weight loss and diarrhea
- **Disease caused by imbalances in nutrition**
- **Disease caused by toxins or poisoning**
- **Disease caused by traumatic episode or incident** — eg, fracture

As well as categorizing the cause of a disease, it is useful to categorise which of the horse's body systems are affected. The major body systems, as identified in Chapter 15, are:

- **The skin**
- **The respiratory system** — lungs, larynx etc.
- **The circulatory system** — cardiovascular system, heart, veins, etc.
- **The nervous system** — brains, nerves, etc.
- **The locomotor system** — bones, muscles, etc.
- **The digestive system** — intestines, stomach, etc.
- **The reproductive system** — uterus, ovaries, testicles, etc.
- **The urinary system** — kidneys, etc.

The following chapter will describe diseases and disorders of these body systems, as well as looking in more detail at some of the specific disease categories.

To be able to judge the health of your horse you need to have a good idea of what to expect and therefore what is out of the ordinary: something experience will certainly help. There are five signs you can look for that will give you a good indication of your horse's state of well being:

Temperature, taken rectally, should be about 100.5°F (38°C).

Heartbeat at rest should be 40 a minute.

Breathing at rest should be unlabored and about 10–15 breaths a minute. Check both heart and breathing together: both should be in relation to each other, so if the heart is racing, the breathing should be faster than usual. If only one of these functions is racing, then there could be a problem.

Feeding: you should know whether your horse is feeding as usual, and you should also be able to tell if the horse is behaving uncharacteristically.

Temperament changes. Abnormalities of this and feeding are factors that, again, experience will identify.

If there are perceptible differences in the physical signs, or marked changes in behavior, call a vet. Don't be afraid to do so: the vet will listen to your assessment and make his own decision as to the likely immediacy of any condition — but let *him* decide; don't put off phoning. This is particularly true for a new horse. When you buy make sure you get the horse's full medical record, in particular of all vaccines and injections; get the animal examined by a vet who will be able to point out any obvious condition; try to talk to the vendor to find out any peculiarities or idiosyncrasies that may be able to give you a clue to the horse's wellbeing.

Just like humans, horses need the right living environment and the horse's mental condition can play every bit as much a part in promoting general health as anything else. Whether stabled or pastured, horses need to be comfortable in their surroundings, they need to be fed well — not overfed but fed sufficiently; they need a good source of fresh water (they will drink between 6 and 12 gallons — 27–54 liters — a day); they may need a salt lick; they need to be well shod and well exercised, if possible in the company of other horses; they need to be kept warm and be allowed shelter from inclement weather. All these things involve common sense on the part of the owner: keep your eyes open and you'll spot problems early.

INFECTIOUS DISEASES

The accompanying tables show examples of infectious diseases to which horses are prone. These diseases are caused by micro-organisms: viruses — minute infective agents which can be differentiated from bacteria by size and their ability only to multiply in living cells; bacteria — unicellular microscopic organisms; and fungi. Each group has further subdivisions — for example, bacteria can be coccus, diplococci, strepto-

BACTERIAL DISEASES

Acne	Sores on skin
Tetanus	Lockjaw. Stiffness, then spasms
Mud fever	Raw areas oozing pus
Rainscald	Raw areas and scabs
Salmonellosis	Diarrhea
Sleepy foal disease	Weakness in newborn
Strangles	Fever, nasal discharge, lymph gland swelling and bursting
Tuberculosis	Wasting

VIRAL DISEASES

African sickness	Pneumonia and enteritis
Equine herpes Virus I	The horse's common cold. Fever, cough, abortion
Flu	Coughing, fever, nasal discharge
Infectious anemia	Anemia, fever and swellings
Pneumonia	Fever, difficulty in breathing
Sarcoids	Growths which ulcerate and bleed
Spots	Ulcers on sexual organs of both sexes
Stable cough	Cough and catarrh
Warts	Growths, usually around muzzle

FUNGAL DISEASES

Abortion	Thickened placenta
Broken wind	Chronic obstructive pulmonary disease. Heaves, cough, nasal discharge
Guttural pouch mycosis	Nasal hemorrhage
Grass sickness	Deadly sickness of nervous systems. Temporary paralysis
Ringworm	Circular patches on skin which scab over, hair loss

ENDOPARASITIC DISEASES

Ascariasis (roundworms)	Diarrhea, colic, pneumonia
Botflies	Gastritis, mechanical obstruction, loss of condition
Lungworm	Cough
Oxyuriasis (threadworms)	Emaciation, bare patches on tail
Pinworm	Tail rubbing
Spasmodic colic	US surveys blame 80 per cent of colic on worm damage
Strongylosis (red worms)	Anemia, debility, intermittent colic, diarrhea
Tapeworm	None
Habronemiasis	Summer sores, nodules on skin or eye
Verminous bronchitis	Cough and emaciation

ECTOPARASITIC DISEASES

Ear mange	Head shaking, rubbing
Lice	Bald patches
Mange	Irritation, loss of hair, scabs
Sweet itch	Rubbing tail and mane
Ticks	Skin irritation

BELOW: This horse has had an allergic reaction to a new brand of feed. The eruptions or hives cover most of the horse's neck and body.

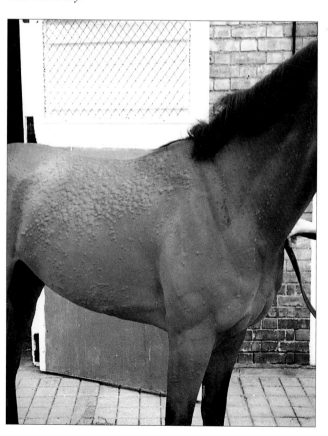

cocci or staphylococcus. Not all micro-organisms are unfriendly — the bacteria in a horse's large intestine serve an important function in the digestion of food.

Other infectious diseases are spread by parasites — either ectoparasites which live on the body of the host or endoparasites which live inside the host. Parasites tend to have to be present in large numbers to lead to disease or to defeat the body's natural defenses. Most parasites spend some of their time outside a host: the first stage tends to be when larvae are produced in the field; the horse crops them along with the grass; they inhabit him, laying eggs which are subsequently excreted onto the field; and so the cycle starts again.

The major internal parasites of the horse (with the exception of the larvae of horse botflies) are worms. All horses may acquire infection with these parasites

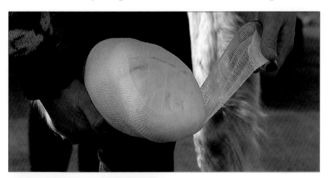

ABOVE: Kaolin poultices are used to reduce inflammation. They are very effective and hold their heat very well, exerting a drawing action to pull fluids like pus out of an abscess.

LEFT: When using a poultice on a horse's leg, use a boot to cover it.

early in life but the development of disease depends on the numbers and species of parasite present, which in turn depends on various environmental and epidemiological factors.

Horses can build up immunity to disease either by creating antibodies which neutralize the attacking microbe or by vaccines, some of which last for some time, others requiring regular boosters.

THE SKIN

As seen in Chapter 15, the skin is the outer protection of the horse. It suffers from cuts and bruises — and the cuts can prove particularly dangerous if they become infected. Painful abscesses can form; as can hematomas — swellings containing clotted blood under the skin — or edema, the collection of tissue in small spaces in and under the skin. As long as you have kept up your horse's booster shots, a tetanus injection shouldn't be necessary after a cut but in any case let the vet decide.

Wounds in general need to be handled very carefully and, if in doubt, call a vet. They need to be cleaned, pressure applied to stop the bleeding and a dressing put on. Wounds heal better on the body and the upper leg than lower down, so it is important to give them time to heal. Cuts which gape or which are over about an inch (2.5cm) should be stitched.

Overreach is a particularly nasty wound caused when the hind feet strike the back of the front heels. As well as causing much bruising, possibly even cutting tendons or muscles they can also be dirty wounds which get infected if not cleaned well.

Because it is the outer surface of the body, skin is directly affected by parasites such as lice, which suck the blood and live on the skin. The most obvious sign

BELOW: Laryngeal paralysis tends to happen on the left side of the larynx and causes the roaring audible when the horse exercises. Here, at left, a healthy larynx and, at right, one with left-sided paralysis.

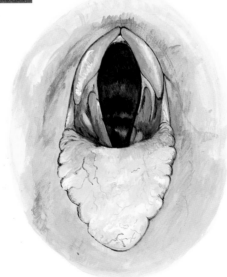
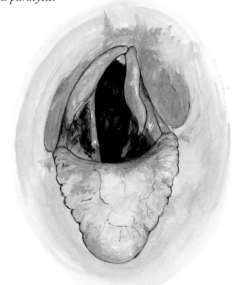

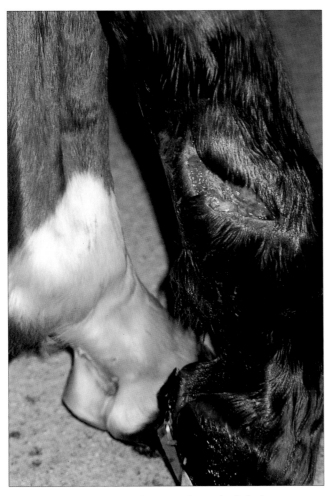

ABOVE: A deep overreach injury above the fetlock joint in a racehorse, caused by the hoof striking and cutting the foreleg while racing. This is a particularly serious injury for this horse because the important suspensory ligament was also severed.

of parasites will be scratching. Flies, too, can irritate and lead to rawness: a hypersensitivity to them is called sweet itch. Once a horse proves susceptible to sweet itch he will remain sensitized and suffer each time flies are out — mainly in the summer.

Other infectious diseases of the skin are: mud fever, around the lower legs, and rainscald on the upper body — both are bacterial and usually easily treated by antiseptic shampoos. Ringworm, the fungal infection common to many mammals, is most common where the skin is rubbed by tack: antibiotics will rapidly clear up the condition.

THE RESPIRATORY SYSTEM

Many problems with respiration tend to be viral and cured by time and a clean environment, which includes no contact with other stables, the vacuuming away of all dust, new dust-free bedding — ie, not hay — and good ventilation. Most lung problems show themselves when the horse starts coughing. If this is not associated with a fever, it could be heaves — Chronic Obstructive Pulmonary Disease — which is a hypersensitivity to fungal spores from hay, or it could be lungworm — the parasitic *Dictyoculus arnfieldi*. Picked up in grazing, horses are often infected with lungworm by companion donkeys, in whom — unless treated — the parasite is endemic. It is very rare for the larvae to reach maturity in horses.

If associated with a fever it is most likely to be the equine equivalent of the common cold: EHV1 (Equine Herpes Virus Type 1), the main problem with which is that it causes pregnant mares to abort. Equine influenza tends to cause an epidemic and can be vaccinated against. The two main strains are Type 1 Prague and Type 2 Miami. It is a serious illness and can cause death, particularly in foals. The infectious bacterial infection called strangles affects the lymph glands around the larynx and jaw. Bursting the abscesses usually causes the condition to improve.

Other illnesses associated with the respiratory system include EIPH (exercise-induced pulmonary hemorrhage) — this is caused by pressure in the top part of the lung in tissue already damaged by a viral infection — and laryngeal paralysis, almost invariably, leads to a roaring noise when the horse is exercised.

THE CIRCULATORY SYSTEM

Problems with the circulatory system tend to center around the blood — anemia or loss of salts through dehydration. Anemia reduces the amount of oxygen reaching tissue and leads to lethargy and tiredness. Sometimes the result of worm larvae damage, an application of a worming agent can help. Dehydration can be caused by the weather, diarrhea or exercise. It's important that the electrolytes lost in dehydration are replaced: this cannot be achieved simply be allowing the horse to drink; you must add the necessary salts, freely available over the counter.

The lymphtic system can become inflamed either by infection caused by bacteria (ulcerative lymphangitis and glanders) or by a yeast (zootic lymphangitis). A non-infective form is often known as Monday morning disease and makes itself known by edema in the lower legs which can be cured by light exercise. Mentioned by Hippocrates, glanders is an infection which can be passed to man, in whom it is nearly always fatal. It is an inoculable disease in the horse and sees nodules form in lungs, liver and other organs. Spread mainly by infected food and water, or as a skin infection, it is treatable but can lead to death.

The liver often shows a disturbance in the form of jaundice, the yellow discoloration of the mucous membranes — eyes, mouth, genitals. In a newborn foal it can indicate an incompatibility between the bloods of his sire and dam which causes hemolytic

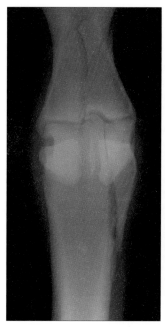
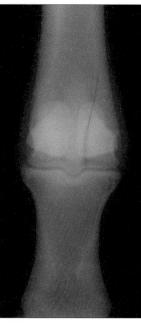

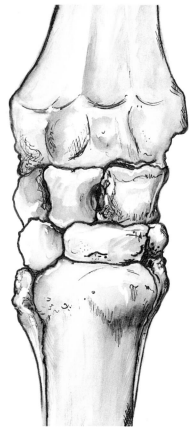

TOP LEFT: X ray showing a catastrophic fracture of the left foreleg of a horse, which was sustained during a race. The cannon bone, a sesamoid and the pastern bone are all involved.

TOP RIGHT: X ray showing a lateral condylar fracture of the cannon bone. This type of fracture can be repaired by screwing the fragment back to the main body of the bone and results in acomplete recovery.

ABOVE: The horse's knee joint.

jaundice. The antibodies created in the mother come to the foal in the colostrum and break down its red blood cells causing not only jaundice but acute anemia. The only treatment is a blood transfusion of up to six pints of suitable blood to the foal, something which requires specialist equipment and must be done quickly. It can be difficult to spot if you aren't expecting it — especially if the mare has foaled before without the problem occurring.

The main liver disease is hepatitis, inflammation of the liver, which can come in acute, suppurative (with abscesses) or chronic forms. It is caused by viruses, bacteria, liver flukes (which can be picked up from drinking infected water), poisons or as part of another illness like tuberculosis.

Finally, the heart itself can suffer from murmurs or arrhythmias: unless they affect the horse at exercise, and many do not, there is little cause for alarm.

THE LOCOMOTOR SYSTEM

Anything that leads to lameness is a problem for the horse: without the easy use of his legs he is useless. There are many problems which can affect leg movement — from obvious fractures through joint problems and on to a range of other ailments.

Joint problems can be caused by arthritis, the inflammation of a joint. In most cases this is caused by wear and tear brought on by age or over use; arthritis can, however, be brought on by infection, vitamin D deficiency or injury. Ringbones around the pastern and coffin joints, spavin (osteoarthritis of the lower hock joints) or navicular disease, all lead to lameness, but all are treatable, as are such obvious injuries as a pierced sole or sandcracks, vertical cracks in the hoof.

Problems involving bones are a common reason for seeking veterinary attention in all types and breeds of horse. Disorders of bone growth such as bowed legs or growth plate enlargement (epiphysitis) are commonly found in horses less than two years old. In older horses, nutritional imbalances can play a role in creating bone deformities such as "big head" where the head bones become soft and distorted.

Most conditions affecting horses's bones, apart from those caused by nutritional problems, can be traced to trauma or infection. Bone is a living tissue and, as such, is continually remodeling itself — its strength or weakness varying with regard to the horse's nutrition and health. It is also important to remember that bone must be regarded in its relationship with surrounding muscles, tendons, ligaments and joints. Bone has an outer lining, the periosteum, and an inner lining, the endosteum. Between these membranes lies the bone substance which is composed mainly of calcium and phosphorus laid down in a system of canals or spaces surrounded by bone cells.

Bone disorders are first noticed as bony lumps, which can be either painful or not, and which may or may not cause lameness. Common terms for these lumps depend on the part of the leg on which they appear. Thus "sore shins" are recognised on the front of the cannon bone; "splints" are recognized in association with the splint bones; high and low "ring bone" is the name given to lumps found on the pastern bone. They are caused by the inflammation of the periosteum. This causes a fibrous swelling and the laying down of new bone beneath the periosteal lining — as happens with splints.

Tendon problems can also lead to lameness: for example, sprains or thoroughpin (a tenosynovitis of the sheath of the flexor tendon above the hock); if the injury comes on quickly it is usually a strain. If it comes on gradually and no heat is present, it is likely that the cause is edema or windgalls — a stretched part of the fetlock joint. If heat is present, there could be an infection or it could be a product of splints.

The stifle joint can cause problems: horses can lock their back legs with their patellas so that they can sleep while standing. This ability can occasionally lead to the joint locking at inopportune moments. The joint also suffers from a specific arthritis — *Osteochondritis dessicans*. Problems with the hooves can cause lameness — sandcracks have been mentioned; thrush also affects horses that are kept in damp conditions.

Fractures are the gross injuries which can bring on lameness or, indeed, affect any part of the locomotor system. There are various types of fracture including:

- **Simple** a clean break with no tissue damage; usually given a direction (transverse, oblique, etc.)
- **Compound** when the skin is injured as well
- **Incomplete** when the bone isn't broken through
- **Fissured** cracks in bone
- **Depressed** when a fragment of bone is pushed below the surrounding area
- **Impacted** when one fragment is jammed hard into another

The key treatment is immobilization, to stop collateral damage from movement of the bone ends.

Other problems with the locomotor system include the many back problems that any animal with such a long neck and back are bound to suffer — and the abrupt equine myoglobinuria (also called azoturia or "tying up") which causes the back legs to seize up, the urine to become wine-red or toffee-colored and the temperature to rise. Often coming on after being well

RIGHT: It can be worth fitting a fly fringe if head-shaking starts, because it seems to be worse when there are flies around. Some horses are more affected by insects than others, as is shown by the incidence of sweet itch, and they may find a fringe helpful—if they will wear one.

fed during a rest period after heavy work, the horse is likely to die if any exercise is continued. Most vets suggest immediate cessation of work, transporting the horse back to the stable by horsetrailer — although take great care: even having to brace itself in a bumpy horsetrailer can aggravate the condition — and complete rest.

Finally, laminitis is a serious ailment affecting feet. It is usually caused by overeating and triggered by excess carbohydrates in the stomach. This excess leads to an increase in the production of histamine, which in turn slows the flow of blood to the feet. The blood that does eventually get to the feet isn't oxygen-rich and the tissues — especially the laminae of the hoof — degenerate. This can lead to the rotation of the pedal bone (which can, in chronic cases, actually penetrate the sole), a slow change in the shape of the foot itself and the inability of the horse to move because of the pain in its feet if it does so.

There are three immediate steps to take: reduce the feed immediately and flush out the carbohydrates with mashes; give the horse painkillers so that he can stand and walk normally — this will stop the the blood circulation problems; finally, visit a farrier urgently — all four hooves may need considerable work to get the horse back to the correct standing position.

THE NERVOUS SYSTEM

Paralysis — the loss of nerve control over a bodily function — usually means a total loss of muscular action; a reduction is called paresis. A symptom rather

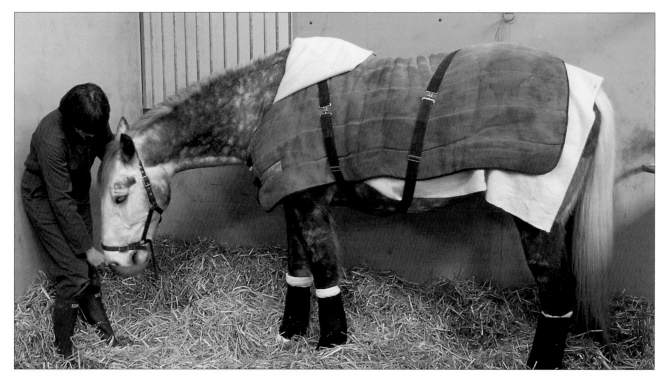

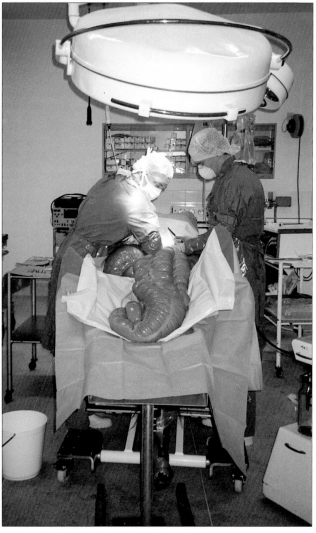

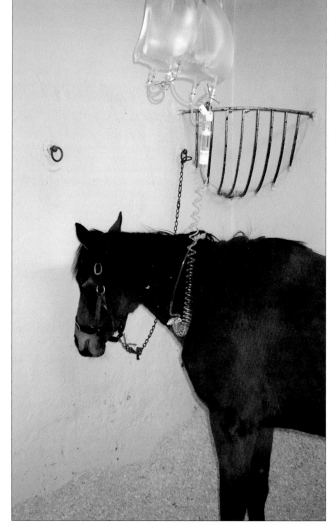

than a disease, paralysis is due to cerebral, spinal or peripheral causes.

- **Cerebral paralysis** results from brain lesions caused by, for example, depressed skull fractures, tumors or encephalitis — the inflammation of the brain caused by bacteria such as strangles.
- **Spinal paralysis** is caused by a severe injury to the spinal cord, generally as a result of a vertebra breakage.
- **Peripheral paralysis** includes such diverse problems as crural paralysis which affects the femoral nerve giving a drop of the hindquarters on the side affected; and paralysis of the external popliteal nerve which results in an inability to extend the foot or flex the hock.

Other nervous system problems include grass sickness — invariably fatal. If a horse gets this disease he must be put down to prevent unnecessary suffering. The problem is caused by the degeneration of the ganglia of the nerves affecting the alimentary tract. A slow virus seems to be the likely culprit because — albeit at some years' or months' distance — there's often more than one case in a stable.

Head-shaking can start quite suddenly and affects the ridden horse. While many diseases could account for this symptom, it's obvious that there are a number of cases for which no obvious culprit exists. It's worth having the eyes, ears and teeth examined and, because it seems to be worse when there are flies around, it can be worth fitting a fly fringe.

Finally, young horses can become "wobblers" — these animals progressively lose the use of their hind limbs, starting with a swaying action of their hindquarters. Caused by a spinal cord injury or deterioration of the cord, the condition is incurable.

THE DIGESTIVE SYSTEM

Whenever a horse has an abdominal pain, it's colic: and by colic most of us immediately assume a twisted gut. You will become aware of the pain in a number of ways — from the horse looking at his flank to lying down and rolling. The pain can be intense, and when it is, the horse will kick at his belly or roll around furi-

ABOVE LEFT: A very unhappy horse with colic — a term used to express the symptoms of abdominal pain which could be indigestion, flatulence, an organic disorder (eg, enteritis or peritonitis), verminous colic (ie, caused by parasitic worms or horse botflies), stones, anthrax, grass sickness, nephritis, uterine rupture, poison or rabies.

FAR LEFT: Surgeons operate to untwist a torsion of the large colon in a horse with colic

LEFT: The patient recovering well.

ously. (There's no truth in the oft-repeated story that letting a horse with colic roll will lead to worse internal twistings.)

There are a number of conditions that can give abdominal pain: acute indigestion is one that will be unlikely if you have been careful with feed. If the horse has had contaminated or bad food then he could well have bad indigestion and flatulence.

Most severe disorders — enteritis, peritonitis, rupture of the stomach, strangulation of the bowel — will lead to abdominal pain as will stones (kidney, bladder, or urethra), worms or horse botflies, anthrax, nephritis (inflammation and then failure of the kidneys), grass sickness, poisoning and, last but not least, rabies.

There are three main types of colic — spasmodic, the continuous pain of obstructive colic and volvulus.

Violently sudden and severe, spasmodic colic — and also flatulent colic — is mainly due to bowel problems often caused by worms damaging blood vessels which feed on the intestine wall. This can lead to death of some of the wall tissues, which can be painful, but nowhere near as painful as the lack of peristalsis — the movement of food from stomach to rectum.

As its name suggests, obstructive colic involves the obstruction of the bowel by partly digested food matter. The horse will often sit or try to sit on something, while keeping its forelegs upright.

Volvulus colic is caused by a twist in the bowels and, apart from being very painful, is often terminal.

When you suspect that your horse has colic, contact a vet at once: much of the time a horse can be saved if he's called early enough. There's little one can do except make the animal comfortable. This is true too of prevention: there's little one can do except worm your horses effectively and regularly since worms do seem to have a major role to play in colic.

WORMS

As shown in the tables on page 117, there are a variety of endoparasites which live inside the horse. Ascarids affect young horses, passing onto grazing land where the eggs can survive for over a year. *Strongylus vulgaris* is the main threat because of the physical damage done as they migrate around the body.

Other troublesome parasites are the pinworm, which lives just inside the rectum and can be seen when adult around the rectum, and horse botflies, Gastrophilus, mentioned earlier. The best defense against these parasites is to control strictly the pasture upon which the horse grazes. Always look for signs of worms; try mowing (it gets rid of a lot of worm larvae which climb to the top of the grass stems); prompt disposal of the horse droppings helps remove the source of the eggs as will grazing the pasture with other animals; finally, regular wormings are essential.

CHOKE

This can be caused by a variety of things, but the most likely is a dry lump of food — for instance a carrot — or by something which expands when it reaches the gut — like sugar beet pulp. This latter is a frequent culprit generally because inexperienced stable hands do not know of its properties. You'll know when there is a blockage not only from the pained expression on the horse but quite possibly because of a discharge through the nostrils of recently eaten food. The horse rarely vomits (there's a secure sphincter at the top of the stomach to stop it from doing so) and so the return of food like this should awaken you to the problem.

RETAINED MECONIUM

The meconium is the feces produced by the foal in the womb. The foal needs to excrete this shortly after birth or it can become impacted. The colostrum produced by the mother acts as a natural purgative to assist this process — but young foals should be watched to ensure the excretion takes place.

Once it has done so, do not relax your vigilance! Any foal that has feeding problems in the first few days should be checked to ensure there is no retained meconium.

THE URINARY AND REPRODUCTION SYSTEM

It is rare for horses' urinary systems to have major problems but genital organs of mare or stallion can often become infected and both the ovaries and testes suffer occasionally from tumors.

The main contagious venereal disease is contagious equine metritis (CEM), a bacterial organism which tends to persist around the clitoris, which is the best place to take testing swabs. It is sensible to test both stallions and mares for CEM before the season. Other infections tend to be due to *Klebsiella pneumoniae*.

Inflammation of the kidneys (nephritis) tends to take place after a blow of some sort, fall or poisoning or in association with another disease like influenza. A suppurating form, when one or both kidneys have abscesses, can either enter the kidneys by the bloodstream or by the bladder, the latter most usual in a mare after having foaled.

Other kidney diseases include parasites and stones.

ESTRUS

In order for breeding to take place, the mare must be in season — usually a 2–8 day period every 21 days between February and July. During this period the mare may exhibit signs of illness — she may be sluggish, irritable or tired and may act strangely — especially when near a stallion or gelding!

FOALING

The main problems in the reproductive system for the mare tend to be associated with foaling. Breeding, foaling and the problems to be encountered after birth are discussed in Chapter 21. There are a number of problems which can be encountered before birth, usually leading to natural abortion. The most prevalent cause for abortions is EHV1 (see p119); bacterial causes are salmonella or, rarely, *Brucella abortus*. Most abortions take place in the first 100 days of pregnancy.

SHOEING

The shoeing of horses and ponies tends to be an unavoidable necessity today because of the amount of roadwork: pavement has a strong filing characteristic and can lead to tender feet. Make sure you keep roadwork to a minimum as far as possible but if you do have to ride on the road keep your speed low, use road studs and make use of the shoulder.

In fact unshod feet are healthier than shod — for example, the frog, which exists to cushion the footfall of the horse, doesn't touch the ground when the hoof is shod and in fact tends to reduce in size. This has a damaging concussive effect on horses' legs.

It's better to keep young horses and ponies unshod while their bones are growing to keep this concussive effect to a minimum. Pads can also be inserted between foot and shoe which can reduce the concussive effects of pavement. They are not to be recommended on soft ground because they reduce the strength of the shoe fixing and, in soft ground, your horse is more likely to throw a shoe.

The frog also helps with blood circulation, acting as a pump. This is particularly necessary for the leg, which can suffer quite easily from poor circulation, the pooling effects of which can lead to laminitis.

TEETH

There are few problems associated with teeth which aren't painful. The most obvious problems are — as with humans — the development of the teeth; peculiar placement or problems with numbers of teeth can cause wear on the surface of the molars. It is important to keep a careful watch on the teeth — particularly when temporary teeth are being replaced by permanent ones (from about 2½ years of age through five years when all permanent teeth are in place) so that correction can take place.

ABOVE RIGHT: A foal born prematurely at 300 days' gestation is intensively nursed through its first critical week, The bandage around the neck protects the intravenous catheter which is used to give the foal fluids and antibiotics.

RIGHT: Vet checking hooves.

FAR RIGHT: Shoeing.

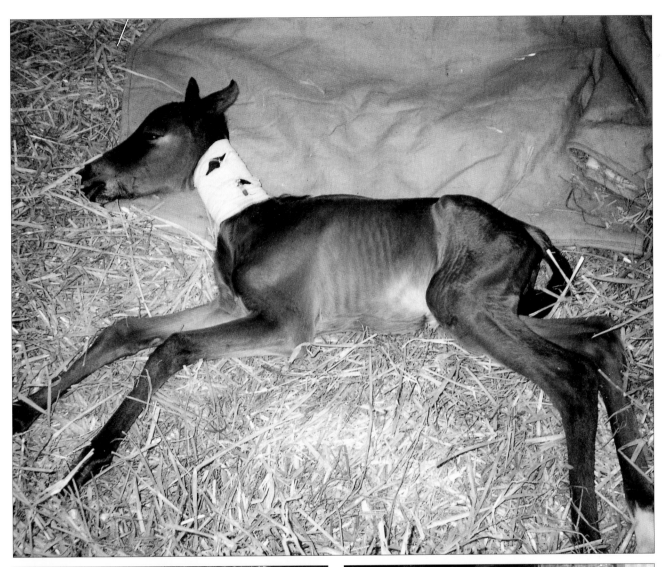

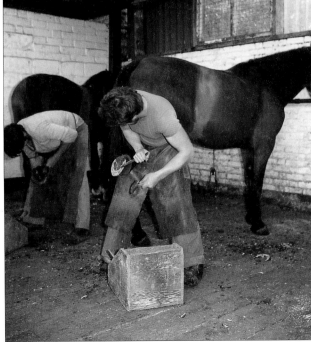

Abnormal wear can be caused by a variety of other problems, including shear mouth (where the upper and lower molars wear on the inner and outer border) and step mouth (where the teeth are stepped), over-hanging jaw or curved tables (when the upper jaw cheek teeth are concave). This can be seen by the horse quidding — forming a ball of food which is then chewed but not swallowed and spat into the manger or onto the floor. Often these problems — and those of sharp or pointed teeth — can be helped by rasping by a horse dentist.

One note of caution: quidding may not be caused by problems with teeth but instead by problems with the mouth, tongue or digestive system — including paralysis of the throat.

RIGHT: A veterinary at work.

BELOW: An elderly horse with parrot mouth.

FAR RIGHT: Teeth rasping; horses, like humans, need their teeth checked regularly for sharp points and hooks which can then be filed off with a tooth rasp — a process which does not hurt the horse at all.

BELOW RIGHT: Dentists and a vet work on a fractured tooth.

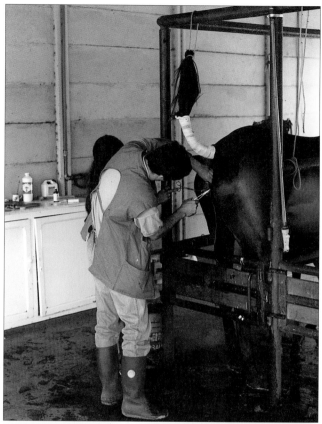

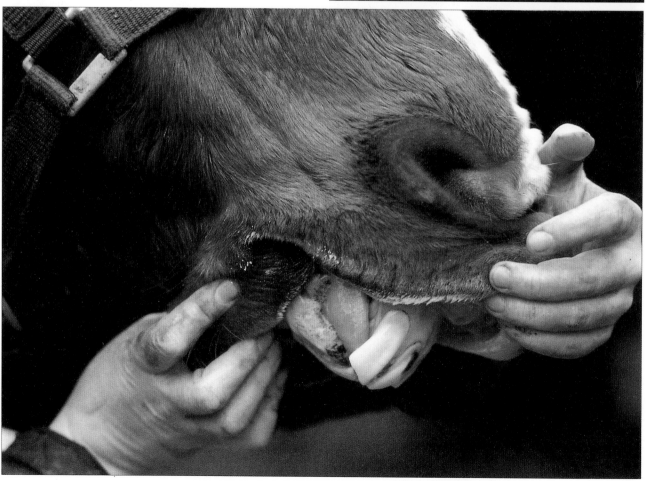

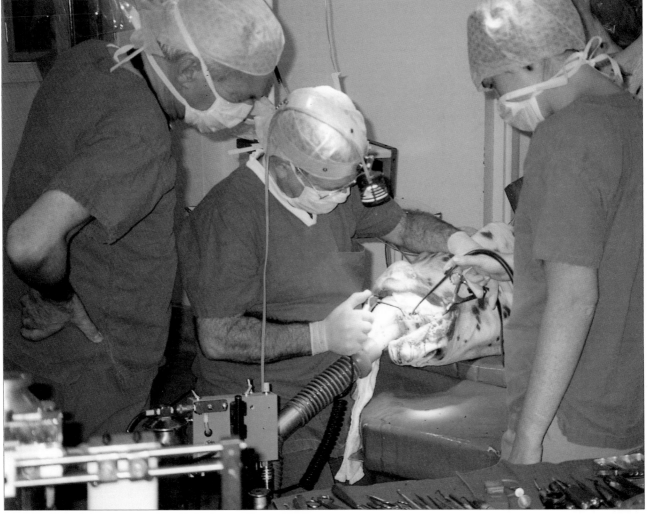

CHAPTER 18

FEEDING

Karen Hampshire

Through millions of years of evolution the horse has adapted to a diet based on grazing and browsing. Its digestive system is ideally suited to that of a 'trickle' feeder, the term used to describe an animal which regularly, and in some cases almost continually, eats small quantities of food throughout the day. There are several fundamental rules of feeding based on understanding the way in which the horse's gut is designed to work.

Always provide plenty of fresh clean water: water may constitute as much as 75 percent of an adult horse's bodyweight, and even more in a foal. It is essential for life and has many vital functions within the body. A horse deprived of water for any length of time may suffer a depressed appetite and, if he should be tempted to eat, may not have enough fluid in his gut to provide the medium needed to move the food through the system. Horses are unlikely to drink water which is in any way tainted, be it because it is offered in a dirty bucket or because it has stood in the stable so long that it has absorbed some of the gases from the bed and become stale. If a constant supply of fresh clean water is always available, it is unlikely that a horse will drink too much, although it is advisable for a horse coming in from work or after a long trip to be offered the opportunity to drink his fill before his feed, providing of course that he is cool. It may be necessary in winter to ensure the water is not too cold; the chill can be removed by placing the full bucket in a warm tack room for a while to bring it up to room temperature. No harm will result from a horse having a short drink while he is feeding or working.

FEED LITTLE AND OFTEN

The horse is a single-stomached herbivore who, when left to his own devices in grass, will graze nearly all the time. The stomach is comparatively small in relation to his size and works most efficiently when kept at approximately two-thirds full. Once the horse has reached this optimum level, food begins to move further down the digestive tract and he will continue to eat at the same rate as the food moves on.

The main process of digestion occurs in the very large hind gut (particularly the caecum). In order for the food to get from the stomach to the hind gut it must pass through the much narrower small intestine — so if large feeds are given, a bottleneck occurs where the stomach leads into the small intestine causing a distension of the stomach and an imbalance in the digestive process which may lead to colic. This is extremely painful for the horse and requires professional advice regarding treatment. Horses eating a mainly bulk diet should not have many problems except when turned out to fresh or lush pasture for the first time after a period of restricted access. However, horses at work will require concentrate feed (also referred to as shorts or hard feed) as well as bulk feeds such as grass and hay in order to provide the extra energy required. It is these feeds in particular which must be given little and often in order to avoid digestive problems. The more concentrates a horse requires, the more feeds per day he will need. Hard feeds based on cereals should not exceed 4lb (1.8kg) but those made up mainly of a proprietary brand of pellets may be as much as 6lb (2.7kg) because the greater fiber content requires more chewing and therefore slows down the eating process.

Do not feed a horse less than an hour before he is worked. There are two reasons for this: the stomach lies very close to the diaphragm on the other side of which are the lungs — if a horse is fed and then asked to work, the contents of the stomach may cause pressure on the diaphragm and so restrict the efficiency of the lungs. This is particularly likely during hard fast work where the movement of the canter and gallop gaits cause the viscera to move forward and down as the forehoof hits the ground. Secondly, blood is needed during the process of digestion but is also essential for muscular activity. Therefore, if the horse is working, the blood will be diverted to the muscles and the digestive process will consequently suffer as a result. For these reasons it is necessary to allow the horse approximately 20 minutes to eat his feed and at least another hour to an hour and a half to move the meal through his stomach and small intestine.

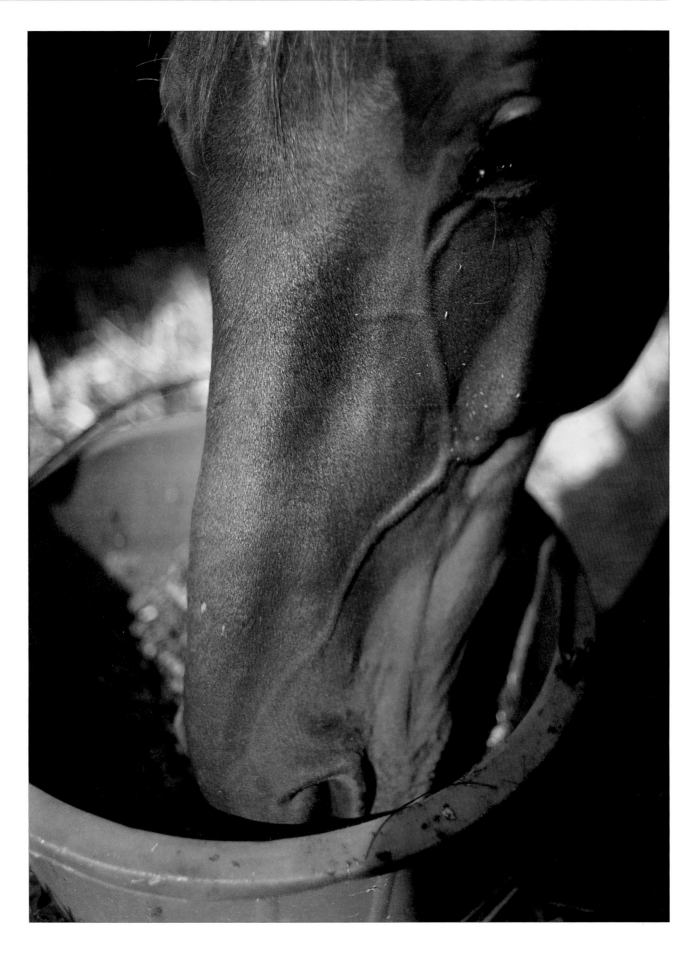

Do not make sudden changes to the diet. Within the gut are food-specific "friendly" bacteria; these micro-organisms are responsible for breaking down particular types of feed. It takes time for the populations of these bacteria to build up and it can cause digestive problems if a new feed type is suddenly introduced before enough bacteria are available. Always make changes in hard feeds very gradually and each time you move on to a new delivery of hay, always mix it with some of the old batch for a few days. If you move on to new grazing, particularly if the grass composition is different, only allow the horse limited grazing time at first.

Horses are creatures of habit, so it is important to feed them at the same times every day. If a horse usually receives a lunchtime feed at 12.30pm, by noon he will begin to anticipate its arrival. If the feed does not arrive, or is late, he may become mentally upset and possibly begin to indulge in some of the noisier and more unpleasant vices; he may also begin to produce the various chemicals needed for digestion. This is particularly likely if there is a "trigger," such as the sound of the feed bins opening or people going in and out of the feed room. If these chemicals are produced and no food arrives, imbalances in the chemical equilibrium of the gut will result.

A BALANCED DIET

To stay healthy, horses require a balanced diet comprising the various nutrients in the correct ratios for their needs:

Protein — essential for growth and tissue repair.
Carbohydrates and fats — needed to supply energy and heat.
Vitamins and minerals — necessary for various processes within the body.
Fiber/Bulk — vital to ensure health of digestive tract and can also provide energy.
Water — essential for life.

Throughout his life the balance of these nutrients required by the horse will change; for example, a young horse will need a higher level of protein than an older horse since protein is needed for growth. Because of the appearance on the market of compound feeds, it has become much easier for horse owners to provide their stock with appropriately balanced diets. Compound feeds come as pellets and mixes. Each manufacturer will have a range of both and every product is formulated to meet different requirements: thus a competition mix or pellet will have a high carbohydrate content and a pasture mix or pellet is designed to be non-heating.

The producers also supply literature explaining their products so that you can evaluate which feed will best meet your horse's needs. These products usually have a good shelf life, do not require as much storage space as conventional feedstuffs and, if from a reputable manufacturer, will be of good quality. These compound feeds are made from a variety of ingredients such as soya beans (for protein) which you would be unlikely to feed a horse as a raw ingredient. However, they also contain feeds which can be fed "straights":

BARLEY
Often referred to as a fattening feed, it is certainly true that barley can help to add or maintain condition. However, it must be remembered that the grain is heavier and contains more energy than oats and therefore is a "richer" feed than oats scoop for scoop — although it does not tend to heat up horses in the same way. Because of its very hard husk, barley can only be fed as whole grains if it is first boiled until the husk softens and starts to split. In common with other cereals, the grain can also be processed by manufacturers, such as by steaming and flaking, pulverising or extruding (all processes which include splitting the husk and cooking the grain in some way) in order to make it more easily digestible.

BRAN
This is a by-product of the wheat milling industry and has for years been fed as a source of roughage. However, the fiber it contains is not easily digested and a further complication lies in the fact that it is low in calcium and high in a kind of phosphorus which inhibits the uptake of calcium from the gut. This can cause problems in young and growing horses and a calcium supplement should therefore be added to a diet including bran. Because bran can hold considerably more than its own weight in water, when fed as a well-made bran mash it makes a useful laxative diet for horses in short periods of enforced rest. Avoid feeding dry bran because it can cause choking — particularly with greedy horses who bolt their food.

CHAFF
Chop chaff or chop is basically short chopped hay and/or oat straw to which molasses is sometimes added as a sweetener. Its main purpose is to encourage the horse to chew his concentrate feed to which it is added.

ABOVE RIGHT: Barley is a richer feed than oats, containing more energy. Because of its hard husk it has to be boiled before eating so that the husk is softened.

BELOW RIGHT: Compound feeds can come as pellets or mixes — this is how pellets look.

CORN

Another high energy feed, corn (or maize) is useful for horses needing a little more condition or for poor-eaters, particularly those who need to be tempted to eat by a very palatable feed. Corn must never constitute the main part of the concentrate ration because it is low in quality protein and fibre and can be very heating. It is usually steamed and flaked since digestion of the whole grain can be difficult.

HAY

Hay usually forms the main fiber part of the diet fed to stabled horses. There are many different kinds available but they usually fall into one of two categories. Seed hay is made from grasses that have been specially selected and grown for the purpose — usually a mixture of rye grasses and timothy, perhaps with a little clover. Meadow hay is taken from permanent pasture and will usually contain a much wider variety of grasses as well as some plants and herbs that would

not be found in seed hay. Not all of these plants may be desirable and care should be taken when checking the contents of the bales. Equally important to the content of the hay is the care taken during its making and subsequent storage. The weather conditions in Britain, for example, mean it can be difficult to cut the crop at the optimum stage of maturity and ensure that it is warm and dry enough to make good hay. These factors, together with the grasses in the hay, will determine its feed value with regard to energy and protein levels. Any bale which upon opening proves dusty, mouldy or smells of tobacco and has brown patches should be discarded, because if fed it may cause respiratory or digestive problems.

HAYLAGE

To make haylage (grass sileage) the grasses are cut earlier than hay and are not allowed to dry out quite as much before baling. When baling does take place, the grasses are condensed and vacuum-packed into tough plastic bags which exclude all oxygen. Due to bacterial activity in the bale, the haylage when fed is virtually dust free, has a higher energy value than hay, and should consequently not be fed in such large quantities. The lack of dust and fungal spores makes this an ideal feed for horses suffering from respiratory diseases.

LINSEED

Although high in good quality protein, this feed is rarely provided in quantities large enough to make a difference to the overall protein balance of the diet. It is usually used to add condition and bloom to the coat through its high oil content. It is essential that the linseed is prepared by boiling in large amounts of water until the grain can be split easily by thumbnail pressure since this destroys an enzyme which otherwise produces toxins. It can also be bought as a pre-prepared oil, but in both cases it is very expensive.

OATS

Perhaps the most common cereal fed to horses, oats can safely make up the full concentrate ration for horses in hard work. They have a relatively high fibre content because of the outer husk but as well as supplying energy can be quite heating, which can turn even the best-mannered of horses into very difficult characters if not fed directly in proportion to the work being done. For this reason oats are rarely recommended as suitable for children's ponies. Naked oats — where the grain comes without the outer husk — are now also available; these require even more care in feeding as they can contain up to 25 percent more energy than conventional oats. Oats may be fed whole to stock over one year of age but bruising or rolling, ie where the husk is slightly damaged, is usually advised as this makes it easier for the horse to chew and digest.

ABOVE: Sugar beet after it has been soaked in cold water. This is a valuable, energy-giving, high-fiber feed suited to endurance runners because the fiber breaks down slowly.

RIGHT: Horses at work will require concentrate feed (also referred to as shorts or hard feed) as well as bulk feeds such as grass and hay in order to provide the extra energy required. It is these feeds in particular which must be given little and often in order to avoid digestive problems.

PEAS AND BEANS

These are often found in small quantities in compound feeds, particularly those designed for horses at very hard work. They can be added to a concentrate ration made up of "straights," but again care must be taken because they are very heating.

It is useful to remember that these heating feeds make useful additions to the concentrate rations of horses wintering out in hard conditions.

SUGAR BEET

Comes as either dried pulp which must be soaked for 12 hours to twice their weight in cold water, or as pellets which must be soaked for 24 hours to three times their weight in cold water. When soaked the beet swells in size and so, if fed dry, can cause blockages anywhere in the narrow parts of the digestive tract. It is a valuable feed which is both energy-giving and fibrous and is often underrated and used only as a feed dampener. The fiber is digested slowly in the hind gut and as a result it makes a useful, slow, energy-releasing feed for endurance horses and those who have long intervals between feeds. The beet should be freshly prepared each day since it can quickly start to ferment and go sour in warm conditions; this can also happen if hot water is used for soaking.

HOW MUCH TO FEED

It is possible to work out mathematically optimal rations for any horse but this is usually only necessary for top competition horses. A general rule of thumb is based around the ration recommended for a 15hh (5ft) horse: 26lb (11.5kg) total of concentrates and bulk per day. From this figure either add or subtract 2.2lb (1kg) as appropriate for each 2in (5cm) of height. The ratio of concentrates to bulk will then be determined by such factors as the condition of the horse, the amount of work being done, the temperament, the ability of the rider, etc. The skill required for judging different rations comes with practice and experience.

CHAPTER 19

THE STABLED HORSE

Karen Hampshire

Horses that "live in" can do so for up to 23 hours a day and may only leave their stables to be ridden rather than turned out. This places a tremendous responsibility on anyone concerned with their management and requires an understanding not only of the horses' physical needs but also of their natural instincts and the psychological effects of this basically unnatural lifestyle. As discussed in a previous chapter, on the whole horses enjoy the company of their own kind and feel safer and more secure if they are able to have physical contact and interact with their own species — in fact their herd instinct is very strong and can explain many problems associated with handling and riding. If horses are to remain content in this artificial environment, it is incumbent on us to remember that, although the horse may not be considered intelligent by some, he most definitely has a mind which he is able to use.

Like humans, horses are individual characters: some are highly strung while others are docile and amenable; some make the most of their intelligence, while others are not so quick. All of them, however, are creatures which live by their nerves through the necessity to survive in the wild. This leads to the instinct either to flee in the presence of danger or, if cornered, to fight to protect themselves and their young. Therefore, if exposed to rough handling from stable hands who shout and bully, or if repeatedly hit and pushed around the stable with a broom handle, the horse will quickly become frightened and difficult to handle. With some temperaments this will result in vicious behavior as a means of defense.

A young horse taught his manners early on will usually have a good quality of life because he will not frustrate his handlers; conversely a youngster allowed to rule the roost, either because his handlers are frightened of him or because he has been indulged too far, will always end up being bullied in order to make him comply. Firm kindness is the golden rule to get the best cooperation from a horse and to ensure their contentment of mind which subsequently contributes to good health. One of the biggest problems with

Stables should be well-ventilated, safe places for their occupants, especially if the horses are only going to leave the stables when they are to be ridden. The horse's living area must be of a decent size, well-lit, preferably with natural light: horses, like humans, are diurnal, in other words they expect to sleep at night and work during the day. Good routines will keep them calm and you on top of your workload.

horses kept in almost constant confinement is bore-dom, leading to the possible onset of such vices as box-walking, weaving and crib-biting. The two for-mer can result in joint problems and the latter in diges-tive and respiratory weaknesses. Good routines which break up the day, together with as many hours spent out of the stable as possible, will go some way to pre-venting such habits from developing.

THE STABLE

In order to remain healthy and happy a stabled horse needs space to move around freely, lie down and roll without the risk of getting injured. A 10x10ft (3x3m) space is adequate for a pony; 11.5x10ft (3.5x3m) for an average 15hh (5ft) horse and 11.5x11.5ft (3.5x3.5m) for larger breeds. Anything beyond this is an advantage to the horse and can make handling easier but the bigger the box the greater the area to muck out and keep clean! In the case of a foaling box this cannot be avoid-ed because an area of at least 15x15ft (4.5x4.5m) is required. Horses dislike dark, dingy conditions just as much as we do and will quickly deteriorate in attitude to life if kept in such circumstances. Lack of natural light can also lead to eye problems since the horse is a diurnal animal: it is in nature an outdoor animal.

The light source within a stable should be protected by a wire-mesh cage and the power supply must be fit-ted with a "trip-switch" in case of fault or accident. This is particularly important in wooden stables.

Good ventilation without drafts is essential if hors-es are to remain physically healthy and the choice of housing must take this very much into consideration. An appropriate combination of louver boards, eaves and ridge vents, open top doors and shuttered win-dows will ensure correct and adequate ventilation in most cases. Stuffy stables can predispose animals to respiratory infections ranging from colds to lower res-piratory tract problems.

The days when as much money and effort were put into providing accommodation for horses as for their rich owners are, on the whole, long gone. Rows of oak-partitioned stables with brass fittings, intricate brickwork flooring and stone-carved mangers can only be inherited or bought as long established stable-yards for vast sums of money. Modern stables are occasionally constructed of brick but, more common-ly, some sort of concrete block or wood is used. The inherent problems associated with wooden buildings are the risk of fire and the lack of security against intruders for both stock and equipment.

The modern style of stableyard is either an L-shape or three sides of a square composed of rows of indi-vidual stables; this provides for good ventilation but can make conditions for both horses and workers cold in winter. Gradually superseding this for stableyards required to house more than a handful of horses is the

ABOVE: Preparing feeds for stabled horses.

BELOW: A vet checks the drip feed of a sick horse. One of the problems of stabling is the speed that disease can spread among the occupants. You also need to keep a careful eye open for potentially dangerous snags and protuberances.

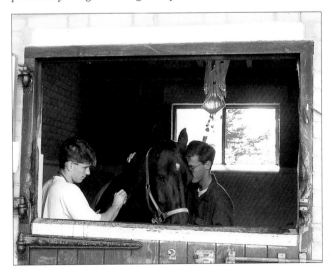

indoor barn system where a row of stables is constructed down each long side of a barn with a central passageway left down the middle and large, usually sliding doors at each end. The partitioning may be of wood or cinderblock and can be fitted to allow for various sizes of box within the rows, with tack and feed rooms and so on also easily accommodated. This method of stabling has become popular because of the comparative ease of converting existing buildings and the attraction to owners and handlers of being able to work in a warm and dry area. This is one of the occasions when available methods of ventilation must be carefully investigated before conversion is undertaken.

The floor and roof must also be checked carefully for suitability: flooring should be solid and non-slip with appropriate gradients to allow drainage. Smoothed concrete is acceptable and easily available but can be expensive, but not as costly as well constructed brickwork. Various materials make good roofs as long as they are quiet when it rains, cool in the summer, able to contain heat in the winter, fireproof and, where necessary, undergirded to prevent objects from falling onto the occupants below. Any stable block no matter what size will need good access and to be in close proximity to power and water supplies and waste water drainage. Costs of linking to such amenities can be prohibitive if great distances are involved.

Thought must also be given to the suitability of storage space for feed and bedding because it will need to be weatherproof and provide protection against rodents. To reduce risk of injury, the fewer stable fittings used the better. Two tie rings on opposite walls are essential for the tying up of not only the horse but also haynets (if used) and are best located at approximately 5ft (roughly 1.5–1.6m) above the ground. A horse tied directly to the ring is in danger of falling if he should panic, but this can be prevented if he is tied to a short loop of rope attached to the ring. Haynets need to be tied up short so that they do not get tangled in the horse's legs when empty and should be removed as soon as possible after being finished. Some people prefer to use galvanized hayracks usually located in a corner high enough to be out of the way of a rolling horse but not so high that the horse has constantly to reach up at an unnatural angle and risk getting seeds or dust in his eyes. It is quite acceptable to feed hay off the floor providing the floor is kept clean — although untidy eaters may end up treading on more than they eat, or mixing it in with the bedding.

There are several systems of watering stable-kept horses, all of which have advantages and disadvantages. The two most often used are either automatic waterers — favorites in large stables because they save a considerable amount of labor — or water buckets which are ideal for a small stable or the single horse owner.

ABOVE: Filling a haynet: be careful to ensure that it is at a decent height — 5ft (1.5m) off the ground is about right — and that it is taken away when empty so that it doesn't get tangled up with the horse's legs.

BELOW: Mixing medicine into feed.

Automatic waterers can cost a considerable sum to install depending on the type of piping chosen and the quality of the watering units. They need frequent cleaning and have a tendency to freeze in the cold, although this is less likely in an indoor barn-style stable. One of the criticisms leveled at automatic waterers is that it is impossible to assess how much the horse is drinking if this needs to be monitored for a short time; for instance, if the horse is ill, the automatic drinking bowl can temporarily be closed off and replaced with buckets. The bucket system works best if they are kept off the ground at waist level, either by means of wall hooks which clip onto the handles of buckets made of specially toughened moulded plastic, or by wall brackets (less popular since brackets present an injury threat). Often the buckets are placed in tires just inside the stable door. This certainly reduces the risk of them being knocked over but does not prevent dirt from the stable contaminating the water.

Feed mangers are not essential since the horses can be fed in free-standing buckets but they are preferable because they are less prone to being knocked over and the contents wasted, and when empty are less likely to be kicked or stepped on, causing damage not only to the bucket but also possibly the horse. Mangers these days are made of reinforced plastic and either sit in corner brackets about 3ft (1m) from the floor, or have fittings which allow them to be hooked to the bottom door. Whatever is decided upon, the utensil must be thoroughly cleaned after each use. Regardless of the materials used in the construction and hardware of the buildings, an amount must be budgeted each year to carry out maintenance work. Otherwise, even the best designed and built stables will quickly deteriorate, becoming health and safety hazards.

ROUTINES

Regular methods are essential when working with any animal. Not only does routine have a calming and reassuring effect, making our charges feel secure, but it is also the only way to ensure that all the tasks relating to the horses' welfare are completed as and when they should be. There will, of course, be times when the routine will have to be altered to fit in with specific requirements, such as on the day of a show or perhaps if the farrier is due. Even the one-horse owner will need to establish suitable daily, weekly, monthly and annual routines, though the composition of these will vary widely depending on the size and type of yard. Certain elements such as feeding, exercising and so on will appear in all daily work schedules.

What follows is a suggested routine suitable for a small livery yard. This basic layout can be adapted for any situation where horses spend the greater part of their day in the stable.

ABOVE: The simplest method of watering stabled horses is by water buckets fixed to the stable wall. Be careful with the brackets, which can cause injury if damaged.

EARLY MORNING

The horses will have been left unattended for several hours overnight and so the first job of the day must be to check for any signs of ill health, injury or discomfort. Careful note must be made of the number of droppings and the condition of the bed because an absence of feces and untidy bedding are two of the easily recognizable signs of colic. Check also that the hay and any late feed has been eaten.

If blankets are being worn, they will probably need adjusting or changing to get the horse ready to be turned out. Ideally the horse should then be watered, fed and hayed and left to eat in peace for at least 20 minutes — in reality this is not always possible and some horses do not object to having someone they know and trust working around them as they feed. However, others will chase any intruders from their box at this time and their feelings must be respected for both the health of their digestive system and the safety of the handler.

Mucking out is next on the list (done with the horse tied up — outside if possible) followed by bedding down if the horse is staying in, then sweeping up and tidying up the manure pile. It is at this point that the water buckets and feed mangers should be scrubbed out thoroughly and, in the case of the former, refilled.

MORNING

Those horses that are going out should be blanketed as necessary and led to the fields. The first string for riding will require brushing off and tacking up. Once the tack is on, they should be tied up if left, otherwise if they roll they may not only break the saddle but there is a strong likelihood of damage to their back. If the weather demands, it may be necessary to throw a blanket over the horse while he waits; in such cases the blanket must be either completely done up or not fastened at all. The practice of doing up the front of the blanket only is very dangerous if the rug should slip.

Returning from exercise, the feet must be picked out and the shoes checked. Depending on the time of year the horse may be washed down after being untacked or, if cool and dry, given a thorough grooming before being warmly blanketed. If for any reason he is wet he will need blanketing, ideally with a sweat blanket under an upside-down burlap or a modern "cooler" one. Now is a good time for a small haynet.

This process of turning out and exercising is repeated as necessary throughout the morning and then, at around midday, the stall should be cleaned, the horses watered, hayed and, possibly, fed. The yard is then again set fair.

AFTERNOON

Turn out any remaining groups of horses and finish off the exercising. Groom thoroughly any animals who have not been ridden, or who were too wet to groom earlier, and blanket them all as required; clean their tack and then complete any odd jobs that may be necessary. Toward the end of the afternoon clean the stall for the final time; water, hay, set fair and feed, finishing with one final check of the horses before washing out the mangers and locking up the stables.

LATE CHECK

This is usually carried out between 9 and 10PM and entails checking the horses, their waters, blankets and that they have eaten. Any late feeds and/or hay can be given then, but try to disturb the horses as little as possible. Many people complain at having to do late checks but it is a crucial part of the daily routine and a time when problems are often detected — the earlier "knock," which didn't seem to be causing any reaction, may now be growing into a worrisome swelling and perhaps the horse is even a little lame. Action can be taken which, if left until morning, may result in much longer-term difficulties. It is also very satisfying to walk around the yard and listen to the contentment of well cared for horses relaxing in comfortable surroundings with total confidence in their handler.

OTHER TASKS

You will need to work other tasks into this overall routine, including: disinfecting floors, cleaning automatic waterers, drains and traps, grooming kits, head collars and rollers, oiling tack, brushing down and washing blankets, pads, etc. The feed and bedding will have to be ordered and possibly picked up, the veteri-

ABOVE: Mucking out.

nary supplies must be checked and the farrier's visits organized. In fact the list seems almost endless but with careful planning the time and labor involved can kept to a minimum.

BEDDING

There are numerous types of bedding currently on the market, all varying in suitability and price. The bedding chosen should provide a warm, dry, comfortable environment and preferably be easy to work with, be cheap and easy to obtain and dispose of, be low in dust content — if not dust free — and be aesthetically pleasing. Straw is perhaps the cheapest form of bedding and for years has been successfully used. It drains well and is still relatively easy to dispose of, although you are likely to be charged for the privilege. Wheat straw is tough and durable and too coarse to be tempting except to the hungriest of horses. It can be difficult to find, however; fortunately barley and oat straw are more readily available from farmers. They are somewhat easier to work with, although tend to be more palatable to most horses.

Modern harvesting methods mean that barley straw no longer comes with the prickly bristles which used to make it so unsuitable as bedding material. The biggest disadvantage with straw is the sometimes high levels of spores found within it. These can exacerbate "heaves", a condition called chronic obstructive pulmonary disease (COPD), which is perhaps most easily described as "equine asthma." A horse suffering from COPD will need an atmosphere as free of dust (including spores) as possible and a bed of either suitably processed woodchips or peat. Of the two, woodchips are somewhat cheaper and provide a better appearance; unfortunately, because of the longer time needed for decomposition, they are less popular with farmers and therefore harder to dispose of.

Peat, although less pleasing in appearance than woodchips, is virtually dust free and considered a highly attractive by-product by rose growers, especially if mixed with horse manure! Both of these beddings are absorbent and will need to have the droppings and wet patches removed regularly throughout the day to prevent them becoming unhealthily dirty and wet. Paper is perhaps the closest to a totally dust-free bedding but acceptable types can be expensive to buy, difficult to work with and a problem to dispose of. All of this renders paper a last choice in most cases.

Whatever the bedding, it needs to be thick: a thin bed is a false economy that leads to less effective absorbency and requires more to be removed each time it is cleaned. A thick bed will also encourage a horse to lie down and rest and prevent him being injured on the flooring when he does so. If laid with thick banks, the horse is discouraged from getting too close to the wall when rolling so that he is less likely to get injured. It is not advisable to allow horses to stand for long periods on concrete or other hard surfaces because it will adversely affect their joints; conversely if horses are to stand on bedding it will alleviate the stress on their joints but will require their feet to be picked out frequently to prevent thrush — a condition of the hoof caused by the warming and softening effects of the bed.

GROOMING

The term grooming means many things to many people but all would agree that it basically refers in some way to the brushing of the horse's coat for the purpose of cleaning, plus the picking out of the hooves. It is in fact much more than this, being an essential part of the stabled horse's routine, encouraging a healthy skin and coat and allowing the close development of the rela-

tionship between horse and handler, particularly important with young or nervous animals. In the wild or if pastured, the horse will undertake his own grooming by rolling, rubbing on trees and bushes, and standing nose to tail scratching with a friend. This opportunity is denied him in the stable and the task must be performed by someone. It involves the expenditure of considerable energy to do the job properly: a gentle stroking with the brush will not suffice to stimulate the circulation under the skin to keep it in good condition.

Quartering is usually done first thing in the morning before the horse is ridden and derives its name from the fact that a rug is only undone at the front and then each quarter of the rug is folded back under a "roller" one at a time and the exposed area is then lightly brushed with a body brush to remove surface dirt and stains. The legs, head, mane and tail are also done and the feet picked out.

Grooming really refers to the thorough cleaning of the horse, ideally carried out immediately after exercise or before going hunting or out to a show, and consists of picking out the feet, removing any dried mud or sweat with a stiff brush (unless the horse is clipped or is particularly sensitive, in which case a rubber currycomb may be tolerated) and by using the body brush with vigor all over and in conjunction with the currycomb. Metal versions of the latter should never be used directly on the horse as they are designed only for cleaning the body brush. Brush out the mane and tail again (preferably with the body brush as it splits the hair less), wipe the eyes, lips and nose with one sponge and the dock with another, where appropriate washing the white leg markings. Finally finish off with a good wipe over with a slightly damp stable rubber and an application of oil to the hooves. If the horse is then wisped or banged, the process becomes known as strapping.

Wisping and banging are both designed to improve circulation and build muscle, as well as for adding shine to the coat. It must be introduced over a period of time, by gradually increasing the number of "strikes" carried out. Only the muscled areas of the shoulders and quarters will benefit from this action and, if done incorrectly, it can easily result in bruising. In order to reduce labor costs, larger stables often use grooming machines which reduce the need for time-consuming strapping, as machines with a rotating brush head combined with suction power have similar effects to wisping. If a field or trace-clipped pony needs to be smartened up for a special occasion, a vacuum-type machine is excellent because it removes the dirt but still leaves much of the protective grease. The disadvantage to such labor-saving devices is that the handler tends not to run his hands over the horse as he would in manual grooming, resulting in the possibili-

ty of cuts, lumps and bumps going unnoticed. The common practice of putting the horse's halter around his neck in order to groom the head is fine, providing that the rope is untied from the string. The rope can be left through the loop but serious injury can result if the horse pulls back while the knot is tied.

The udders of a mare must be kept clean by carefully wiping them over with a clean damp sponge. The sheath of a male horse also needs regular washing, a rather more time-consuming and difficult job but essential if the build-up of potentially infectious dirt and grease is to be avoided.

CLIPPING AND BLANKETS

Horses change their coats twice a year — in spring and autumn. This process can be helped along by regular use of the rubber currycomb. The summer coat is fine, silky and short in contrast to the rougher, thicker, longer winter hair. Such a coat is perfect for warm summer months and only the thinnest skinned animals being prepared for shows will need any kind of blanket when a cotton summer sheet will usually fit the bill. The winter coat, provides excellent protection for pastured horses, can be a problem to horses at work. The heavy coat causes the horse to sweat up when exercised and then prevents him from drying off quickly; this leads to loss of condition and makes him

TOP and ABOVE: Grooming is an essential part of the stabled horse's routine, encouraging healthy skin and developing the relationship between animal and handler. As well as brushing, make sure that the feet are picked out.

very susceptible to colds and chills. Clipping is the best answer since it removes as much or as little hair as appropriate for each case. There are four basic clip styles around which several variations have evolved depending on requirements:

THE TRACE CLIP

This removes the hair of the belly and comes a little way up the sides of the horse, between the thighs and forearms, across the chest and from the underside of the neck. It suits horses and ponies living out that are required to do light exercise.

THE BLANKET CLIP

If the trace clip is extended to take out all of the neck and head hair, it becomes known as the banket clip. This is useful for horses that are expected to do a reasonable amount of work and so are perhaps out for most of the day but in at night.

THE HUNTER CLIP AND THE FULL CLIP

The hunter clip leaves only the hair of the legs and saddle patch and can be extended to removing the coat in its entirety when is it called a full clip. Leaving the saddle patch helps to prevent saddle sores and the theory is that leg hair left on protects against scratches from thorns. etc. These are the only alternatives for horses in hard, fast work and, besides removing the stress equivalent to running the mile in a fur coat, it makes grooming a much easier task.

Clipping normally begins in October and it may be that for this first time only a blanket clip is needed. The number of clips will depend on the growth rate of the individual coat and its natural density. The final clip is best completed before the end of January so that it does not interfere with the growth of the summer hair. Once the coat has been removed it becomes necessary to provide the horse with an alternative means of keeping warm while at rest. For all but the most expensive of racehorses, centrally heated accommodation is out of the question and blankets are the only affordable alternative.

Wool-lined burlap blankets, either with a padded bellyband or crossed belly girths, used to be the favorite night blanket and are still a relatively cheap option. They are especially useful to have around if the horse comes in wet because, when turned upside-down, they allow the horse to dry off while keeping warm. Many patented variations of this style, made out of modern fabrics, are on the market, providing sometimes expensive but preferable alternatives since they are lighter weight, more durable, easily washed and dried and considerably warmer. They can sometimes eliminate the need for any underblankets during moderately cold spells.

Many blankets now come shaped and fitted with crossed belly girths, which reduce the likelihood of pressure sores developing as they are prone to do under a roller. If finances allow, it is a good idea to have two blankets, one for daywear and the other for nighttime because the night blanket is almost guaranteed to get fairly dirty.

Underblankets can be added as the temperature drops and the horse gets colder at night. In severe weather as many as three may be needed, but this is the exception rather than the rule, depending on climate. Anyway, this will vary according to the individual horse; just like us, some feel the cold more than others. The best quality underblankets are made of pure, soft wool and have plenty of length which can be folded back to be held securely in place by the roller. Those that are designed to go under the more modern roller-less rugs will often have their own crossed girths and many these days are sown up the front requiring the horse to be taught to accept it being put over his head.

Common sense comes into play when deciding exactly how many and when blankets and underblankets should be used; for instance, warm winter days may dictate a blanket only, but by 4PM this alone may not be enough. Specially designed hoods are also available for use with certain night blankets, offering even greater warmth. A similar weatherproof article can be employed with some New Zealand rugs for outside wear. All blankets need to be shaken out and brushed off daily; some require fairly regular washing and repairs must be expected and made as soon as necessary. Because of their price, the very neat bound-edged woolen day blankets are often reserved for wear at shows and events with many forming part of a total color coordinated look.

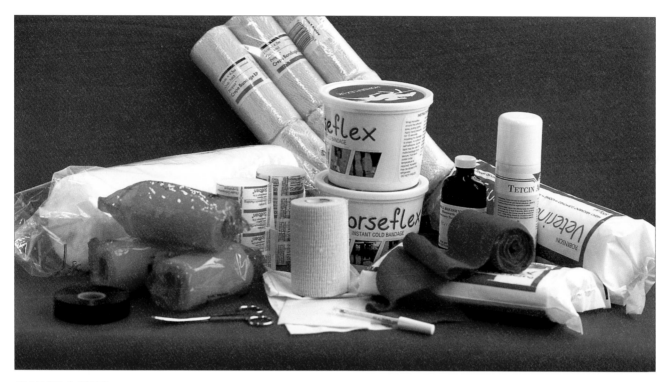

BANDAGES

Used on a daily basis, a tail bandage, usually made of elasticated cotton/stockinette and about 4–6in (10–15cm) wide, can help to "train" an unruly tail to lie flat. It should be applied after grooming but not left on too long because it may cause chafing and possibly even circulatory problems. This type of bandage is also used when traveling to protect the tail hair from being rubbed on the back of a trailer or along the sides of a horsebox. Again, recent invention has produced several alternatives, most of which are easier for the uninitiated to apply, but the same points must be born in mind.

Exercise bandages are made of similar material but are 2–4in (5–10cm) wider and, if good quality, somewhat longer. They are applied to the lower leg from just under the knee to halfway down the fetlock joint, level with the ergot. Either gauze covered with cotton or a modern felt-type equivalent must be carefully positioned underneath because the bandage alone cannot provide enough protection and may even cause "ridges" in the horses legs. Much practice to perfect the art of application is essential to prevent permanent damage being done to tendons and even joints. Their function is to supply support and protection. Stable bandages are made of either wool or flannel, up to 15½in (40cm) wide and are used to assist in the drying off of wet, muddy legs when they can be fitted advantageously over straw. They are also used in the stable for extra warmth and when traveling to guard the legs against knocks; in each case either gauze or felt must be applied underneath.

ABOVE LEFT: Plaiting a mane before a show.

ABOVE: First aid kit; as a rule of thumb, it's better to call a vet than try any but the most basic treatments. You should have antiseptics for small cuts — although often salt water will do just as well — and poultices for swellings and bruises as well as a range of bandages and paddings.

THE MEDICINE CHEST

This will not actually consist of many items because only the most basic treatments should be carried out on horses by anyone but the veterinary surgeon. Either a clinical or digital thermometer is indispensable. At the first signs of trouble an abnormal temperature can quickly confirm that the vet should be called (the "norm" being 100.5°F or 38°C for an adult healthy horse at rest). Salt water makes as good an antiseptic wash as one is likely to need; additionally, it is much more difficult to do damage with salt water than with many of the proprietary alternatives.

An antiseptic, or better still an antibiotic powder and/or cream, should be stocked for treating small cuts and scratches, and some sort of poultice (either kaolin or other linament) for more severe cases and as cooling dressings for bruises and swellings when applied cold. A selection of bandages and under-padding should also be stocked along with a pair of rounded end, curved scissors. There are many other items which may prove useful but the best advice is to keep it simple to start with: increase and vary your stocks as you gradually gain experience over the years.

CHAPTER 20

THE PASTURED HORSE

Karen Hampshire

Comparatively few horses today can be described accurately as totally grass-kept, although many will spend some of their time living out. Wild and feral horses living a very natural life need large areas of terrain over which to roam for food, and will have adapted to the environment in which they live in order to survive. Even the hardy, tough little ponies of the New Forest need help to endure the British winters.

Horses are often turned out for the better months of the year, when grass and herbage are at their best — particularly if they are at rest, such as hunters off season or mares with a foal at foot. Otherwise they are turned out for a couple of hours per day, blanketed if necessary, in order to exercise themselves lightly. There are, of course, many variations along these lines and much will depend on the amount and quality of land available, the breed of horse, whether or not the horse is at work (and if so what kind) and the time and availability of the owner. It is universally acknowledged that horses benefit from being turned out on appropriate grazing not only from the fact that the fresh air helps to keep their respiratory system clear and healthy, but also from the point of view of the horses' psychological health. Time spent in the company of others of their kind roaming around with the opportunity to kick their heels if they wish has a very calming effect on most horses and can greatly improve their attitude to work and their generosity to the rider!

It must be remembered that, in any group of horses living together, the imprinted herd instincts will be emphasized; a hierarchy will very soon emerge, which will alter each time the group composition is changed. This may mean that some horses become bullies and may try these tactics out on their owners; others may get bullied and become nervous and stand miserably waiting at the gate to come in. It may be that removal of the bully, or if possible a complete change of group, may make life in the field more pleasant for these characters. Many people find that keeping mares and geldings in separate fields reduces some of the likely problems. Few horses enjoy being turned out alone and, if a companion horse cannot be found either, a goat or a donkey should be considered; however in the case of the latter it will be necessary to check to ensure there is no threat of lungworm because donkeys are commonly carriers of this parasite.

THE COMBINED SYSTEM

This is the term applied to the most common form of keeping horses partly pastured and consists of the animal spending a number of hours during the day in the field, possibly blanketed in inclement weather or having access to shelter if required, but being brought in overnight. Very often these horses are in work of some kind and will be receiving supplementary concentrate feed, at least through the winter. In very hot summers this regime may be turned around and the horses allowed to stand in during the day to avoid the worst of the heat and flies. The combined system is a very good method, which is much less labor intensive than a system where the animals are kept in most of the time and as such, it usually suits the owner-rider very well.

BLANKETING

When the temperatures begin to drop, out in the field horses may need to wear a well-fitted New Zealand rug in order to keep their condition and health. This will be essential for Thoroughbred type horses and others with thin skin and coat. There are many types of New Zealands available on the market, but whichever you chose, it should be weatherproof (rain and wind) and have a thick, warm, lining material. They will all have front fastenings and legstraps and those which are either shaped to stay in place or have crossed girths are strongly recommended, as the much cheaper rugs with the sewn-in girth are prone to slipping and rubbing. Whichever type is chosen, the most important thing is that it is well fitted. It may be necessary to have two such blankets in order to allow one to dry out or be cleaned while the other is being used. In the better weather no clothing should be necessary

unless a summer sheet is worn to offer some protection against flies or to keep a freshly groomed horse clean before a show.

DAILY ROUTINES

Horses living out 24 hours a day should be checked for lumps, cuts, lameness and other signs of ill-health at least twice a day, with a quick head count ensuring everything is "on its feet" and still within the confines of the field. This need not necessarily involve bringing the horse in as in many cases checks can be made in the field, although since a light grooming is also recommended it may be easier to take the horse out of the field where neither he nor you will be pestered by the other stock. The feet must be picked out at these times and the blanket removed, checked and reapplied. This is also the ideal time to cast an eye over the shoes if they are still being worn and, if not, to check and see if the foot is getting too long or beginning to break and crack. Remember that the feet will still need regular attention every six to eight weeks even if the horse is not at work — in fact good grazing will encourage the horn to grow quicker.

If the horse is coming in for any part of the day, then the number and timing of checks can be adapted as necessary. The field itself should also be checked daily

ABOVE: Protection against the weather is well provided by a waterproof New Zealand rug, warmly lined. They must be well fitted so that they don't chafe. When feeding hay make sure that there are more piles than animals in the field so that even the lowest in the pecking order gets enough.

BELOW: It is essential to check pastured horses carefully and regularly and to worm them every six to eight weeks.

for any breaks in the fencing, signs of poisonous plants, problems with the watering system or evidence that garbage has been dumped over the fence and so on. Depending on the size and lay of the field and the times of your checks, it may be necessary to walk around the area in order to be sure that all is well.

VETERINARY

When the horse is pastured it is very easy to overlook a vaccination booster and yet it is just as important that flu and tetanus immunisation is kept up to date. It will also be necessary to have the teeth checked and rasped twice a year, because they continue to grow and wear throughout the horse's life, creating sharp edges which, if left unattended, will eventually cause sores in the mouth and stop the horse from eating.

In spring and summer there are several likely problems for which the owner should be on the look out: from January onward it will be necessary to check the root of manes and tails and the feathers for signs of lice, which are often not spotted until considerable damage has been done. At the first signs contact your veterinary surgeon for advice on the best method of treatment. Sweet itch can also affect some horses and ponies at this time; it can be very unsightly as the horse will scratch himself voraciously, developing sores around the base of the mane and tail. Hogging the mane and shaving the tail are sometimes necessary in order to treat this difficult condition and, again, veterinary advice may well be needed. Ensuring that the horse is stabled and lightly blanketed from well before dusk to some time after dawn, particularly on still days, may help since this is the time when the evening midge, which causes the problem, is most active. This season also heralds the arrival of often large numbers of tiny sticky yellow botfly eggs on the hair, particularly on the shoulders and legs; these are best removed with a special botfly scraper. A good worming program will help with the limitation of possible internal damage caused by the larval stages.

Winter may bring its own problems such as rainscald, which appears as a sore rash usually on the horses back and quarters, and will often require antibiotic treatment. The frogs are especially prone to thrush in the usually muddy conditions of winter; these conditions also predispose to mud fever (found on the legs and occasionally the belly) and cracked heels, all conditions which are very painful and can lead to lameness. The affected areas should be well washed, thoroughly dried and then one of the several available creams or lotions applied. If the horse is thereafter kept in dry conditions the infection should clear up. If it does not or if it is not noticed until it is rife, which may happen with horses with a lot of feather, then veterinary advice should be sought.

WORMING

A good worming routine is important to all horses, but those living out for large portions of the time are more at risk as their dung constantly reinfects the pasture. All horses living on any given area of land should be wormed at the same time every six to eight weeks, using the same brand of wormer. This helps to prevent horses reinfecting each other and also ensures that the same kinds of worms are being attacked at the same time, as each brand has a different range against which it is effective. Resting paddocks or, even better (from a worm-control point of view), rotationally grazing the pasture with sheep and/or cattle will help to break up the parasite infestation cycle since these animals are able to consume horse worm larvae with no ill effect.

Cattle will also eat the coarser, rougher parts of the foliage which the horses ignore, thus helping with pasture management. Frequent collection of droppings on small fields is an essential control measure. In larger areas where this is not feasible regular harrowing to break up the droppings and expose the eggs and larvae to the elements can be helpful. It is advisable to vary the wormers from time to time, not only to ensure that the whole range of internal parasites is treated, but also to prevent problems with worms becoming resistant to certain active drug groups.

FEEDING ON GRASS

Horses not at work will normally do extremely well on good pasture during spring and summer, requiring no supplementary feeding; indeed some of those at light work will also flourish. This will depend on the quantity and quality of the pasture available, the climatic conditions during the season and the standard of paddock care both before and throughout the time the horses are on the land. It may be necessary to supplement the diet with a mineral or salt lick — a deficiency is usually indicated either by the horses eating their own or each other's droppings or by the stripping of bark from available trees, and sometimes even uncharacteristic chewing of wooden fencing. The dangers of laminitis must always be remembered as the overfeeding of any carbohydrate can cause this painful and debilitating disease: lush grass (especially if not gradually introduced) can also quickly cause the onset.

There are several popularly held beliefs concerning laminitis which should be disregarded. Firstly, latest research shows that the problem is carbohydrate-related rather than attributable to high protein levels. Secondly, it is not just children's ponies that are likely to succumb. Thirdly it can affect either the front and/or the hind feet. So if you discover your horse standing in the field with his front feet pushed out in front of him and his weight on his heels, you will need to seek veterinary assistance as soon as possible in order to prevent permanent damage. Unfortunately those of us lucky enough to have access to lots of really good grazing may find ourselves putting our horses on "starvation" paddocks or severely restricting access.

When it becomes necessary to feed hay it is best done either in a rack in a shelter or in long wooden freestanding racks originally designed for cattle. Haynets can be a useful alternative but they must be tied high enough so as not to present a hazard when hanging down empty; because of this, the top rail of the fence is rarely adequate. Where there are a lot of horses in a large area, it is sometimes more appropriate to place piles of hay on the ground even though this can lead to waste with the hay getting trampled or blowing away in the wind. It is helpful if the piles are always placed along one fence line in the least muddy area, if possible protected by a good thick hedge. The horses will soon learn to avoid walking on this area so much. The hay is less likely to be blown away if put out in slices rather than shaken out and there should be gaps of at least 13ft (4m) between piles to discourage bullying. Uneaten hay must be cleared away frequently to prevent a build-up of inedible forage which will contaminate any placed on top of it.

Whether piles or haynets are used, there should always be at least two or three more than the number of horses in the field, so that those at the bottom of the pecking order get their fair share. It must be remembered that the amount of hay needed will increase as the quantity and quality of available grass decreases and extra rations will be needed in freezing conditions, not only because the horses will be unable to eat any available grass, but also to provide the fuel to produce the extra energy needed to keep warm. Should it be necessary to feed concentrates to horses at different times, the individuals should be taken from the field to avoid fighting. Where they are all fed simultaneously, a long wooden trough may prove useful, although it means that all the horses will get the same type of feed which may not be appropriate. Portable mangers which hook onto the top rails of wooden fences or gates are excellent for feeding two or three animals together.

The practice of taking buckets of feed into fields of several horses is most strongly not recommended — the infighting which usually results often ends in not only the horses but owners or workers getting hurt. Do not feed pastured horses this way!

WORKING THE PASTURED HORSE

Most pastured horses are used for light to medium work, although with care, sufficient knowledge and experience it is possible to keep horses at hard work in

ABOVE: Ensure that all the horses in the field get fed, and that horses down the pecking order don't get bullied out of their feed by putting down piles. Try to do so in the same place each time, along a hedge if possible so that there's some wind protection to stop it from being blown away.

147

this way throughout the summer. Whatever the work, the horses will need to be brought in at least two hours before, so that they are not too gorged with grass. It will also allow a wet horse time to dry off before being groomed and tacked up. Tacking up a wet horse, if absolutely necessary, will not cause harm, but if the horse is also muddy skin damage will result. It is essential that the horse is cool and dry before being turned out again.

PASTURE MANAGEMENT

Horses are very selective grazers and, as a result, any land they use constantly needs very careful management. Even fields where there are relatively low numbers on the acreage the pasture will develop "lawns," areas where the horses graze quite close to the ground, and "roughs," the areas where the horses defecate and urinate. Only if there are very few options will horses graze the roughs, so over a period of time the size of the rough areas increase and the grazing lawns diminish. Places that undergo particularly heavy use, such as gateways and ground surrounding troughs, will quickly become devoid of grass and turn into poached areas that are dust bowls in summer and mud baths after rain. Bearing in mind that many grazing paddocks also have to double as exercise arenas, the demands made on modern grazing can be very severe; good management is essential to provide conditions which promote the most productive and palatable forage with the minimum of weeds, and furthermore ensure that the land does not become an eyesore inviting complaints from neighbors and possibly even environmental protection groups.

The first step to good management is to undertake a soil analysis immediately on arrival at new grazing and then regularly every four or five years. It is important that soil samples are taken from both lawns and roughs, as the results will vary because of the use of roughs for urination. Local government agricultural extension services can help. They will advise you of companies qualified to carry out soil analysis for an appropriate fee. The results will indicate whether potash, lime, or phosphate should be applied and in what quantities. Breeding establishments find that more specialist advice is needed since the youngstock rely to a much greater extent on the uptake of essential trace elements from the grazing. Lime, potash and phosphate can be applied at any time of year but usually to better effect if done during either summer or autumn. With any application, give particular thought to the possible effects on other stock if cross-grazing.

To take full advantage of the chosen dressing, the field should be rested after application and it is best if horses are not allowed back onto the land until there has been some rain, or at least a heavy dew, to aid the breakdown of the granules. A light dressing of nitrogen may be appropriate in mid to late February, with a second, slightly heavier, application eight to ten weeks later. Once the field has been fertilized the grass should be allowed to become established and reach a height of about 4in (10cm) before any serious grazing takes place. If this sort of growth isn't allowed, the development of strong root growth will be adversely affected, resulting in a quick deterioration of the pasture. Poached areas can be harrowed and reseeded, either by broadcasting suitable mixtures, or over large areas by direct drilling and then rolling. The plowing and reseeding of horse grazing land is usually reserved for pasture considered beyond reclaim by any other means.

Regular and frequent cutting of weeds such as nettles and thistles will discourage their growth — if the problem is very widespread it may be necessary to spray the entire field. If topping (cutting) is to be carried out, the field must be carefully searched for the prolific and poisonous ragwort first, as a mechanical cutter is apt to spread the plant as it does the job. Once the field has been topped the cuttings must be forked up, removed and disposed of to avoid problems with colic and also to ensure that the regrowth of the underneath grasses is not inhibited.

There is considerable regulation relating to the use of herbicides and sound advice must be sought before use. In practical terms the application should take place when rain is not expected for at least 24 hours and on a still day to prevent spray drift. Stock should not be returned to the fields for some time since herbicides are often toxic and horses tend to be much more vulnerable to their effects than other stock. Always refer to the product label. Poisonous plants too can be treated by spraying; perhaps the most well know in this category is ragwort, a tall yellow-flowered plant with tough stems and lots of foliage. Small clusters of ragwort can be dealt with by being pulled up — providing the roots are also extracted and all the bits collected up and removed from the field since any left behind will become even more toxic as it wilts. Allowing sheep to graze the pasture in early spring can also discourage ragwort growth. Other poisonous plants commonly found in horse grazing areas are foxglove, yew, ivy, deadly nightshade, bracken, most evergreens and buttercups when growing in large quantities. Where the pasture is bordered by residential properties, care must be taken that laburnum and other toxic garden plants are not within the horses' reach and where there are oak trees the acorns must be removed. Windfalls from apple and other fruit trees must be regularly cleared away to prevent gorging leading to colic.

The number of horses and/or ponies that can be successfully grazed on any area will depend upon several factors, including the soil type and its subsequent fertility, climatic conditions during the growing season, the number of hours per day the field is grazed and the quality of management. As a rough guide, good grazing should support one horse per acre or up to three ponies, but supplementary feeding will be necessary during the winter months and don't forget that the horses' workload will have a significant influence. Grazing rotation will help pasture management where there is sufficient land available. Divide the field into a minimum of three one-acre (half-hectare) paddocks and rotate the horses around at intervals of approximately three weeks. This will allow the grazing of up to nine or ten horses (or slightly more ponies) during the growing season. A similar system can be implemented using one-acre (half-hectare) paddocks for a couple of horses.

THE FORAGE

The grasses used in horse pastures need to be palatable and fairly hard wearing, with good bottom. Obviously some grasses are better suited to some soils and growing conditions. Although a mixture of perennial rye grass, smooth meadow grass, creeping red fescue and chewing fescues is generally considered ideal, they will not be a good choice where the growing conditions do not suit them. If hay is also to be taken, then timothy is often added. There are many herbs which are of value to horses and they are usually eaten with great relish providing nutrients not always found in grasses. Ideally they should be planted in a strip in one area of the field so that if the pasture at some point needs to

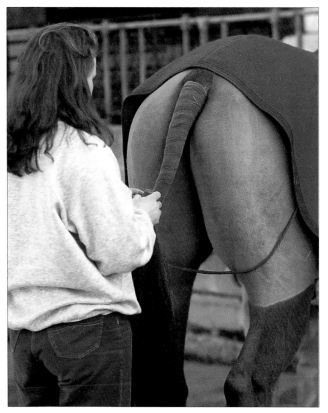

ABOVE: Tail bandaging.

BELOW: Hungarian half-bred foals grazing. Pasture management is essential to ensure the best possible foliage with a minimum of weeds, palatable grazing and even wear. Horse droppings should be removed from the pasture to reduce the possibility of worm transmission. If you do use fertilizers, do not graze until there has been a reasonable rainfall.

be sprayed for weeds, this area can be avoided. Some herbs can be difficult to establish and will be easier to tend and encourage if in a restricted area. Favorites include comfrey, dandelion and yarrow.

THE FIELD

Many of us have little choice when selecting grazing for our horses and very often have to make the best of less than perfect conditions, but before buying or renting, various factors should be considered. Poorly drained, marshy land predisposes health problems in winter and makes working the land with machinery very difficult. The grass which grows in the summer tends to be poor quality but may suit stock which tends to get overfat. Very steep fields can cause joint and back problems due to the constant strain placed upon them. Exposed fields offer no respite from harsh winter conditions or from the heat of the summer sun. Good access to the field all year-round will also make management of the animals easier.

A good supply of fresh clean water is obviously essential. Unfortunately, very few streams today remain unpolluted throughout their course and therefore are unlikely to be a suitable water source. Those with sandy bottoms also pose a threat of colic and if the sides are steep youngstock can get stranded. Ponds should always be fenced off as the water in them will be stagnant and an unwary foal may end up out of his depth. Ideally a galvanized water trough, sited a little way away from the gate and well away from overhanging trees or hedges, should be used. It will need to be in a well drained area, either in the fence line or at least 33ft (10m) in from the fence and well away from the corners so that horses cannot get trapped behind the trough and kicked. The supply pipe must be laid deep enough to ensure it does not freeze in winter. The water level is best controlled by a well-greased covered ballcock system.

If an old bath is used, raise it on blocks to allow easy emptying. Box it in so that no protruding edges can cause injury; for the same reason remove the taps. In winter the water may well freeze so the trough should figure in your twice daily checks and should be cleaned out regularly throughout the year. Mounting the trough on a concrete or limestone base will help to prevent poaching but can be expensive.

Outdoor shelter can be provided in various ways — a thick hedge, a sleeper-wall windbreak or a three-sided, usually wooden, shelter. The shelter must be positioned either flush with the fence or well away from it with the back of the shed towards the prevailing wind. The quality of the drainage and the likely level of use will determine whether or not the shelter will need a foundation. Either way the floor should be kept well bedded down and frequently cleaned. Sizes and shapes will vary depending on the number of animals to be sheltered, but they should be open-fronted to prevent horses becoming trapped and bullied.

Keepers of stock are legally responsible for ensuring that their boundaries are secure; otherwise they are held liable for any damage caused by strays. Owners and keepers of quality competition horses and breeding stock will need to take particular care with their choice of fencing but all owners should erect the best quality fencing they can afford to meet legal responsibility and guard the safety of their stock. Walls of a suitable height, or with an affixed top rail, make good boundaries and in some parts of the country are very common and cheap to maintain well. Banks alone, although providing shelter, are not enough to be stock-proof and will need to be topped with either a hedge or a fence. Hedges themselves should be tall and thick and correctly trimmed to ensure good growth at the bottom. If gaps have already developed, the hedge may well benefit from being well laid by an expert; an alternative is to put good quality wire through with solid well-sunk fence posts.

Post and rail is ideal but very often prohibitively expensive as well as needing regular maintenance with a wood preservative. A wire fence can be a cheaper alternative which requires less maintenance, does not split and cannot be chewed; unfortunately whichever color you chose — white, brown or green — they do not seem to blend into the countryside and are often considered unsightly. Being made from 3¾in (10cm) plastic strips threaded through with high-tensile wire top and bottom, the fence is very durable and tough but will need exact and regular re-straining. Either plain or, preferably, the more expensive high-tensile wire erected on wooden posts is most commonly seen these days and provides an economic answer to a sometimes difficult and costly problem. To make the fence more visible to galloping horses the top rail is often made of wood or stud rail with the wire rails underneath. This fencing is not as substantial as some of the others mentioned but to prevent damage from stock a single line of electric fencing can be off-set to the inside.

Electric fencing tape or the modern more visible electric wires can be used to divide paddocks either with wooden fence posts for permanent divisions, or with metal fencing rods for temporary boundaries. Electric fencing on its own is not recommended as a satisfactory method of securing a perimeter. Barbed wire is not recommended to fence any area containing horses for the obvious injury hazards it presents; however, it is cheap and fairly effective and good maintenance together with judicial use can reduce the risks.

Whichever fencing is chosen, it is important that the bottom rail is no less than 11in (28cm) high to reduce the danger of horses getting a foot caught.

ABOVE: Good pasture and plenty of exercise are necessary to help a young foal to grow up fit and strong. The foal will be weaned at around six months if the mare is in foal again, othewise more usually, at a year.

Furthermore the top rail should be high enough to deter the horses jumping out and other stock jumping in. The most effective gates are hung, so that they open both ways and have the hinges either welded or turned so that the gate cannot be lifted off. All hinges and fastenings should be of galvanized steel to prevent rusting and of sufficient strength for the weight of the gate. Hardwood gates, although more expensive, are preferable to softwood since they don't warp or split to the same extent and, if well maintained, can last up to 50 years. Metal gates are acceptable but when they start to become damaged care must be taken that no sharp edges appear. The gateway may need to have stone or crushed limestone laid in winter in order to provide a good safe surface.

ROUGHING OFF AND BRINGING UP

These are the terms used to describe the processes of preparing a fit horse for a period pasture rest and taking an unfit horse from rest in the field and getting him ready for his fitness levels to be improved.

When roughing a horse off, his concentrate feed, exercise, grooming and, where appropriate, the number of blankets he is wearing, are all gradually decreased over a period of two to three weeks.

Simultaneously the number of hours out in the field per day are increased. At some point during this period the horse's teeth, vaccinations and shoes should be checked and, if necessary, remedied and, finally, he should be wormed.

These last points should all be checked during the two- to three-week period needed to bring a horse up from grass, but the rest of the process is reversed — in other words, grooming, exercise, concentrate feed and blankets are all introduced and gradually increased as the time spent in the field is gradually decreased. Once the horse starts to spend some length of time in the stable, a careful watch must be kept for legs that "fill" and for a "stable cough," both the result of the change of environment; very often initially feeding wet hay may help to prevent the latter, as will turning the horse out while his bed is being mucked out. Filled legs may indicate that either the horse is not getting enough opportunity to exercise in the field or that the concentrate feed has been increased too quickly.

151

CHAPTER 21

BREEDING

Leisa Crook and Michael Hurley

STALLION MANAGEMENT

Most stallions are selected for breeding based on their conformation and pedigree and their prowess on the racetrack or in the arena, with very little consideration given to their actual reproductive potential. The task of the stallion manager is to maximize the stallion's reproductive efficiency regardless of the horse's inherent fertility.

A stallion may be unsuitable for stud work if he is found to have defects such as cataracts, navicular disease or imperfect genital organs. Conformation and action should be as near perfect as possible since the stallion is required to improve any shortcomings the mare may have. A stallion can be put to stud purposes surprisingly young: a two- or three-year-old colt can sire 20–25 foals even in his first year of covering.

Normal and functioning genitals are necessary for the stallion to cover the mare successfully. He needs to have visible, level testicles of the same size. If a testicle remains inside his body he is probably infertile; in such case he is called a "rig" and if he does manage to inseminate a mare any male descendants are liable to inherit his defect.

It is the turf record of a racehorse stallion that is important — conformation is secondary. To get the best from a stallion he has to work with a handler that he trusts. A "stallion man" is needed; he will guide and reassure the stallion and once a good relationship has been established between man and horse they should work together for the season. Additional help will of course be needed with handling the mares.

To be able to serve mares all season a stallion must be kept in the best possible environment as well as being in tip-top physical condition himself. If at all possible, he should be kept company by stablemates and, as much as possible, participate in the general routine of the stable. However, he needs his own loosebox and some good pasture to run around. The covering yard should be nearby with tying and teasing equipment handy.

The stallion should have a good program of adequate grooming, foot care, teeth care, vaccination and worming. It is important to have the stallion fit and healthy for the entire breeding season. With Thoroughbreds, this typically extends from February 15 to July 15 each year (northern hemisphere). The stallion cannot be ill or lame and must be capable of breeding every day. Feeding the best quality forages available will result in maintenance of excellent body condition, attitude and breeding performance with fewer digestive upsets. It is a good idea to weigh the stallion regularly and monitor body condition and hair coat in order that any necessary dietary adjustments may be made. Overfeeding can lead to digestive problems and painful feet disorders, such as laminitis.

Regular exercise, apart from normal stud duties, is essential to keep the stallion fit and in good condition. Some stallions require no forced exercise. When they are turned out all day in a small paddock they will run and play, thus getting adequate exercise. Other horses, however, will only graze or stand in one spot for most of the day, essentially getting no exercise. Such horses require forced exercise to remain healthy and fit. This may take the form of riding under tack at a slow canter, or driving in a jog cart for about one to three miles (2–5km) every day. Lunging at a fast walk or trot for 15 to 30 minutes or being hooked to an automatic walker for 30 minutes to an hour a day are other common forms of forced exercise.

The amount of time a stallion is kept in a paddock must be tailored to his personality. Some stallions tolerate being in a paddock next to another stallion, others do not. Times when stallions are due for paddock exercise must be coordinated with their individual preferences. Everything possible must be done to keep the stallion in a happy and balanced frame of mind.

COVERING THE MARE

The mare may not be willing to be covered and considerable care has to be taken so that neither animal is damaged in the process. The stallion is best harnessed on a long leather lead of lunging length to give him some leeway should he rear up. The lunge is then run through the nearside ring of a straight mouth metal bit, taken under the jaw and attached to the offside ring. The bit should be attached to an 18in (45cm) long chain attached to the bridle. The stallion is controlled through pressure on the lead which can be strong enough to be painful when it tightens across his jaw. Should the stallion be too excited at the thought of the mare and refuse to be bridled, then his halter can be left on and the bit buckled through the side rings when needed.

The stallion and mare have to be introduced very carefully. Let them meet safely apart on opposite sides of the teasing gates or boards. If either horse is not ready, or conversely is overeager, one or the other animal can inadvertently be harmed, so the teasing gate is to stop the stallion mounting the mare before she is ready by being teased or prepared with hobbles (see Mating).

It is not always easy to tell if a mare is ready for servicing and rather than over excite the stallion by bringing him in before the mare will accept him, a "teaser" is used, this is often a "rig" or inferior stallion. He flirts with the mare until it becomes clear whether or not she is ready to see the stallion. It is for the stud groom to decide whether to continue with the planned cover.

Overbooking a young stallion may lead to "psychological" problems, even to the point of impotence — at which time he becomes useless for stud purposes. At four years and older a stallion with a good libido, mating ability and fertility can readily breed a book of 60 or more mares. With these same characteristics, a stallion used in an artificial insemination program can efficiently breed over 200 mares. To breed a book of 60 or more, the mares must come to the stallion after a veterinary inspection for covering at the optimum time in their estrus cycle, thus economizing on his number of services.

CHOOSING THE RIGHT MARE

As with most things to do with horses, finance is an important factor with breeding. Money will dictate the chance to breed to a good pedigree, but other issues need to be considered. The stallion is usually credited with contributing speed to the foal, while the mare brings stamina and staying power. Research and time must be put into finding a suitable pairing which will perhaps produce a spectacular foal. The type, temperament, conformation and action of the mare must be related to the intended appearance of the offspring and the purpose for which it is intended — racing, jumping and so on. The careful selection of the right stallion can improve upon a few imperfections in the mare's conformation or action.

Before a mare can go to the stallion she has to be checked out thoroughly by a vet: other than in good health, she has to be fit and able to travel to the stallion — who can be a considerable distance away. All this costs money, as does the traveling expenses, livery charges, extra feed, plus of course the stud fee which can be considerable depending on the sire. A groom also has to be paid to look after her. And then there are all the costs of feeding and stabling the foal once it arrives.

BELOW: At Banstead Manor Stud FARM, ENGLAND and, they have all the facilities necessary for the successful covering of mares. Before the mare goes to the stallion she must be checked out thoroughly to ensure that she is in good condition.

Finally the mare has to be in good condition before being taken to the stallion — in essence this means being relaxed and healthy. An unfit, overweight or underweight animal can be hard to get into foal; at the other end of the scale, a mare who is too fit can prove difficult to foal.

Prior to sending her to stud, and to avoid delay in getting the mare covered and in foal, her genital organs can be checked by an equine veterinarian. This is done to determine if the mare's internal and external reproductive organs are normal and if there are any signs of damage or infection. Mares going to stud should have been regularly wormed, vaccinated for influenza and be unshod. Before covering, some studs may require swabs to be taken to ensure the mare is free from infectious disease such as contagious equine metritis (CEM), pseudomonas or klebsiella infections.

The mare's estrus cycle must be monitored and recorded to ascertain that she comes into season regularly every 18–21 days — this time is called "horsing" — and the days between when she is in heat. From this information a vet will establish as closely as possible exactly when she will ovulate so she can be booked for the stud on precisely the right day. To coincide her visit to the stallion at a time when she is ovulating and at her most fertile is vital. Artificial lighting is used routinely in breeding programs to induce mares to restart their normal sexual cycle early in the breeding season. Mares with abnormal cycles may be treated with hormone therapy.

Once introduced to the stallion on the other side of the teasing rail, the mare is closely watched to see whether she appears willing. If she seems ready for covering by standing still, and not responding violently to the stallion's advances, she can be led to the covering area. The mare is usually twitched and hobbled to prevent her striking out at the stallion, but the hobble is removed as soon as the stallion enters the mare. When the mare is ready, the stallion approaches from behind: she needs to be held calmly but firmly, with her head held right up high at his approach. Once he has mounted her and his penis is securely inside her, the mare must be kept as still as possible for sometimes as long as one or two minutes so as not to spill any semen after the stallion has ejaculated. The stallion then dismounts and the mare can be led quietly away.

PRE-NATAL CARE OF THE MARE

It takes three weeks after covering before a mare is clearly in foal by not coming into season as usual. Pregnancy may otherwise be diagnosed with the use of ultrasound scanners as early as 12 days after conception. Using this technique, the embryo is seen as a tiny cyst-like structure in the uterus. Rectal palpation can be used to diagnose a pregnancy accurately after 30 days gestation. A blood test is also available which is accurate between 40 and 120 days. This method is often used in smaller horses in which rectal and ultrasound examination may not be possible. The foal will be born between 335 and 350 days after fertilization of the egg. To calculate when the foal is likely to appear, count 11 months and four days from the last covering. Thus a mare serviced on August 1 will probably foal on September 5 the following year.

It is advisable to confirm the mare's pregnancy by one of these methods, so that the horse's diet, facilities and vaccinations can be tailored to her requirements. It may be necessary to consider supplementary feeding, bearing in mind that the pregnant mare must maintain her own physical condition, whilst at the same time providing the fetus with sufficient nourishment to develop and grow.

If early pregnancy occurs in late spring/early summer then the mare can be fed as usual. The fetus requires proteins for forming tissue and muscle — good sources of high protein food are oats, corn, linseed, beans, good hay and alfalfa. Protein and trace elements are absorbed into the body system by the consumption of fibrous roughage or bulk (hay, chaff and bran) — accordingly between half and two-thirds of her diet must constitute roughage. Vitamins, and minerals are essential for the development of the embryo and, if suspected to be lacking, can be supplemented in powder form in the feed.

A pregnant mare must not be allowed to get too fat. Let her graze and feed her supplements according to her temperament. A quiet animal won't need anything extra until the end of summer, at which time give her a mixture of 1.1lb (0.5kg) of bran and 2.2lb (1kg) of high-protein pellets every day. As the pasture stops growing with shorter autumn days, give her additional hay at night — up to 7.7lb (3.5kg). All being well this need not change until spring. However, should the brood mare appear to be looking for more food, or is starting to lose weight give her an extra morning feed of bran and stud cubes and increase her hay ration to 11lb (5kg). Her protein intake should stay the same as before but with additional hay and bulk depending on whether she looks as if she needs it or not.

For a larger mare or a Thoroughbred the quantities need to be greater: a 17hh (5ft 8in) Thoroughbred needs about 7.7lb (3.5kg) of oats, 4.4lb (2kg) of stud cubes and 4.4lb (2kg) of bran twice a day, plus as much as 15lb (7kg) of good hay throughout winter if there is no suitable grazing. To put it simply: as long as a broodmare can gather her protein from grazing grass she is fine: however, when the grass stops growing and

ABOVE LEFT: Mares quietly waiting out at pasture at Banstead Manor Stud Farm. The visit to the stallion must be made at the precise time each mare is ovulating and at her most fertile.

TOP: Sperm can be collected from the stallion with the use of an artificial mare.

ABOVE: The sperm is then decanted into a large test tube for removal, storage and later use. This is particularly useful if the desired dam is abroad, temporarily incapacitated or too young to foal.

starts to disappear, then she needs replacement protein foods but she also needs the hay and bulk to fill her stomach up and make her feel full.

For a happy confinement the mare needs to be in a good frame of mind. First of all she needs a large and comfortable stall. If she is to foal there it must have electric lighting, be draft-proof and have any potentially dangerous objects removed. The stall should be about 11x20ft (3.5x6m) to give her and her foal plenty of room to maneuver. She needs clean and fresh bedding every day and plenty of clean water to drink. She needs to go outside to stretch her legs every day after breakfast, somewhere she can peacefully graze and get a little exercise until being brought in again in late afternoon for an evening feed and a browse at her haynet. Brush her over once a week — don't bother her with daily grooming — but make sure her feet are regularly trimmed. Worm her every two or three months. A broodmare doesn't usually need a blanket but she will appreciate it on cold nights and will keep in better condition accordingly. In the coldest depths of winter a New Zealand rug during the day will help to keep her happy.

Above all the mare must not be overexerted — that is, allowed to sweat or become short of breath — by being asked to do fast work or climb steep hills. Jumping must not be attempted and all riding should be stopped at the beginning of the seventh month of pregnancy. A mare gestates for anywhere between 10 and 12 months, although her official time is 340 days. Around the tenth month her teats will become prominent and her udder will begin to spring. As time goes on the udder will swell considerably and eventually produce globules on the extremities of the teats. This last sign usually means that the foal will arrive within the next 24 hours. Watch her closely, look to see when the globules fall off and milk starts to appear; at round the same time the muscles on her quarters will sag on either side of her croup. Her vulva will start to distend and foaling will begin.

FOALING

The mare should, as much as possible, be left to foal without interference, although a careful watch should be kept on her throughout delivery, so that assistance may be given if she needs help. Although some of the hardier breeds, eg native ponies, may be best left to foal outdoors, most mares and foals will benefit from delivering in a large, clean, well-lit stall.

Labor occurs in three definable stages:

- Stage 1: the uterus contracts involuntarily, repositioning the fetus for expulsion. The cervix is gradually relaxed.
- Stage 2: begins with the "breaking of the waters" (fetal membranes rupture) and the delivery of the foal.
- Stage 3: expulsion of the fetal membranes (afterbirth).

An observer will notice the following behavior in a natural birth:

- With the onset of the first uterine contractions, the mare paces around the field or stable, swishing her tail and continuously looking round to her sides. The length of time between the contractions will gradually shorten and they will become more intense. All this can take anywhere between one and eight hours. The mare may lie down and get up again and may start to sweat as the contractions become more painful.
- Her water will suddenly burst and a rush of water will gush from her vagina indicating the rupture of the bag of amniotic fluid surrounding the foal.
- The mare is obviously in pain and will lie down and begin grunting and straining.
- The forefeet of the foal appear at the vulva. To ease her discomfort the mare may decide to get up and walk around between contractions.
- The tip of the nose and then the head of the foal appears lying on the forelegs, while the mare continues to strain. The head is covered in membranes and these need to be cleared immediately from around the nose and mouth to allow the nostrils to draw their first breath.
- As soon as the shoulders are clear of the mare the membrane-covered foal will slip out easily. The foal is still attached by the umbilical cord which should be left to break naturally as the foal moves of its own accord.
- The exhausted mare will stay lying down to recover her strength for up to half an hour before getting up to lick the foal and mother it.
- At this stage the remaining fetal membranes or afterbirth are expelled from the mare. It should then be inspected by a vet before disposal to ensure that it is complete and nothing is left to fester inside the mare.
- The foal attempts to stand after about half an hour, so that it may start suckling from the mare. The first milk is called colostrum; it is especially enriched so it is vital that the foal drinks some within the first couple of hours after birth.

DANGER SIGNS

At any significant deviation from the above schedule the vet should be called, particularly if the foal fails to present head first with extended forefeet. Anything else is considered abnormal. Sometimes the hind feet and tail appear first in what is called a posterior presentation; this is not usually a problem and the foal can be delivered without help. However, the danger is that the foal will drown in its fetal fluid, so speed is of the essence — pull down on the hind fetlocks during contractions as the mare is expelling the foal and remove the mucus from the foal's nose as soon as possible.

Sometimes the umbilical cord has to be cut if it does not break naturally. To do this, tie some sterilized cord tightly around the umbilical about 2in (5cm) away from the foal's belly, and then again about 1in (2.5cm) further along. Using a sterilized knife or scissors, cut the cord between these two points and treat the raw ends with iodine or antibiotic spray.

Occasionally a mare will strain so much during labor that her womb prolapses. This is immediately apparent as the uterus will appear at the lips of the vulva as a huge, bright red, pear-shaped mass. Call the vet immediately as the mare will require sedation and stitching.

The foal may sometimes have problems feeding. Weakness in the newborn when it is unable to stand to take milk may be solved by taking the colostrum from the mare and feeding it to the foal in a bottle with a teat, or with a stomach tube. As the foal gains in strength, it can gradually be introduced to the mare's teat. On the other hand, the mare may be at fault — for example, a maiden mare sometimes refuses to let the foal suckle. Solutions include twitching the mare or pushing her against the stable wall and bracing her so that her foreleg is raised. This restricts her movement and allows the foal to suckle. She should come around to letting the foal suckle after three or four times; then try holding her headcollar until she is willing to let the foal suckle unaided.

After a normal foaling the mare will need to rest and recover before she is inspected by the vet. Her foal also needs to be checked for any congenital defects or malformations. The vet will need to establish that the foal has passed its first bowel motion or meconium. Routine injections such as that for tetanus may be administered. The vet will also check the mare for any tearing of the vulva and will stitch or restitch the animal as necessary. The afterbirth will be examined for completeness and treatment will be commenced immediately if any parts are retained in the uterus.

POST-NATAL PROBLEMS AND DISEASES

INFLAMMATION OF THE VAGINA

After a difficult labor, particularly if the foal had to struggle to get out, there may be severe bruising around the mare's vagina. The lips of the vagina will be swollen and dark red or in bad cases black. The vet will prescribe antibiotics and anti-inflammatories, to prevent an infection becoming established. If left

ABOVE: Taking a vaginal swab. Some studs require swabs to be taken to ensure the mare is free from infectious diseases such as CEM, pseudomonas and klebsiella.

BELOW: Foaling boxes at Banstead Manor.

untreated, a foul-smelling discharge will develop, her pulse and temperature will rise and the mare will have difficulty passing urine.

LACK OF MILK

A small udder does not always mean a low milk supply, but a hungry foal who is not growing is a sign to be concerned about. It might be that the mare has a milk shortage, her diet could be at fault, so increase her intake and encourage the foal to continue sucking. Give the mare plenty of clean, fresh water and high quality and good grazing should be sought; otherwise add milk pellets or powder to good rations of oats and flaked corn. Also give her plenty of clover and meadow hay. If her milk doesn't improve the foal will need supplementary feeding.

DIARRHEA

There are may infectious forms of diarrhea caused by microbes in the digestive tract. Scouring may begin two to three days after birth, with foul-smelling, yellowish liquid forcefully expelled from the foal. Veterinary treatment is necessary since replacement fluids and perhaps antibiotics. will be quickly required. This condition causes rapid dehydration. The mare and foal will need to be isolated if the cause of the illness is infectious. The stable will need to be kept disinfected and clean, with soiled bedding removed frequently.

RETENTION OF MECONIUM AND CONSTIPATION

Meconium is the green-black first excreta of a foal. If this does not appear soon after birth, or after the first milk feed, it may still be inside the animal. The foal will be obviously uncomfortable and unable to pass anything although it is straining to do so. It may also show signs of colic. An enema needs to be administered. This should quickly clear up the problem, but if it persists, call the vet to look for other causes such as a blockage.

JOINT ILL OR INFECTION OF THE NAVEL

Joint ill or blood poisoning is mainly caused by inattention to the navel following foaling. The area around the navel swells up and is full of pus which in turn causes abscesses. Otherwise joint ill can also happen if the foal hasn't had his mother's colostrum and it hasn't been able to build up natural resistance to infections.

Treatment requires antibiotics: in fact some vets as a matter of routine like to treat newborn foals with antibiotics to prevent joint ill. If left untreated the foal will become listless, show no interest in suckling and in time will lose the use of one or both hind legs. The foal's joints will be stiff, swollen and painful, with abscesses in the joints which rupture causing an unpleasant discharge. The foal becomes virtually motionless and usually dies.

MASTITIS

Inflammation of the udder, can occur at any time during the suckling period and immediately following weaning. It has many causes. Sometimes it's because the mare has been lying on cold, wet or hard floors, her teats have been either injured or obstructed somehow or even that she has too much milk supply. Her udder becomes engorged and she will be in obvious sharp pain if her udder is touched. If the milk is drawn, it will be clotted and blood-stained. Treatment includes rest from the foal, hand milking of the udder, warm bathing and antibiotics, all carried out under supervision by the vet.

INFLAMED WOMB

Initially everything seems all right, but between two and 10 days after giving birth the uterus still has not contracted back satisfactorily into the womb. This can be because some of the afterbirth or fetal membranes are still lodged within her. The mare becomes stiff in her movements, loses her appetite, has a foul smelling vaginal discharge, plus a high temperature and pulse rate. Also, she may stop producing milk and laminitis may occur. Treatment includes removal of the retained matter, thorough cleansing and antibiotic treatment. If not caught in the early stages, this inflammation will cause the death of the mare.

ORPHAN FOALS

Sadly sometimes the mare dies during or after foaling. If her foal survives he will need to have a foster mother to care for him. Sometimes this mare has just foaled herself, in which case rub the orphan foal with her afterbirth before placing the foal next to her, and hope she accepts the orphan alongside her own foal. If the mare has lost her foal, then put the skin from the dead foal over the orphan in the hope that the mare will be fooled into accepting it as her own offspring. Sometimes this works and sometimes it doesn't.

If the mare is unwilling to accept the new foal, try again, but this time to be on the safe side separate the two with a partition so they can still see and smell each other. Milk the mare and then bottle feed the foal, with time and luck they will grow to love each other.

Occasionally a non-lactating, barren mare will "nanny" a foal, allowing him to grow up naturally so he can develop along normal lines, although the foal will, of course, have to be bottle-fed. Commercially manufactured milk powder is the best substitute for a bottle-fed foal. However, in all cases, every effort must be made to obtain colostrum and feed it to the foal immediately, since it contains vital antibodies which protect the foal's early days of life. Bottle-feeding should initially take place at two-hour intervals, gradually extending to every four hours by the time the foal is three to four weeks old. By the time a healthy foal is four or five months old it should require only two milk feeds a day and may even be considered for weaning.

A mare who has lost her foal at birth needs to be kept on a low protein diet of hay and bran mash until her milk supply dries up. She needs as much exercise as possible within reason, but don't let her get on to any lush pastures. In particular her udder will need regular checks to make sure she is not contracting mastitis.

FEEDING AND EXERCISE

After an easy natural birth and providing both animals are in good health, mare and foal can be allowed out for a little gentle exercise after a day for recuperation. As summer goes on mares and foals will do splendidly on good pasture. If the grazing is sparse, give the mare a high protein diet of crushed oats, flaked corn and bran plus a good supply of hay, so she can continue producing good quality milk for the foal.

To grow up healthy and strong the foal needs plenty of exercise to promote muscle development. Both animals need particularly close observation until weaning. This can happen at about six months if the mare is in foal again, but left for another six months if she is barren but in good health.

Providing the foal is healthy and eating well then it is time to wean. To make this easier it is best to separate the pair completely for three weeks. This means keeping them well out of each other's earshot and hidden completely from sight. Then they can be put back together again.

Providing the mare recovers well physically from the foaling and has had no bruising, stitches or discharge, she can be taken to the stallion again on her foal heat the following year.

RIGHT: The end product of all the hard work — a healthy happy foal.

BELOW: A foal can be weaned from six months onward providing it is fit and healthy and otherwise eating well.

159

CHAPTER 22

BUYING

Zoë Nicholls

Anyone who has ever bought a horse knows what a hit or miss venture this can be. If you are lucky, you have a horse already lined up; perhaps friends are selling their ever-so-genuine equine and he is perfectly suited to you — not to mention your bank balance. Furthermore you will already know him well, so are used to all his little ways. Unfortunately this is unlikely to be the case. Most of us, once we have decided to buy, have to set out with money in hand and hope that we find our dream horse. But, before signing that check there are definitely one or two things worth considering.

WHY OWN A HORSE?

To those of us who were born horse-mad, this hardly seems a question worth asking: well it is obviously a natural progression that once you have learned to ride and care for other people's horses, that you should want one of your own to care for.

Many people find their way around the buying problem by having a horse on loan from someone else or perhaps sharing with a friend. It can be a very real problem finding time to do everything if you lead a busy life, and for people who work long or difficult hours, having a reliable friend to split mucking out shifts with can be a real bonus. Stress the reliable part, because, as everyone is aware, sharing any task with people who do not pull their weight can ruin even the firmest friendships.

No matter what it is that you intend to do with your new horse, there can be few things as satisfying as seeing him healthy and happy in your care. Horse ownership can be incredibly rewarding for both parties and with the correct attention a real partnership should develop.

Anyone who has seriously decided to set out in search of their perfect horse will have their own reasons for doing so and being able to do so. Perhaps you have recently moved to a property with an amount of pasture and now you can finally have your horse; or maybe you had a pony as a child and would like your children to have the chance. Having a horse or pony in the family can often be a real benefit, and many a child has gone from strength to strength in the equestrian world with the encouragement of family behind them.

The most important thing when buying a horse is to know exactly what you are looking for. Let us assume that you are starting from scratch, with nothing lined up and only your horsesense to guide you.

WHERE TO GET ADVICE

Unless you are very knowledgeable, it is essential that you ask as many people as possible for their advice. In truth, much of what you will be told will not apply to your situation, and may even be downright useless, but if you get one really useful piece of information from all of this then you are getting somewhere. The equestrian world can be a strange one at times and you will do well to exercise a little caution now and then. Try not to let yourself be swayed too far in the opposite direction by well-meaning strangers. If you are looking for that nice 15hh working hunter then there is little point in allowing anyone to persuade you that what you really want is their 16.2hh ex-racehorse.

Without a doubt the most important aid you can possibly take with you on your quest is the "knowledgeable friend." He or she should be someone whose opinion you value and whose company you enjoy. Many miles may be traveled before you find what you are looking for and spending each journey in stony silence can only add to the pressure.

A good plan if you have been taking riding lessons from qualified riding instructors is to arrange for them to come along with you. In theory they will know what you are looking at and should have a fair idea of your level of competence. They may also wish to ride your prospective purchase — this way you get to see how the horse goes for someone other than his regular rider and your instructor can pick out any hidden problems and report them back to you.

Likewise it is well worth asking your local riding club if any of their members are thinking of selling their mount; very often good animals often change hands without ever being advertised. Good children's ponies are always in demand and some will remain in the same branch of the pony club for years, just going on to a new member when the last has grown too tall. So it is a good idea to keep an ear to the ground.

Looking for a more specific type of horse or pony presents you with more opportunities to explore. For

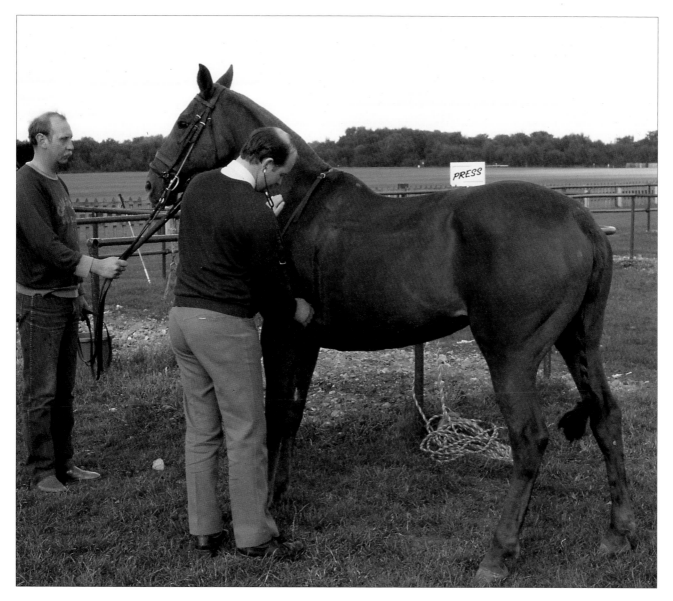

ABOVE: Always get a vet to check the horse and make sure it's not the vendor's choice of vet!

those who wish to take up a certain discipline or are looking for a particular breed there are many, many societies which will have access to any information you require concerning the breed or type that they promote. Very often they will also provide a sales list and can put you in touch with breeders, who — even if they do not have anything suitable themselves — might know someone who does. As the saying goes, forewarned is forearmed, so once you have gathered all that priceless information, you and your "knowledgeable friend" are one step ahead.

LIKELY COSTS

The type of horse you will eventually buy will, to a large extent, be decided by how much money you can afford to spend, not only on the initial purchase, but also on his day-to-day upkeep. At this point you need to be really honest with yourself. Remember, the one

ABOVE: Always get a vet to check the horse and make sure it's not the vendor's choice of vet!

thing you can guarantee where horses are concerned is that you will end up forking out more money than originally intended and probably more than you can afford. Of course it is all for a good cause, but it really does pay to plan ahead. Can you afford to keep your 16.2hh ex-racehorse in the manner to which both you and he would like him to become accustomed? This will most likely involve good stabling, sheltered grazing, frighteningly expensive amounts of hard feed and no end of other expenses. While it is possible to keep a Thoroughbred out all year round, it is not always practical should you want to ride, and you would still need to supply him with fairly large amounts of extra feed. If you have been honest and know that you have neither the time nor the funds to care properly for such a horse, then you are better off looking elsewhere. Find a horse that can live outside all year, then when you want to keep him in and get him fit you can, but at least *you* have the choice.

It goes without saying that you can expect to pay more for a highly schooled type of horse — you are buying his experience and, to a certain extent, a guarantee that he is good at what he does. Always remember that any horse, no matter how able, is only as good as his rider's ability. A young or very green horse will cost less than its well-schooled and experienced counterpart. You may well like the idea of starting with a clean slate, but young horses are a handful and demand a lot of hard work. The attraction of the price may be a strong one but could turn out to a false economy; young animals are easily spoiled and unless you are confident in your ability to train a young horse correctly you would do well to steer clear of this area.

Be sure to plan well into the future before you buy — perhaps work out the cost of one year with your new horse. Included in this plan should be things like insurance, shoeing, boarding costs if you cannot keep him at your home, worming, vaccination and any other veterinary costs. Also his feed costs, bedding, tack plus any blankets he might need and all those little extras that you do not already have if you have never owned your own horse before — buckets, haynet, grooming kit . . . the list goes on.

While it may seem tempting to cut corners in order to cut costs, it is advisable to stick to the basic rules of stable management. You could get away without vaccinating your horse or perhaps forget the worming routine, but in the end is it really worth risking your beloved horse's health to save money? If you are planning to keep your horse at a commercial stable, you will most probably find that they require that your horse be regularly wormed and vaccinated anyway.

PREPARING TO BUY

For the sake of your health and the health of those around you, I strongly advise that you do your homework first. Everyone goes about things in their own way but it's a good idea to be prepared. I have a friend who set out to find her daughter the perfect 14hh pony, armed with a notebook filled with ads. Once they had seen a pony she would write down the details beneath each ad, allowing them to compare prices and details; after viewing what seemed like hundreds of ponies, they had a comprehensive record of their likes and dislikes and any mistakes made. Not everyone finds it necessary to go this far, but if it helps you find your perfect horse, then so be it.

Be sure that you have in your head a firm idea of exactly what you want. More often than not the horse you go to see will bear little relation to the ad in the magazine, and sometimes you can find yourself glossing over his faults just because he is pretty or you are

starting to think that you will never find a horse to suit you. There are some points you can afford to be a little flexible on; it would be a shame to miss out on the right one because you wanted a bay rather than a gray. In the end it all comes down to what you are happy with — there is no point in buying a gelding if you had planned on producing a foal in the future.

Should you be in the position to keep your horse at a boarding stable, arrange a stall for him in advance; buying a horse on the spur of the moment and then having to rush about like a lunatic trying to find somewhere to keep him can be more than a little stressful. The number of stables in your vicinity depends on the part of the country you live in: very "horsey" areas have many and depending on how much you wish to pay each month, to some extent you can shop around. Be aware, though, that the chances of finding a place for him in the winter months are fairly slim.

Whether or not you decide to insure your horse is entirely up to you; there is no legal requirement for this but it does bring peace of mind, especially in a crisis. If you are going to insure, arrange to be covered as soon as possible, even for the journey home. You have no way of knowing how your new arrival is going to travel or how he might behave in the excitement of moving to a new home.

WHERE TO BUY

Classified advertisements in the horsey magazines immediately spring to mind. There are alternatives but it is as good a place to start as any, if only to give yourself an idea of price. The details given in private ads can sometimes be a little short on details, so if you are planning to travel far, it can be very helpful to get the seller to send you some recent photographs of the horse before you go. Occasionally they may be able to send a video of the horse, which can be a real help. Should you decide that the horse is not for you, then let the seller know in good time and do be sure to send back the photographs.

Papers and magazines are not the only place to find ads; it is well worth trying the local feed merchants and saddlers. Most of them have bulletin boards filled with all sorts of information. The advantage of buying privately is that generally the seller knows something of the horse's background and may even have bred him themselves. Usually this means plenty of information and perhaps a chance to view the sire and dam. If at any time you feel that you are not being given straight answers to your questions, be a little wary. The seller is obliged to let you know of the horse's nasty habits in the ad, so it is worth asking for a written receipt before you take your new purchase home with you. At least that way you have some form of recourse should anything untoward occur.

One alternative to the classifieds is the dealer. Contrary to popular belief, not all dealers are crooked; if you make your living from buying and selling horses, it pays to keep your clients happy and not cheat them. Obviously the only way to do this is to make sure that you find them good horses.

The best way to find out about a dealer's reputation is to ask people who have bought a horse from him, or anyone else with a tale to tell. Are they pleased with their purchase, or do they feel ripped off? From all that you hear you can then form your own opinion. Once it gets around that you are horse-hunting you may well find that one or two people mention the same dealer and suggest that you give him a call. Usually a dealer will have a selection of horses and can tell you if any of them might suit your needs. If not, he can probably set about finding you one. The advantages of buying as horse this way are that you are likely to be able to see more than one horse at a time and there are usually better facilities available for trying the horse. Should you decide to buy this way you are least covered by the commercial code (Sale of Goods Act in the UK), so if the horse turns out to be totally unsuitable you should be able you exchange him.

As you scour the pages of your equine magazine, very often you will come across ads for agencies offering their services. Basically agencies keep lists of horses for sale: if you are selling then they will charge you for adding your horse to their books, but for buyers there is no fee. Once you contact them wanting to buy, the agency can supply you with the details of any animals that you might be interested in.

Alternatively you could arm yourself with an envelope full of cash and take yourself off to a horse sale. Buying a horse at auction is a hair-raising business at the best of times and is only recommended for the extremely brave. The quality of sales varies enormously as does the size. There are hundreds going on all year round and while some are of the very highest standard, attracting only the best animals to be sold, there are others you would do well to avoid if you really want to find a decent animal.

Large sales, selling quality stock, will usually send out catalogs a couple of weeks in advance on receipt of a stamped self-addressed envelope. On arrival at the sales ground you usually only have a very limited time in which to look at and possibly ride any horses that you liked in the catalogue. It is this pressure that makes this way of buying a horse so difficult. You have to make a fairly major decision in a very short space of time and, more often than not, the facilities provided for trying out horses under saddle are sorely inadequate.

However you go about buying your horse, the same basic rules apply when you are looking him over:

- See him in the stable or at least tied up in the yard — this way you can get an idea of how he behaves.
- Does he stand patiently or fidget all the time while being groomed?
- Watch him being handled, always an excellent way of assessing his temperament.
- Find a nice level piece of ground and ask the seller to lead him away and then back towards you in a straight line, both at walk and trot so that you can see how he moves without a rider.
- Stand him up square: study his shape. A well-made horse will please the eye and if he has correct conformation then, in theory, he should also move well.
- Once you have had a good look from afar, check his feet and feel down his legs for any lumps and bumps. Whether or not you are prepared to put up with a blemish or two depends entirely on what uses you have in mind for your horse.
- If you have any doubts about the horse's health and are still interested in him, then contact a vet. The vet will come to examine your potential purchase at a time that suits the seller and then will let you know the results. It is well worth the extra cost to have your horse examined. However good you are at spotting faults, problems such as with the heart, for example, do not always have symptoms visible externally.

If you do buy at auction or sale, then you can usually find a staff vet who will examine your horse for a fee once you have bought him. In the event of anything being wrong, or your purchase beginning to show signs of unpleasant behavior which you were not warned about in the catalog, then you are entitled to return the horse and claim your money back.

Once you have decided that you wish to buy the horse, lumps and all, it is up to you and the seller to settle on a price. Try not to take too long haggling because you may find that someone else comes along with cash in hand and buys your carefully chosen horse out from under you — leaving you back at square one!

So, your horse has passed the exams and you have settled on a price: all that remains is for you to arrange transport to get him home. When he arrives and you have turned him out into the paddock to settle down then you can finally relax and enjoy the feeling of owning your own horse. Do not relax too much though, the fun has only just started!

CHAPTER 23

THE WORKING HORSE AND
WORKING WITH HORSES

Karen Hampshire

Through the past century the role of the horse in society has undergone a dramatic change; the arrival of the motor car has brought about the gradual decline of use of the horse as an everyday means of transport and in many parts of the globe has significantly reduced its role in the cultivation of land and the control of farming stock. It would have been logical to conclude that this would herald a serious demise in the popularity and prevalence of the horse, especially as it is expensive to maintain such large creatures properly. In reality, man's love and respect for this majestic and loyal animal has ensured not only its survival, but also its strengthened place in today's society as part of our leisure and sporting industries.

The type and number of jobs available with horses varies widely around the world. In parts of both North and South America ranching still demands that workers spend all day in the saddle riding the range and moving stock over large tracts of land. By contrast, in Hong Kong almost the only opportunities lie within the highly popular racing industry. In many countries the greatest scope for employment is within the leisure industry, as more and more people take up riding, owning or breeding horses and competing in the various disciplines creating requirements for first class grooms and instructors. There will usually be a recognised governing body or society to ensure that high standards of training and qualification are available in each sphere.

As an example of the size of the equine leisure industry, take Britain: with an estimated quarter of a million people employed in the equine industry there are not just jobs but many varied and highly rewarding careers available if you want to work with horses. These range from work in stables and riding schools through to stud farms, the racing industry, manufacturing — saddlery, clothing and and all the accoutrements of riding including farriery — not to mention veterinary science.

In most cases a remunerative career with horses

ABOVE: A thing of the past — the mechanization of farming and, more significantly, personal transport means that sights like this are few and far between. Haymaking with Lipizzaners.

RIGHT: Sport can provide the very best performers (here Nick Skelton negotiates the bank at Hickstead in the south of England) with a good living — but for the majority it is always going to be in the ancillary areas of care and management that most jobs will be found in the equine industry.

requires dedication, ambition and well prepared plans. As with any industry, most of these requirements are the same. Common sense dictates a good education, not only because it is needed for entry into many areas of the industry but also to provide a good fall-back position should an accident occur in what can be a dangerous profession. It is also imperative that you find out what specific qualifications are required within your chosen field — and then achieve them. Qualifications make job acquisition easier and lead to better scales of pay and working conditions but in many cases — like veterinary science — these qualifications can take years to achieve and may not be directed purely toward horses.

LEFT: There are still many areas of the world in which ranching and wrangling are ways of life. Here Brumbies are collected in the Australian bush.

BELOW LEFT: Heyday, an Olympic Games mount: only very few riders reach this level of competition.

THIS PAGE: Many police and military forces have mounted sections. These photographs show: men of the British Royal Horse Artillery, whose performances on horseback today are restricted to ceremony and sport (BELOW); and mounted policemen, used in urban areas the world over for both ordinary policing and crowd control.

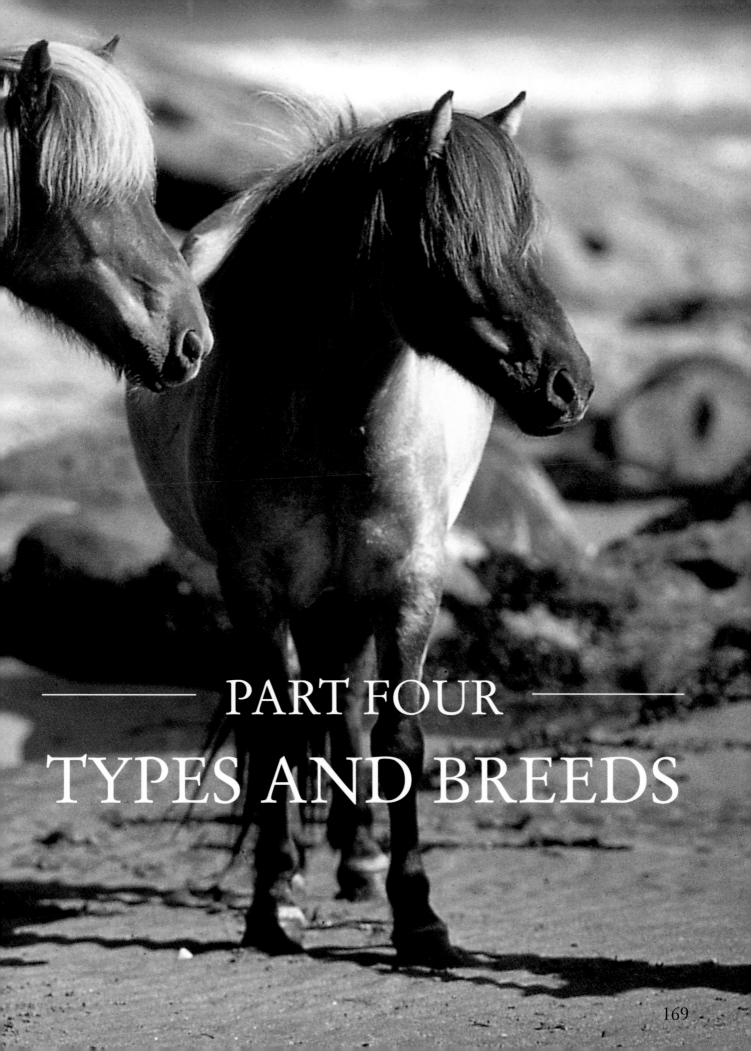

PART FOUR
TYPES AND BREEDS

CHAPTER **24**

PRINCIPAL HORSE BREEDS OF THE WORLD

Lynda Springate

ABOVE: Egyptian and Shagya Arabian foals.

BELOW: A Criollo polo pony.

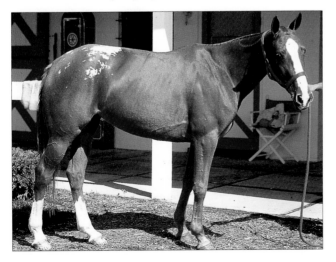

AFRICA

ARABIAN

Arabians, together with the Mongolian horse, are direct blood descendants from the horses of ancient times. The purity of the Arabian blood line has influenced other horse breeds worldwide — even Queen Victoria lent her Arabian stallion to run wild in the New Forest in the south of England in the hope that the local stock of ponies would be improved. Horses that appear Arabian in type can be seen in illustrations that go back 3,000 years to the time of Noah's great-great-grandson.

Arabians are known as hot-blooded horses, with eager and fiery natures, yet good-natured at the same time. They are light-boned and quick, with beautiful concave or dished faces, with enormous eyes and wide forehead. Although no bigger than 15hh (5ft) and more often 14hh (4ft 8in), the Arabian can carry large weights for long distances.

ARGENTINA

CRIOLLO

The native pony of South America, the Criollo is related to the Spanish Arabian and Barb horses taken there by the conquistadores. The horses later ran wild after Buenos Aires was invaded by the Indians. Only the toughest and most adaptable horses were able to withstand the extremes of climate and the Criollo is outstanding in terms of toughness, a quality which made them favorites of the South American Gauchos. The Criollo also helped to start the Argentinean polo pony. Two famous Criollos were Mancha and Gato, the horses that accompanied A. F. Tschiffely from Buenos Aires to New York — a journey of 13,350 miles — an expedition that was immortalized in the book *Tschiffely's Ride*.

The Criollo's usual color is dun; height stands between 15hh and 16hh (5ft–5ft 4in).

AUSTRALIA

AUSTRALIAN STOCK HORSE
Australian Walers were famous as brave cavalry mounts. From this base stock, more outcrosses were made during the 20th century — the Australian Stock Horse Society includes Appaloosas, Thoroughbreds and Arabians in their stud book in addition to Walers — to produce the Australian Stock Horse. Used on farms and sheep stations, it also makes a good eventer and polo pony. Height varies between 14hh and 16hh (4ft 8in–5ft 4in). All colors are allowed.

BRUMBY
The Brumby is the wild horse of Australia, usually of mixed blood. They tend to adapt to their surroundings, and can be found in two distinct environments. Toughest of the lot is the desert type, found in outback Australia. They have to contend with drought, flood and extremes of temperature; meanwhile the mountain Brumby has access to plenty of water and grasslands.

WALER
A crossbred, the Waler is a mixture of the breeds which existed in colonial Australia. The name is derived from New South Waler, a horse bred in New South Wales, Australia's first colony. The foundation stock was based on animals sent from the Cape of Good Hope, and later English horses such as Thoroughbreds, Clydesdales and Timor ponies (interestingly, some of latter, the last in existence, are said to live in the Kimberley area). The Waler was used as a remount for the British army in India. Rajahs also bought them for military uses and as polo ponies. Their endurance as remounts for the Australian army became legendary during the Boer War and during World War I.

AUSTRIA

LIPIZZANER
The name immediately brings to mind images of the elegant Spanish Riding School of Vienna, so called because the founding stallions were from Spain. The Spanish were acknowledged as fine breeders of horses, and during the 16th and 17th centuries it became fashionable for royal courts to import them. The Lipizzaner breed was founded in 1580 by the Archduke Charles II, son of Ferdinand I, who chose Lipizza or Lipica as the base for the new stud farm. Nine stallions and 24 mares were imported from Spain and bred with selected local horses. The stud flourished and more imports were made from Italy, Denmark and Germany. After the end of the Austro-Hungarian Empire, the Austrian school stud was moved to Piber in southern Austria. Lipizza came

ABOVE: *Australian Stock Horse.*

BELOW: *Brumbies.*

BOTTOM: *Lipizzaner.*

ABOVE: Pinzgauer-Noriker.

BELOW: Ardennes heavy horse and foal.

back into its own again when it became part of Yugoslavia at the end of World War II. Piber itself was taken over by the German Army and the Lipizzaner mares were sent to Bohemia, where they were rescued by the US Army and were returned at the end of the war. They are still bred there.

To this day Lipizzaner stallions are named for six sires introduced in the late 18th century: Pluto, Conversano, Neopolitano, Favory, Maestoso and Siglavy. The Austrian Lipizzaners go through a three-year training period gradually leading up to the exercises known as the "Schools on the Ground" and the "Schools above the Ground" — the movements of Haute École. Hungarian and Yugoslavian Lipizzaners are also trained as dressage and harness horses. The Lipizzaner is intelligent, usually gray in color and has a reputation for longevity; their height is 15hh–16hh (5ft–5ft 4in).

NORIKER

The name is a corruption of Noricum, what the Romans called the region of today's Austria. The Noriker became the best known of the Alpine work-horses, evolving into a general purpose workhorse, and it is still used as an army horse and as a light draft horse. There is another version — the Pinzgauer-Noriker, a spotted horse. One of the requirements of the Noriker stud book is that the girth should be not less than 60 per cent of the height at the withers; this makes for an exceptionally deep body. The usual colors are chestnut, brown or black.

BELGIUM

ARDENNES

An ancient breed that may have been used by the Romans, the Ardennes comes from France and Belgium. Later they were used as cavalry horses and as artillery wheelers during World War 1. The breed has seen several changes in its history, including attempts to make it larger by crossing with the Brabant.

The Ardennes is noted for its hardiness and for being economical to feed. It has a small straight head, with a short stocky body and short legs. It is popular in other countries, especially Sweden, where a smaller version exists. Roan is the usual color. Height stands at 15hh–16hh (5ft–5ft 4in).

BELGIAN HALF-BLOOD

Also known as the Belgian Warmblood, the Half-blood was developed for use in competition work to be distinct from Belgian heavy breeds. To achieve this the lightest of the heavy breeds was crossed with imported stock from France — the Selle Français, Arab and Thoroughbred proved most influential. Later in the 1960s the Half-blood Society was given permission to call itself "Royal." Belgian Half-bloods of recent years have performed well in events such as show jumping.

The head is alert and refined, with a long neck and sloping shoulders. Much emphasis is placed on the straightness of limbs and soundness of feet. The breed is noted for having a willing temperament.

BRABANT

Related to the ancient heavy horses of Flanders, the Brabant or Belgian Draft Horse is an important breed that has hardly ever been influenced by outside bloodlines. Many examples have been exported worldwide, particularly to the United States. There are three versions of the breed: Big Horse of the Dendre, Gray Horse of Nivelles and Colossal Horse of Mehaique.

The breed survives in large numbers today and is noted for the strength of its massive shoulders and quarters. It has a very calm temperament; its usual coloring is chestnut or roan. Height is 16hh–17hh (5ft 4in–5ft 8in).

DENMARK

DANISH WARMBLOOD

The Danish Warmblood is one of the most recent of the world's horse breeds, a stud book opening only in the 1960s. Ironically it was developed from one of Denmark's most ancient breeds, the Frederiksborg. Horse breeding is very much an ancient Danish tradition but, in spite of this, the Danes found themselves relying on imported riding horses after World War II. Using the Frederiksborg as foundation stock, a careful breeding program was started. The first crosses were with Thoroughbreds, then Trakehners and Anglo-Normans. The result is an enviable competition horse, an example of which won the silver medal for dressage in the 1984 Olympic Games.

The Danish Warmblood is similar in looks to the Thoroughbred. In conformation, everything looks near perfect: the head is intelligent, the body has great strength with excellent limbs. The Danish Warmblood is bred by private breeders, who have between them produced horses capable of winning many of the major dressage and three-day events. Many are now exported abroad.

The Danish Warmblood is an intelligent horse with a kindly nature. All solid colors are permissible, but bay is most common. Height stands between 15.3hh and 17hh (5ft 1in–5ft 8in).

FREDERIKSBORG

King Frederik of Denmark was an enthusiastic horse breeder and in 1562 he founded the stud farm that was to bear his name. Andalusian horses were one of the first of the foundation breeds. At that time every

ABOVE: Brabant heavy horse stallion.

BELOW: Danish Warmblood.

ABOVE: Frederiksborg.

BELOW: Jutland heavy draft horse.

European Royal Court had its own equine high school that could perform dressage and exhibit skill at arms before guests. The Frederiksborg excelled at such events and was also unbeatable as a saddle, harness and cavalry horse.

A Frederiksborg stallion was used to improve the most famous of the high school breeds, the Lipizzaner. Later in the 19th century Frederiksborgs were crossed with Eastern and British half-bred stallions. Indeed, the quality and popularity of the Frederiksborg has very nearly brought about its extinction. Many horses were exported and breeding stocks were heavily depleted resulting in poorer examples, although this could also be blamed on an attempt to breed lighter animals more like the Thoroughbred in looks. The royal stud was forced to close after 300 years and it was left to private breeders to carry on. Danish breeders are now trying very hard to preserve the original Frederiksborg.

The head of the Frederiksborg could hardly be called handsome: it is large with big ears, but it does have an intelligent look. The body is long with powerful shoulders that aid the horse's high action. Chestnut is the most usual color. Height stands at 15.3hh–16hh (5ft 1in–5ft 4in).

JUTLAND

Denmark's breed of heavy horse is named after its home region of Jutland, where it has been bred for centuries. From Jutland it travelled to the other Danish islands and found great favor as a warhorse in medieval times. The modern Jutland began to emerge during the 19th century, when it was crossed with British breeds such as the Cleveland Bay and Suffolk Punch. The best stallion lines are related to Aldup Munkedal, Fjandbo and Lune Dux.

The Suffolk Punch influence can be seen in the shape of the Jutland. An important difference is the mass of feathering that the Jutland has on its legs, whereas the Suffolk Punch has none. The usual color is chestnut, but roan is also seen. Height stands between 15hh and 16hh (5ft–5ft 4in).

KNABSTRUP

The Knabstrup is a horse which is bred specifically for its unusual spotted coat. History tells us that the Knabstrup developed from one particular mare called Flaebehoppen, left in Denmark by a Spanish officer during the Napoleonic Wars. Used by a butcher named Flaebe on his delivery round, the mare was noticed by Major Villars Lunn, owner of the Knabstrup estate and a keen riding horse breeder whose stock was based on the Frederiksborg. Lunn admired the mare's chestnut coat which had "blanket" markings and a white mane and tail. He bought her and began a line of spotted horses. In 1812 she was mated with a Palomino Frederiksborg stallion, and produced a colt named Flaebehingsten. It was rumored that the colt's coat had "more than 20 colours." Much crossbreeding has taken place since then to produce different color patterns. This caused the breed's conformation to suffer at one time, but the modern Knabstrup is an animal of great quality, similar to the Appaloosa.

The Knabstrup is kind and gentle, very strong and a good riding horse. The breed is very popular in the circus. Height stands at 15.2hh–16hh (5ft 1in–5ft 4in).

EUROPE

PRZEWALSKI

Discovered by Russian explorer Col. N. M. Przewalski in 1881, it is unlikely that many of these ancient ponies survive in the wild today. They were found in the Tachin Schara Nuru Mountains at the edge of the Gobi Desert. It was once thought that this breed was the common stock from which all horses were descended. We now know this is not the case; that honor must go to the sole surviving breed of a type of horse known as the Plateau Horse, which was one of four ancient and primitive ranges of horse to survive the Ice Age. The cave paintings of early man, however, do show them hunting creatures very similar to the Przewalski.

Przewalski horses are strongly built and thickset with a short neck. A hardy and enduring animal, groups survived for many years in Mongolia. The Przewalski has no forelock and a short almost hogged mane. Sandy or dun is the usual color with a black stripe down the center of the back. The Mongolian and Chinese type of ponies are direct descendants of the Przewalski.

FINLAND

FINNISH

The Finnish horse is a breed which splits into two distinctive types. Although small (height stands between 14.1hh and 15.2hh — 4ft 8in–5ft 1in), one version is a powerful light draft horse, and the other more lightly built animal is used as a trotting or riding horse. Either version is basically similar in conformation. Special breeding programmes have been set up to refine the trotting horse for racing. The heavy horse is still the most effective way of hauling loads through the Finnish pine forests. A stud book was first opened for the Finnish horse in 1907; since then select breeding guidelines have been maintained.

Although the head of the Finnish horse can be said to be plain, in appearance the breed is well proportioned and muscular, with a long mane and tail. As a breed, the Finnish horse has a delightful temperament,

ABOVE: Knabstrup.

BELOW and BOTTOM: Przewalski.

ABOVE: Breton stallion.

BELOW: Camargues.
.
BOTTOM: Percheron.

TOP RIGHT: Selle Français stallion.

CENTER RIGHT: Young Bavarian Warmbloods.

BELOW RIGHT: Young Hanoverian horses.

steady yet intelligent. They are a long-lived breed well adapted to existing in the extremes of the Scandinavian climate.

FRANCE

BRETON

The Breton horse of northwest France was developed to meet a variety of demands. At one time there were several types of Breton, used for heavy draft work, light draft work and riding.

The modern Breton is divided into a heavy draft type and a lighter type. The Lighter Postier Breton is sometimes used as a coach horse. The heavier type was developed from crossbreeding with the Ardennes, Percheron and Boulonnais and is still used as a work-horse.

The head is square with a short thick neck. The body is short and strong with short limbs. The tail is usually docked. The Breton is also used for meat. The usual colors are roan or chestnut. Height is 15hh–16hh (5ft–5ft 4in).

CAMARGUE

Home for the Camargue horse is the swampy area between Aigues-Mortes and the Mediterranean. Known as the "White Horses of the Sea," the coat of the Camargue is always white, although the foals are often born dark gray, brown or even black.

The breed is hardy as most of its diet is of salty water and tough spiky grass. The horses are highly maneuverable at the gallop making them ideal for the job of working the famous Camargue black bulls in the bullring.

The conformation of the Camargue is far from perfect because they tend to have an oversize head on a short neck. However they have good bones and action and a short, strong back.

FRENCH TROTTER

Harness racing as a sport gained popularity in France during the 19th century. In response to the demand for good trotting horses, breeders took Norman mares as their base stock and crossed them with suitable British breeds. Major influences were an example of the now extinct Norfolk Trotter — The Norfolk Phenomenon — and Heir of Linne, a Thoroughbred. The resulting breeds were the Anglo-Norman and French Trotter. American harness horse blood was added later.

France also holds mounted trotting races. As a result of all this breeding the French Trotter is very strong, with more stamina than other breeds used purely for harness racing. The horse has powerful hindquarters with correspondingly hard and robust limbs.

PERCHERON

The Percheron is one of the most popular of heavy horses, and can be found worldwide. It is an elegant horse, showing Arabian influence. It takes its name from the Perche area of Normandy. The breed was founded on the big Flemish horses and Arabians. The world's biggest horse was a Percheron — Dr Le Gear, standing at 21hh (7ft).

For such a heavy horse the breed has a very free action. The head is intelligent and slightly Arabian-like; it is very deep chested with a compact body and there is very little feathering on the legs. Usual colors are gray or black; height stands at 16hh (5ft 4in) and upwards.

SELLE FRANÇAIS

One of the more recent of the French breeds, the Selle Français was developed after World War II. French breeders of the 18th and 19th centuries decided to refine the Norman horse with the introduction of Thoroughbred and Arabian blood. Breeding was further influenced by the Norfolk Trotter. The Anglo-Norman was a product of this selective breeding, as was the French Trotter. Bred in the area around Caen at Haras du Pin, the Anglo-Norman itself became a major influence on French regional breeds. As these breeds became more alike, it was decided to amalgamate them under one common name — Selle Français. The more heavyweight of them make good general riding horses. Others are used to great effect as competition horses and cross-country eventers.

Standing at 16hh (5ft 4in), the Selle Français is a strong, well-muscled horse, with strong limbs and good bone. It is noted for having free and active paces. All solid colors are allowed, but chestnut is the most common.

GERMANY

BAVARIAN WARMBLOOD

Formerly known as the Rottaler, the Bavarian Warmblood was originally a warhorse. As with many of the older heavier breeds, a lighter blood was added during the 18th century. British horse breeds were a notable influence, the principal ones being the Thoroughbred and Cleveland Bay. The breed today is best known as a riding horse, but is also making a successful competition horse, helped by a calm temperament. Height stands at 16hh (5ft 4in) and its usual color is chestnut.

HANOVERIAN

Most famous of the German breeds is the Hanoverian. It has its origins in the German great horses of the Middle Ages. These heavyweight animals dated from the pre-Christian era and can also be traced back from a tribe called the Tencteri, who lived along the left

ABOVE: Holstein.

BELOW: Oldenburgs.

bank of the Rhine. The Hanoverian continued as a warhorse until the use of armor died out. The breed was altered in 1735 when King George II of England founded the Celle stud. This was done to create a lighter farm and harness horse. Holstein stallions were crossed with the local mares, then English Thoroughbred blood was added.

The "new" Hanoverian became popular as a coach horse. Strict rules were made to ensure that only stallions passed by a selection board could be used for breeding. Private breeders founded their own society in 1867 with the intention of producing animals that could also be used as army horses. The requirements were changed again between the two world wars. Then the emphasis was on an animal that could be used as a utility horse on the farm and as a quality riding horse.

The postwar years have seen the Hanoverian develop into an elegant competition horse. Strong and powerful, with a showy action, yet with a good temperament. Height stands between 16hh and 17hh (5ft 4in–5ft 8in). All solid colous are allowed.

HOLSTEIN

Another excellent German breed of horse, the Holstein is also the oldest, possibly dating back to the 13th century. It is believed to have Andalusian blood and some Oriental. The Holstein was bred on good pasture ground along the banks of the Elbe River. During the 16th and 17th century, the breed became popular as a powerful riding and coach horse. Many animals were exported abroad, particularly to France. The Holstein proved to be too heavy for military purposes and it was decided to refine the breed by the use of Thoroughbred blood, notably through the introduction of three Yorkshire Coach Horses in the 19th century. The resulting animal was one that was elegant enough for riding and driving, yet was strong enough for light farm work.

A central stud, which stayed open until 1961, was formed in Traventhal. Holsteins were once again exported, many of them to South America. Numbers declined again after World War II — farms were rapidly becoming more mechanised and the Holstein was still considered too heavy as a competition animal. Once more English Thoroughbreds were imported from Britain. Consequently, the present day Holstein is a much lighter and elegant animal. The neck is long and arched with high withers and a strong back. Height stands at 16hh–17hh (5ft 4in–5ft 8in). All solid colors are permissible.

OLDENBURG

Named for Count Anton von Oldenburg, this breed originated in northwest Germany. It used to be the heaviest of the German horses, related to the Friesian.

But, as with many other heavyweight breeds, much effort has been made to lighten it. Von Oldenburg was responsible for putting Spanish and Italian stock to the local mares in the 17th century. This resulted in a powerful coach horse noted for maturing early. Later in the 19th century, a breeders' society was established for the Oldenburg. A lighter horse was developed through the addition of Yorkshire Coach Horses, Thoroughbreds, Cleveland Bays and Normans. These made superb coach horses, which were also capable of use as farm horses. Recent breeding programs using Thoroughbreds and Hanoverians have further refined the Oldenburg. At 16.2hh–17.2hh (5ft 5in–5ft 9in) the modern day Oldenburg is still Germany's tallest horse, and also one of the most powerful. Examples of the Oldenburg are now being used for competition work.

Oldenburgs are known for having an even temperament with a kind head, strong neck and shoulders. Limbs are short in relation to its deep and well-muscled body, with good bone. All solid colors are allowed.

RHENISH-GERMAN/RHINELANDER

Almost 100 years ago the Rhenish stud book was founded; the best known sires were Albion d'Hor, Indien de Bievene and Lothar III. The breed quickly became a useful heavy draft horse, used by the farmers of Westphalia, Rhineland and Saxony.

Because of farm mechanisation there are very few examples of the Rhenish left today, and efforts are being made to produce a riding horse — the Rhinelander — using the heavy draft as foundation stock.

The Rhenish is not unlike the Belgian Heavy Draught, with a plain head, short neck and deep muscular body. Height stands at 16–17hh (5ft 4in–5ft 8in); the usual colors are chestnut and red roan.

TRAKEHNER

The Trakehner has a fascinating history. Originally from East Prussia, the breed developed from the Schwieken, a tough little horse native to East Prussia. In 1732 Frederick William I of Prussia founded the Trakehnen Stud. He supplied an area of marshland in the northwestern area of East Prussia which was drained to became perfect pasture land. Frederick also donated horses from the royal studs and imported Arabians from Poland. Thoroughbred blood was added later, one of the most influential stallions being Perfectionist, son of the famous race horse Persimmon. Such careful breeding produced an excellent riding horse, the pride of the German army.

Only the best stallions were kept at the Trakehnen Stud. The three-year-olds were sent to the resident training stable and kept there for one year. As four-

ABOVE: Rhinelander.

BELOW: A coach drawn by two Trakehner horses.

179

ABOVE: Württemburg.

BELOW: Anglo-Arab stallion.

BOTTOM: Cleveland Bay.

year-olds they underwent trials which included hunting with a pack of hounds and cross-country courses. Second best animals went to state stud farms, third class went to private breeders. The rest were used as remounts by the German army. This practice continued up to the end of World War I. In a drastic attempt to keep the best animals from the advancing Russian Army a number were trekked across country to the west. The rest were left behind in what eventually became Poland, their famous stud destroyed. The Trakehner is good tempered with excellent conformation, very similar to the Thoroughbred in outline. Height stands at about 16hh, although taller examples are not uncommon. All solid colors are permissible.

WÜRTTEMBURG

The Württemburg is bred at Germany's state-owned stud at Marbach. This warmblood breed was founded when Arabian blood was mixed with German mares; later Anglo-Norman blood was added. The Anglo-Norman blood proved to be very important, and an Anglo-Norman is credited with being the founder of the modern day Württemburg breed. Trakehners proved to be an important later influence. The breed was originally intended as a light general purpose horse but is now used extensively for competition work. The Württemburg has good limbs and a sensible, intelligent head. The usual color is chestnut, but brown and bay are also common. Height stands at 16hh (5ft 4in) and upward.

GREAT BRITAIN

ANGLO-ARAB

The Anglo-Arab is a well-established breed, which originated in the UK although it is now particularly well known in France. Indeed, the French Anglo-Arab has been bred at stud farms for the last 150 years. The Anglo-Arab is an amalgamation of the best of Arabian and Thoroughbred, more solid looking than the Arabian and more Thoroughbred in appearance. Arabian blood has given more stamina and a spirited but kindly nature.

As the Anglo-Arab became a more popular riding horse in France, races especially for them were started. In later years as the Anglo-Arab became more successful as a competition winner a number were used to found the Selle Français. While not as fast as the Thoroughbred, the Anglo-Arab has excelled as a dressage, race and competition horse. Height standards have recently been changed from 15.3hh (5ft 1in) to 16.1hh (5ft 4in).

CLEVELAND BAY

This is the most ancient of the English horse breeds. The Cleveland Bay is often used today as an ideal mating partner for the Thoroughbred. Originally from Cleveland in Yorkshire the horse has been exported abroad in recent years to improve native stock. Clevelands were useful for two purposes: as agricultural workers and carriage horses. Furthermore, a Cleveland Bay/Thoroughbred cross makes an ideal hunter. In England the Cleveland has often been used as a ceremonial carriage horse in displays and royal processions. As a farm horse, it had the advantage of being clean-legged (no feathering on the legs), unlike the larger heavy horses, and so could work more quickly.

Color should be bay or bay brown; the body wide with a deep girth and strong shoulders. The head should be large and convex in shape. Height is usually 16hh–16.2hh (5ft 4in–5ft 5in). The Cleveland Bay is particularly noted for its stamina, presence, action and intelligence.

CLYDESDALE

One of Britain's heavy horses, the Clydesdale breed was founded in Lanarkshire. (Clydesdale is the old name for Lanarkshire.) The 18th century saw considerable commercial demand for use of the horse in the Scottish coalfields. To improve the breed and give it more weight, Flemish stallions were imported and crossed with the local mares. The Clydesdale Horse Society was formed in 1877 and published its first stud book shortly afterwards. A great number have been exported abroad.

The usual colours are bay and brown, although black is also seen. White markings are allowed, and are most often seen on the legs and face. The most important aspects of the Clydesdale are its feet and limbs. The forehead is wide and open and the face flat. Clydesdales are very active movers for their size, and have a kind and gentle temperament. Heights range up to 16.2hh (5ft 5in).

COB

The Cob is actually a type rather than a breed of horse: a popular riding horse, well known for having a placid temperament and good manners. Although not particularly fast, it gives a comfortable, safe ride and is a useful hunter, particularly for novice riders or the less mobile. In appearance the Cob is short-legged, with a deep body and small intelligent head on an arched neck. In the past it was fashionable to show the Cob with a hogged mane and docked tail. Tail docking is now illegal, but many people still prefer to show the horse with a hogged mane. Height should not go higher than 15.2hh (5ft 1in).

HACK

Not to be confused with the Hackney Carriage Horse, the Hack, like the Cob, is a type, rather than a breed.

ABOVE: Cob and Pinto pony.

BELOW: Hack.

181

TOP: *Hackney.*

ABOVE: *Hunter.*

BELOW: *Shire horse and foal.*

A refined riding horse, many successful Hacks are Thoroughbreds. Because of this many of the conformation points needed to make a good Thoroughbred also apply to the show Hack. The Hack must have perfect manners and stand absolutely still while the rider mounts and dismounts. The rider must appear to be in complete control at all times. The breed society for the Hack is the British Show Hack and Cob Society. Height should be up to 15.3hh (5ft 1in). Any color is allowed.

HACKNEY

Hackneys are mostly to be seen driven in the show ring. They are descended from the Norfolk Trotter and, in particular, the Norfolk Roadster, an 18th century trotting horse, the most famous example of which was the "Norfolk Cob," alleged to have done two miles in 5min 4sec. Hackneys have a mixture of Thoroughbred and Arabian blood: nearly every Hackney can trace ancestry back to the Darley Arabian, through his son Flying Childers. With their high-stepping stride and high-set tail, the obvious impression of the Hackney is one of alertness. Usual colors are brown, chestnut, bay and black.

HUNTER

The first hunting horses were required to carry a man while he was hunting a number of different quarries. These days a Hunter is a horse which is usually ridden with a pack of hounds and over the years the best form of Hunter has evolved. Notably it has Thoroughbred blood, good conformation and action. The Hunter needs to be up to carrying weight all day and over a variety of obstacles, if need be, during the season. So stamina and conformation are important. When being shown, Hunters are judged according to the weight that they will be asked to carry: lightweight, middleweight and heavyweight. In the US, unlike Great Britain and Ireland, the horse will be asked to jump in the show ring, to prove its ability over fences.

SHIRE

One of Great Britain's best known and best loved heavy horses, the Shire was originally bred in the Huntingdon, Lincoln and Cambridge areas of England. It traces its beginnings to Elizabethan times and may well be descended from an older breed — the Great Horse of England — as any horse in those times would be required to carry a man in a suit of armor, which could boost the weight carried to about 450lb.

Although one of the slower breeds of heavy horses — it can weigh around 2,000lb — the Shire can actually pull loads of 10,000lb. Fortunately, the breed avoided extinction despite the invention of the tractor and it is still a popular sight at many agricultural shows and plowing matches with its harness decked out with horse brasses and terrets. Breweries still keep teams to haul their drays for publicity purposes and no working farm attraction would be complete without at least one pair of Shire horses on the farm. The most common colors are bay, brown, gray or black. With long well-feathered legs, height can be up to 18hh (6ft). The Shire has a gentle, placid temperament.

SUFFOLK

Known previously as the Suffolk Punch, the breed started in Suffolk and is said to trace its roots back to 1506. Modern examples can all trace their male bloodline back directly to one horse, which was foaled in 1760. It is also one of the few breeds of heavy horse to have "clean" legs — that is to say, no feathering; this has the advantage of making the horse more active over heavy ground and making it easier to groom.

The Suffolk is a handsome horse, does well on relatively poor feed and is long-lived: in working life they can live well over 20 years. Strong and compact in shape, this conformation combined with short legs gives the horse a great deal of "pull." Many years ago the problem of unsoundness of the feet was associated with the Suffolk. There is now no foundation to this rumor, and the breed is generally as sound as any other drauft horse. The horse is always chestnut in color, although there are obviously variations in the shade. In height the Suffolk stands at about 16hh (5ft 4in) and has a great width in front and in the quarters.

THOROUGHBRED

One of the best-known and most beautiful horses in the world: mention the word racehorse, and you will almost certainly think of the Thoroughbred. The very name epitomises its standing: it is taken from the Arabic word *Kehilan* meaning "pure bred." All Thoroughbreds, as is well known, trace their roots back to three Arabian sires, the Darley Arabian, the Godolphin Arabian and the Byerley Turk. Through these three fathers, the purest blood lines were developed and some of the most famous racehorses produced — like Eclipse, born during a solar eclipse, who won 18 races with great ease and went on to establish an important blood line. As time went on, less Arabian blood was introduced into the breed.

The English Thoroughbred is a superb racehorse, it also makes a good show jumper or event horse. The Thoroughbred has long been used to improve other breeds. Many Thoroughbred lines have been established in the United States and Europe, each country having slightly different requirements for the horse. Any solid color is allowed, although the usual colors are chestnut, brown or bay. In conformation the Thoroughbred has an intelligent head set on an elegant neck, very sloping shoulder, clean hard legs, deep body and short back.

ABOVE: Suffolk Punch.

BELOW: Thoroughbred.

TOP: *Dutch Warmblood.*

ABOVE: *Friesian.*

ABOVE RIGHT: *Groningen.*

BELOW RIGHT: *Nonius.*

HOLLAND

DUTCH WARMBLOOD

Most modern of the Dutch horse breeds, like its Danish counterpart the Dutch Warmblood breed was founded during the 1960s. It was produced in response to a demand for athletic horses with speed and endurance that could also be used for competition work — primarily three-day events — and show jumping. The base breeds were the Gelderland and Groningen and this combination was then refined with further breeding to Thoroughbred stock. The result is a keen performance horse, exported all over the world. Governing body for the breed is the Dutch Warmblood Society, which oversees the breeding of the various types of Warmblood, whether they be for riding, competition events or riding and driving. There are many famous Dutch Warmblood show jumpers, notably Marius and his equally famous son Milton, and one of the best-known current dressage horses is Jennie Loriston-Clarke's Dutch Courage. In 1980 a team of Dutch Warmbloods won the bronze at the World Carriage Driving Championships.

The competition Warmblood has a Thoroughbred type of head, a shorter body than the Gelderland and sound strong limbs. Any solid color is permissible; height stands at 15.3hh–16hh (5ft 1in–5ft 4in).

FRIESIAN

One of the oldest of the European breeds, the Friesian was used by the Roman legions and in the Middle Ages became a warhorse. Highly popular because of its willing and gentle nature, it was used extensively for farm work as farmers could leave unskilled labor to handle the horse without mishaps. The Romans took Friesian horses with them to Great Britain, where they had a great influence on the way that the Dales and Fell developed. Other breeds also influenced by the Friesian were the Dole Gudbrandsdal, Clydesdale and Shire. The Friesian is noted for its very high action fast trot, which makes it an ideal harness horse. Friesian blood was also used to help develop breeds of trotting horses. Too much crossbreeding, however, corrupted the pureness of the breed, and steps had to be taken to control breeding stock. To this end the Friesian Stud Book was founded in 1879. Before they can be entered in the Stud Book mares and stallions have to meet high standards of pedigree and conformation. Farm mechanization caused a decline in numbers, except during World War 2, when they were heavily in demand as farm horses again. Today the Friesian is used as a carriage horse, and does well in competition work. Its color and appearance also made it a popular choice for undertakers.

The long alert head has short ears carried on an arched neck. Shoulders, back and limbs are strong; the legs are feathered. Height stands between 15hh–15.3hh (5ft–5ft 1in). Friesian horses are always black, although a small white star is allowed. Another characteristic of the Friesian horse is an exceptionally long, thick mane and tail.

GELDERLANDER

Named for the Dutch province, the Gelderland is probably best known for being one of the foundation breeds of the Dutch Warmblood. It has its origins in a very old native breed that was crossed to other breeds such as the Norfolk Roadster, Holstein and Oldenburg. Later breeding crosses were made to Thoroughbreds and Arabians. This resulted in a distinctive horse with stylish action, a breed which has found a home in several royal stud farms, Great Britain's included. The Gelderland could be used for light farm work, yet was also an outstanding carriage horse, that could be also be used as a heavyweight riding horse. It is still a popular carriage horse. In common with other Dutch horse breeds, it has a docile and willing nature. The head is large and plain, but softened with a kindly expression. The body is wide and deep with strong shoulders. Usual color is chestnut, height stands at 15.2–16.2hh (5ft 1in–5ft 5in), although larger animals are sometimes found.

GRONINGEN

In essence a Dutch agricultural horse, the Groningen is the second breed in the partnership that provided the foundation stock for the successful Dutch Warmblood, and originally came from the Groningen region of Holland. The present Groningen is a light draft horse, but until fairly recently it was considerably heavier in action and shape. As a farm horse it could also be used as a carriage horse, but it lacked the pace of the Gelderlander. Later influences used to lighten the breed were the Oldenburg and Friesian.

The modern Groningen has kept the bone and height of its ancestors. The head is plain and sensible with a shortish neck and long body. Color is usually brown or bay. Height is 15.2hh–16.2hh (5ft 1in–5ft 5in).

HUNGARY

NONIUS

The Nonius owes its name to a stallion foaled in France and taken to Hungary with a group of other Normandy horses. Nonius's sire was Orion, an English half-bred, his dam a Norman mare. Nonius proved highly successful as a sire when put to the local mares, and also some with Arabian, Turkish and Lipizzaner blood. Used extensively by the military and by farmers, as with many Hungarian horses of the 19th century, the Nonius proved highly popular and many were exported abroad as cavalry remounts.

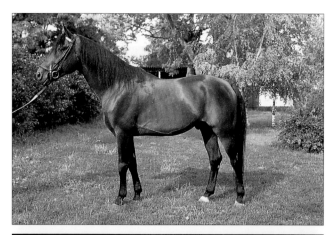

TOP: *Furioso.*

ABOVE: *Shagya Arabian.*

LEFT: *Irish Draft horse.*

ABOVE RIGHT:
Maremmano.

CENTER RIGHT:
Murgese.

BELOW RIGHT: *Barb*

The latter half of the century saw the Nonius being influenced by more Thoroughbred blood, causing the breed to develop into two types. One is heavier and taller, standing at 15.3hh–16.2hh (5ft 1in–5ft 5in). It was once used as a horse artillery wheeler, but is now used for driving. The other is a lighter riding horse of about 14.3hh–15.3hh (4ft 9in–5ft 1in). The Nonius is a well-built horse with a gentle temperament. The commonest colors are dark bay, brown or black.

FURIOSO

The Furioso is a relative of the Nonius. Two Thoroughbred English stallions, Furioso and North Star, were imported into Hungary. There they were bred with Nonius mares and founded their own bloodlines. North Star was the son of Touchstone, a St. Leger winner. He in turn sired some fine harness horses. The two bloodlines eventually merged, with the Furioso becoming the more dominant. The breed is used as a riding and competition horse, although it is also a popular harness horse. The Furioso has a strong compact body, standing at 15.1hh–16.2hh (5ft 1in–5ft 5in). All solid colors are permissible.

SHAGYA ARABIAN

As with all of the Hungarian breeds, the Shagya Arabian takes its name from the foundation sire. In 1836 an Arabian stallion of that name was imported from the Bedouins to the state-owned Stud of Babolna. The chief aim of the stud was to breed a special type of Arabian with which to supply riding horses to the famous Hungarian Light Cavalry. Some Shagya stallions were exported to Poland, once the breed had become established. They proved to be of enormous help in refining Polish breeds. The Shagya Arabian made an excellent riding and cavalry horse, but it was also used as a harness and light farm horse. The modern-day Shagya Arabian makes a good competition horse.

The original Shagya was tall for an Arabian at over 15hh (5ft). Selective breeding produced a breed of horse with the same shape and character of the Arabian, but one that was bigger and broader. The Shagya Arabian has more bone and more correct hindlegs. It is also hardier and thrives on poor food. Height usually stands at 14.2hh–15hh (4ft 8in–5ft). All solid colors are allowed, but the usual color is gray.

IRELAND

IRISH DRAFT

More of a lightweight than a heavy draft horse, the Irish Draft makes an exceptional hunter. They may be descended from the Connemara, although no research has actually proved this. The first stud book was opened in 1917. During this period many examples of this breed were sent to war, where they suffered heavy losses. Since the curbing of export to the Continent in the mid-1960s, this breed is beginning to flourish in greater numbers in its native Ireland. Some examples are crossed with the Thoroughbred to produce show jumpers. Height stands between 15hh and 17hh (5ft–5ft 8in). All solid colors are allowed.

ITALY

SALERNO
The Salerno used to be popular as a cavalry horse; it is now greatly reduced in numbers and is used for competition work and as a general riding horse. The breed originated in the Campania region of Italy. During the 18th century it was known as the Persano, after the stud farm founded by Charles III of Naples. The foundation horses were crossed with Andalusian and Neopolitan blood. The stud closed when the Italian monarchy was abolished, but breeding was re-established during the early 1900s, and this time the Persano was known as the Salerno. The Salerno is a good-looking horse, showing later Thoroughbred influences. Height stands at 15.3hh–16hh (5ft 1in–5ft 4in). All solid colors are permissible.

MAREMMANO
To be found in Tuscany, the Maremmano is well-liked for its general versatility and because it is economical to keep. It is used for a number of purposes in Italy: as a farm horse, riding horse, police and army mount. No one quite knows how it came to its present type.

There have been several examples of crossbreeding, including some English blood. Height stands at 15.3hh (5ft 1in). All solid colors allowed.

MURGESE
From the well-known horse breeding area of Murge, the modern Murgese is a light draft and riding horse. It developed from two earlier types, one of which has died out. A strong horse and a good worker, Murgese mares are sometimes used to breed mules. The usual color is chestnut, but black is often seen. Height stands between 14.3hh and 16hh (4ft 9in–5ft 4in).

MOROCCO

BARB
A horse native to Morocco and Algeria, the Barb is an ancient breed that may be descended from a group of wild horses that escaped the Ice Age. Few other breeds have had as great an influence on horse bloodlines than the Barb: the Thoroughbred in particular owes much of its development to the Barb. Examples were imported into Great Britain during the 17th and 18th centuries and were used to help create the

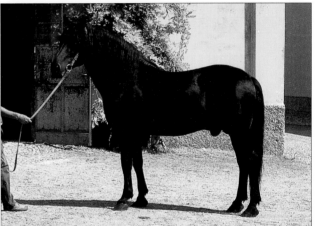

187

ABOVE: Herd of Alter Reals.

BELOW: Alter Reals.

BOTTOM: Young Lusitanos.

Thoroughbred racehorse. However, after a while its popularity in Britain began to decline, probably because it could not compete with the Arabian. In its homeland the Barb is held in high esteem by Berber tribesmen who called it the "Drinker of the Wind."

Although it highly likely that the Barb has at sometime been crossbred with the Arabian, there are still great differences between the two breeds. The Barb has a much more primitive head and more sloping hindquarters. All solid colors are allowed; height stands at 14hh–15hh (4ft 8in–5ft).

NORWAY

DOLE
Originally found in the Gudbrandsdal valley in the center of Norway, the Dole is similar in looks to the British Fell and Dales ponies, which may be due to Friesian blood being present in all three breeds. There are different types of Dole, although all are noted for their trotting ability. Some are heavily built and best used as draft horses – the Dole Gudbrandsdals. A lighter version, known as the Dole Trotter, is used for harness racing. The Trotter was heavily influenced by a Thoroughbred stallion imported to Norway in 1834. Another much earlier influence on the breed was a now extinct cold-blooded type of heavy horse. The Dole is also well known in Poland and Sweden.

The Dole is not overly tall, standing at between 14.2hh and 15.2hh (4ft 9in–5ft 1in). It is, however, extremely powerful, with a strong body and muscular hind quarters. The heavier version is noted for having more feather on the legs.

POLAND

WIELKOPOLSKI
The Wielkopolski is a combination of two Polish breeds, the Poznan and the Masuren. Both had a great deal of Trakehner blood, particularly after the Poles gained control of the Prussian Trakehnen stud and were able to amalgamate the remaining bloodstock. The Wielkopolski has many uses: heavier examples can be used for light farm work, lighter animals in harness, riding and competition events. There are now several Polish state studs, some of which specially breed the Wielkopolski for eventing.

These horses are noted for their good temperament and powerful conformation. Height stands at 16hh–16.2hh (5ft 4in–5ft 6in). All solid colors are permitted; chestnut is one of the most common.

PORTUGAL

ALTER-REAL
To keep up with the fashion for court Haute École

demonstrations in the 18th century, the Portuguese started their own royal stud. Andalusian stock was imported from Spain and the Alter breed was founded. The resulting horses were noble looking and intelligent, well suited to Haute École work but the stud was overrun by Napoleon's troops and shortly after was disbanded. The Alter breed was nearly destroyed with subsequent attempts at crossbreeding, but happily was saved when more Andalusian horses were imported. Modern attempts to reintroduce the breed were begun in the 1930s, when the Portuguese Ministry of Economy took over the breed's welfare.

The modern Alter-Real stands at 15hh–16hh (5ft–5ft 4in); the usual colors are gray, brown or bay.

LUSITANO

The Portuguese have their own version of the Spanish Andalusian — the Lusitano. Agile and athletic, well suited to the movements of Haute École, the Lusitano is the favorite of mounted bullfighters and is often used in demonstrations. It was also a favorite of the Portuguese cavalry. As a breed the Lusitano is becoming more popular, especially in the US.

The Lusitano is very similar to the Andalusian in general appearance, with the same convex-shaped head, and the same characteristic full mane and tail.

SPAIN

ANDALUSIAN

Many people believe that Spanish Iberian horses were crossed with the Barb to produce the Andalusian; others believe that the breed had been extinct for thousands of years before this took place. Whether or not it is true, the Andalusian was one of the premier breeds of Europe. No important European court was complete without its own high school of horse performing Haute École, and the Andalusian was perfect for this work. Their blood is to be found in nearly all of the great breeds of horses, including the world famous Lipizzaner. The Andalusian was particularly important in the US. Examples of the breed were shipped to the States with the colonists. Many American breeds, such as the Appaloosa, were based on Andalusian horses. The Carthusian monks of Jerez de la Frontera, Seville and Castille maintained lines of pure-bred Andalusians, when elsewhere crossbreeding was threatening the breed.

The Andalusian is an athletic horse with high stepping paces and much presence. Height stands at about 15.2hh (5ft 1in). The usual color is gray.

SWEDEN

NORTH SWEDISH

North Swedish horses share much of their develop-

ABOVE: Lusitano stallion.

BELOW: Andalusian.

TOP: Swedish Warmblood.

ABOVE: Appaloosa.

BELOW: Morgan.

ment with their Norwegian neighbor, the Dole. Towards the end of the 19th century a breed society was formed and devised strict performance tests, such as log-hauling, for breeding stock. The North Swedish horse is a small draft horse, used by the Swedish army and foresters.

The breed has a large head with a short neck and strong shoulders. The quarters are strong and rounded with a sloping croup. They have a kindly temperament and are a long-lived breed. All solid colors are allowed; height stands at about 15.3hh (5ft 1in).

SWEDISH WARMBLOOD

The Swedish Warmblood was developed from local stock crossed with warm-blooded breeds such as the Hanoverian, Thoroughbred and Trakehner. Today the Swedish Warmblood is a powerful competition horse, but it was originally bred to fulfil the Swedish army's need for cavalry remounts. Indeed, the Swedish government owns its own stud farm at Flyinge where breeding programs have been in place for over 300 years. A stud book was opened in 1874 and strict standards were set to qualify for entry. To qualify these days, stock must undertake a number of tests, including riding and harness tests. Other important points are conformation, performance, veterinary history and action. A full breeding license for stallions is only granted after examination of their first offspring after they reach three years old. Such rigorous attention to detail has worked well for the Swedes, as the Swedish Warmblood is in great demand not only for the ridden disciplines, but also harness events.

The head is well-proportioned, with big, bold eyes and an alert expression. Shoulders are strong, the body is compact and well muscled with plenty of girth. Limbs are short and strong with sound feet. Height stands between 15.2hh and 16.2hh (5ft 1in–5ft 5in).

UNITED STATES

APPALOOSA

An American saddle horse, the breed goes back to horses found in the Palouse country of central Idaho and may have originally been bred as a warhorse. Its origins go back to the horses left by the Spanish conquistadores. The Appaloosa is best known for its spotted coat, which may be all-over spotted, loins and quarters only spotted or light spots on a dark background (leopard). The Appaloosa is known as a popular riding horse and, because of its unusual and rather glamorous looks, is often used in parades and circuses.

The Appaloosa ranges from 14.2hh to 15.2hh (4ft 9in–5ft 1in). The breed has good strong shoulders, strong legs with plenty of bone. Arabian influences have also given the horse an attractive head and good carriage.

AMERICAN SADDLEBRED

The Saddlebred was founded in Kentucky and was at first called the Kentucky Saddler. The requirements of the breed's founders were that the horse should be smooth enough in action to ride around farms as well as be able to race and look good in harness. Influences were the Narragansett Pacer, Morgans and Thoroughbreds. Three-gaited and five-gaited horses have several eye-catching gaits: including the spectacular rack. The modern American Saddlebred makes a superb show horse, and consequently is often used in parades and demonstrations.

Height stands at 15hh–16hh (5ft–5ft 4in). All solid colors are allowed.

MISSOURI FOXTROTTER

Another of the American gaited breeds, the Missouri Foxtrotter originated in the Ozark mountains during the 19th century. Settlers of the area needed a mount that could be used to cover long distances comfortably: as a result the Missouri Foxtrotter gives one of the most comfortable of rides. The ambling gait needed to accomplish this became known as the foxtrot — where the horse walks in front but trots with its hind legs. This gait enables the Foxtrotter to proceed at speeds of up to 8mph.

The Foxtrotter is noted for having a gentle nature and is very popular today for trail riding. Its body is wide with a short back and muscular hindlegs. Height stands between 15hh and 17hh (5ft–5ft 8in). All colors are allowed, but many are chestnut.

MORGAN

One of the smaller US horses, the Morgan can trace its beginnings back to just one stallion — a little bay named Justin Morgan after his owner. Little is known of the horse's origins: it may well have had Arabian or Barb blood, while others suggest that he was sired by a Welsh Cob. Justin Morgan was famed for his ability to pull great weights and win races. Luckily his owner decided to try him out as a stud horse before having him gelded. Whatever mare he was put to, the resulting foal always took after the sire. Demand for his services grew and he was eventually bought by the United States Army. A Morgan Stud farm was founded in Woodstock Vermont. The little bay stallion lived on into his 20s.

The Morgan is a popular all-rounder with a kindly and tractable nature. Although robust, its maximum height stands between 14.0hh and 15.2hh (4ft 8in–5ft 1in) making it an ideal mount for a child or adult.

MUSTANG

Initially the term Mustang or Bronco was given to the semi-wild horses that roamed the plains of America, based on the horses imported by the Spanish in the

TOP: American Saddlebred.

ABOVE: Missouri Foxtrotter.

BELOW: Mustang.

TOP: Palomino.

ABOVE: Pinto.

LEFT: Quarter Horse.

ABOVE RIGHT and
CENTER RIGHT:
Standardbred.

BELOW RIGHT:
Tennessee Walking Horse.

16th century. Inevitably some of the conquistadores' horses escaped and bred in the wild; many in turn were captured by the American Indians. Original Mustangs showed their Spanish origins and were fine examples. As the breed grew wilder, its quality degenerated and although the animals were noted for their toughness, they grew scraggy in appearance. During the 20th century many Mustangs were shot because they were thought to be a nuisance to cattle.

The breed is now protected, and efforts are being made to increase the numbers of the original "Spanish" Mustangs, those animals that have obvious Barb origins. All colors are allowable, height ranges from 13.2hh to 15hh (4ft 5in–5ft).

PALOMINO

There have been gold Palomino horses since the time of the Ancient Greeks, although the name is later and could either come from a golden grape variety or Juan de Palomino. Horses of this color were highly sought after in Spain, particularly since Queen Isabella, sponsor of Columbus, favored them. Certainly the Spanish were responsible for introducing the color type into the US. In turn, however, the US was one of the first countries to establish a breed society: the American Palomino Horse Association sets the standard by which a Palomino can be registered. To be accepted one parent must either be Arabian, Thoroughbred or Quarter Horse, and the other already registered. Today the Palomino is popular as a saddle and show horse; they are also seen in Quarter Horse racing.

Palomino identifies a color rather than a true breed. To qualify the coat must be the color of a newly minted gold coin, or three shades lighter or darker. The eyes must have dark coloring. Height should be over 14hh (4ft 8in).

PINTO

The eye-catching Pinto or Painted Horse of America is divided into two color types. The Ovaro has white patches starting from the belly, and colouring is usually dark. The Tobiano's white patches start elsewhere, usually from the back. There are two registers in the US for the Pinto: the American Paint Horse Association and the Pinto Horse Association. The Pinto has its origins in the Spanish horses brought to America during the 16th century. The Pinto is a color type rather than a breed, but there are certain points such as sound limbs and hard feet that are preferable. There are no height limits.

QUARTER HORSE

Founded on English and Spanish horses during the 18th century, the American Quarter Horse is now the most numerous of the American breeds. The breed began life as a racehorse, and that is how it got its name. Early racetracks in America usually had to be cleared specially for racing and the usual race distance was a quarter mile — and thus the name quarter horse. Further developed by crossing Mustang and Thoroughbred blood, in addition to sprinting quarter-mile racetracks, the breed made a useful cowpony.

The Quarter Horse is noted for having an easy temperament and great acceleration. The quarters are exceptionally powerful. The Quarter Horse is very popular and has a large following outside the United States as well. All solid colors are allowed. Height stands at 15hh–16hh (5ft–5ft 4in).

STANDARDBRED

Harness racing is one of the primary horse sports in America and the Standardbred was developed solely to meet the demand for a good trotting horse. The breed was fathered by Hambletonian, a direct descendant of English Thoroughbred Messenger, who was the son of the Norfolk Trotter, Bellfounder. Officially the name Standardbred dates from 1879, when the American Trotting Register set a speed standard as an entry requirement. Modern rules admit horses on blood rather than speed alone. Standardbred horses either race by trotting conventionally or pacing – using a lateral movement. Pacers are more popular in America.

In appearance the Standardbred is heavier set than the Thoroughbred, with hind legs set behind the horse, giving greater propulsion. The usual colors are bay but other colors are also found. Height stands at 14hh–16hh (4ft 8in–5ft 4in).

TENNESSEE WALKING HORSE

A breed developed to meet the needs of American plantation owners, the Tennessee Walking Horse was also known as the Plantation Walking Horse. As with the Morgan, the breed was founded by one stallion – Black Allan — a Standardbred. The Walking Horse is famous for its unusual gaits: the flat walk, running walk and the rocking chair canter. Although unusual, the gaits are natural – show horses, however, are often shod with heavyweight shoes to show off their paces. Together with many American breeds, the Tennessee Walking Horse is known for having a docile temperament. The Tennessee Walking Horse Breeders' Association was founded in 1935.

All solid colors are permitted. Height stands at 15hh–16hh (5ft–5ft 4in).

The Former USSR

AKHAL-TEKE

The Akhal-Teke is one of the world's most ancient breeds, bred by the Turkoman tribes, and noted for having an almost metallic sheen to its coat.

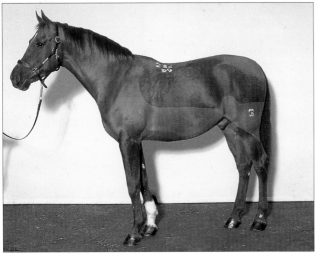

TOP: *Akhal-Teke.*

ABOVE: *Don gelding.*

RIGHT: *Orlov Trotter.*

Turkmenistan is an arid desert region surrounded by mountains: these rough conditions have produced a horse with incredible stamina, able to withstand great extremes of temperature, used to being tethered and fed a mixture of barley and alfalfa. One of the best recorded examples of the breed's endurance was in 1935, when a group of Akhal-Tekes travelled 2,500 miles (4,000km) from Ashkhabad to Moscow, in just 84 days.

Domesticated for centuries, no one is quite sure if the Akhal-Teke is an example of a totally purebred breed or a descendant of the Turkoman horse from Iran. The Akhal-Teke itself has influenced a great many breeds including the Trakehner. Extremely elegant, with large intelligent eyes, long ears, good legs and feet, chestnut is the most common color. Height stands at 15hh–15.2hh (5ft–5ft 1in).

DON

The Don is best known as the warhorse of the Cossack cavalry, renowned for its hardy constitution that enables it to live out the harsh Russian winters. This stamina contributed to the resilience of the Russian cavalry in pursuing Napoleon's troops in their retreat from Russia: the Don was able to survive where the French horses could not. It is bred in the area around the Don and Volga Rivers. Major influences in the breed's development have been the Akhal-Teke, Arabian and Thoroughbred. The modern Don is often used in long-distance endurance riding.

The usual colors are chestnut and bay. Height stands between 15.3hh and 16.2hh (5ft 1in–5ft 5in).

KABARDIN

This breed is to be found in the Caucasus region, and is noted for being sure-footed and hardy. Often used as pack horses as well as riding horses, the breed was founded when tribesmen crossed Mongol stock with Persian blood. The breed was upgraded in the 20th century when Thoroughbred blood was introduced. This has resulted in a faster and taller horse — the Anglo-Kabardin. Bay is the most common color, height stands at 14.2hh–15.2hh (4ft 9in–5ft 1in).

KARABAKH

This is a beautiful breed from the Caucasian region; it shares the metallic coat of the Akhal-Teke and is very similar to the Arab in conformation. It has previously been crossed with the Persian, Kabardin and Akhal-Teke. It is noted for being extremely agile and is used in the mounted games that are held in the region. Economical to keep and with a kindly nature, the Karabakh was used to further develop the Don horse, the famous mount of the Cossacks.

The usual colors are dun or chestnut. Height stands at 14.2hh (4ft 9in).

ORLOV TROTTER

The Orlov was founded by Count Alexis Grigorievich Orlov, a Russian nobleman who may have been involved with the murder of Czar Peter III. Orlov began by importing an Arabian stallion and putting it to a Danish mare. This resulted in a stallion named Polkan; he in turn fathered Bars First. These animals formed the basis of the Orlov Trotter. The next step was the introduction of English, Arabian, Dutch and Danish blood. The Orlov became the world's best trotting horse. Originally intended as a racehorse, the Orlov Trotter is also used for general harness work. The Orlov is a handsome horse; the best have an Arab-like head, are tall and lightly built. Quarters are strong and the legs have good bone. Height stands at 16hh (5ft 4in) but larger animals are known. The usual color is gray.

CHAPTER 25

PRINCIPAL PONY BREEDS OF THE WORLD

Lynda Springate

ARGENTINA

FALABELLA

This is a miniature horse rather than a small pony. Named for the Falabella family, who own the Recreo de Roca Ranch in Argentina, the story goes that a small Indian stallion appeared on the land of an ancestor of Señor Falabella. He kept it and decided to breed it because he was curious to see what would happen. The dwarf gene was dominant and any foals sired by the stallion were noticeably smaller. The Falabella breed was gradually evolved by the use of other ponies, such as very small Shetlands, and also very small Thoroughbreds. Today many small breeds are crossed, and these produce many different colors.

The Falabella exhibits several differences from all other equine breeds: the gestation period is two months longer than other horses or ponies, being 13 months; foals are tiny when born, a mere 16in (41cm) long; Falabellas also have two fewer ribs and vertebrae. On top of this, as it is a miniature horse, there are certain complications. Although some Falabellas can be used in harness, their bones and feet are miniaturized and as a result the breed cannot be ridden since it is too delicate. Although they have some Shetland blood in their veins, Falabellas have to be cosseted when the weather is cold.

Inbreeding has led to poor conformation in some specimens, which may have crooked hocks, large heads and ewe necks. Height stands up to 7hh (2ft 6in); one of the smallest Falabellas recorded was Sugar Dumpling, only 20in (51cm) high.

AUSTRALIA

AUSTRALIAN PONY

The Australian Pony Stud Book Society was formed in 1929 and came into being after much crossbreeding had taken place in Australia to produce a children's riding pony. As more settlers arrived, they brought their own breeds and gradually the Australian Pony evolved. One of the first ponies to be imported in to Australia — a Timor — arrived in 1803. The dominant influences in today's Australian Pony are the Welsh Mountain, Arabian, Shetland and Hackney. A Welsh Mountain stallion was imported in 1911.

The Australian Pony looks very like the Welsh ponies, and could easily be taken for one of the British breeds. It has a compact and well-built body, elegant to look at. The head is slightly dished like an Arabian with big eyes and a wide forehead. It is an intelligent pony with a very kind temperament, making it ideal for children. The height varies between 12hh and 14hh (4ft–4ft 8in). All solid colors are permissible.

AUSTRIA

HAFLINGER

The Austrian Haflinger is also known as the Edelweiss pony. An immensely strong, long-lived breed, many survive happily well into their 30s. The Haflinger's ability as an all-round working pony is well known: it even has had a tractor named after it. Typically, a Haflinger pony is not worked until it is at least four years old. This restrained approach to breaking in contributes to such a long working life. The main breeding area is Hafling in Austria's Etschlander mountain area. As with all mountain ponies, the Haflinger is sure-footed and can be used in harness or as a riding pony. In winter they are sometimes used to pull sleighs for the tourist trade.

THIS PICTURE: Australian Pony.
LEFT: Falabellas.

ABOVE: Haflingers.

LEFT: Ariegeois.

A Haflinger is easily recognized by its striking coloring, which is usually Palomino, but chestnut coloring is also found. The neck is muscular and strong, with a long body and a deep girth. The head has an intelligent and lively look, showing traces of Arabian influences in the breeding.

CANADA

SABLE ISLAND

Semi-feral ponies have lived on Sable Island, Nova Scotia for at least 300 years. They are thought to be the descendants of French horses taken to the island in 1739. If the claim that Norman horses were their ancestors is true, it is from this breed that the island ponies get their height. The ponies are very hardy: they have to be – the surroundings on Sable Island are very desolate. They can be trained as saddle horses, but lack conformation.

The body of a Sable Island pony is narrow and not very well muscled. Height stands between 14hh and 15hh (4ft 8in–5ft)

FRANCE

ARIEGEOIS

An Ariegeois pony is invariably black and closely resembles the British Dales pony. The foundations of the breed date back to prehistoric times and, over the centuries, the Ariegeois has been improved by breeding with the oriental Barb horse. The breed is named after the Ariegeois river in France and can be found in the eastern Pyrenees. This location has fostered many tales of Ariegeois ponies being used for smuggling over the Franco-Spanish borders. True or not, the breed's most notable feature is its feet, the horn of which is unusually strong. The fact that the Ariegeois can work happily without being shod, would certainly have helped its smuggling activities considerably. A hardy breed, the Ariegeois was used initially as a pack pony.

In height the pony can range between 13.1hh and 14.3hh (4ft 4in–4ft 9in). Face, mane and tail have thick hair to protect it against cold weather.

LANDAIS

The French Landais was first found on the Barthes plains and Landais marshes alongside the Ardour River. These grazing conditions led to a tough pony, able to do well on very little. An ancient wild pony, there was a larger version of the Landais called the Barthais. Domestication has meant strong Arabian influences. Early this century, in 1913, an Arabian stallion was turned out to run with Landais mares. This much improved the breed as a riding pony, although since then the numbers of Landais have sadly declined.

To combat this French breeders now use Arabian and Welsh Section B stallions to help keep the numbers steady and keep the quality of the bloodlines. The principal use of the breed today is as a riding pony for children; consequently, Landais are often to be seen at French Pony Club events.

The back is short and straight, the neck long with an Arabian look to the head. Accepted colors are usually chestnut, brown or bay. In height they stand between 11.3hh and 13.1hh (3ft 9in–4ft 4in).

GERMANY

DULMEN

The Dulmen is virtually Germany's sole native surviving pony breed. The other is the Senner, which is now found only in extremely small numbers. This hardy breed dates back to medieval times, having its origins in the Westphalia district of Germany. The usual colors are brown or dun; average height stands at around 13.2hh–13.3hh (4ft 5in– 4ft 6in).

GREAT BRITAIN

CONNEMARA

The Connemara is named for the area of Connaught on the west coast of Ireland of which Connemara is a part. The only pony breed indigenous to Ireland, it has been suggested that the Connemara, together with the Highland, Shetland, Icelandic and Norwegian ponies, may be a descendant of ancient Celtic ponies. Certainly the Connemara has had to be a tough breed to survive in its natural habitat. It is one of the most beautiful of the mountain ponies. Besides the Celtic theory, there are many legends about how the breed evolved. Some say that horses swam ashore from shipwrecked Spanish ships during the Armada of 1588. Others say that the Connemara gets its oriental looks from horses bought from the Spanish by Galway merchants. The Commission on Horse Breeding in Ireland, set up in 1900, received a report on the Connemara pony by Prof. J. Cossor Ewart. The Connemara Pony Breeders' Society was formed in 1928, to protect and improve the breed.

As a show pony the Connemara can hardly be bettered. It combines refined looks with speed and great jumping ability. When bred away from their natural home — and they have been bred in England for some years — they have a tendency to grow larger. Sometimes Connemaras are crossed with Thoroughbreds to breed larger competition animals. The head should have the look of an Arabian, the sloping shoulders aiding a comfortable riding action. The body is compact with short limbs having good bone. Height is between 13hh and 14.2hh (4ft 4in–4ft 9in).

ABOVE: Connemara.

BELOW: Dulmens.

ABOVE: Dales.

LEFT: Dartmoor.

ABOVE RIGHT: Fell.

BELOW RIGHT: Hackney.

DALES

Native to the north of England, the Dales belongs on the eastern side of the Pennine range, while its relative the Fell inhabits the western side. Originally the two breeds were very similar, but the Dales evolved into the larger by about 2in (5cm). Unsurprisingly, the Dales was used as a weight-carrying pony, to carry ore from the lead mines across the hills to the docks. The ponies walked in convoys carrying about 240lb (110kg) for distances of over 200 miles per week.

The Dales has often been crossbred with heavy horses such as the Clydesdale, giving it a stocky build. Another important cross was the Welsh Cob. A stud book was opened by the Dales Pony Improvement Society in 1916. This helped to conserve the Dales when mechanization led to the decline of the pack pony, but the breed went into decline again in the early 1950s. This situation was helped with the formation of the Dales Pony Society in the 1960s. The modern Dales pony is an extremely capable all-rounder, as useful in harness as it is a riding pony. Its heritage has given it a calm temperament, sure-footedness and strength, making it ideal as a competition pony.

The head of a Dales should be neat and alert; the shoulders are sloping, contributing to the famous raised knee action of the breed. The quarters are strong, limbs short and powerful. Height stands at 14.2hh (4ft 9in).

DARTMOOR

Southernmost of the mountain and moorland breeds is the Dartmoor. Ponies have roamed Dartmoor for hundreds of years but, unlike neighboring Exmoor, Dartmoor's position made the breed much more accessible, particularly as it is close to the sea. They were used extensively locally — for example to carry metal from the Cornish tin mines to the towns.

As a result of this accessibility much crossbreeding has taken place. In the early years of this century, an attempt was made to define the Dartmoor as a breed. It was decided that ponies which had a more than quarter of outcross blood in their veins could not be entered in the stud book. The most noteworthy influence on modern Dartmoor ponies was a stallion called The Leat, sired by an Arabian stallion: most of today's Dartmoor ponies can trace their lineage back to him. Today many of the show Dartmoors are bred at stud farms throughout the British Isles. Dartmoors make superb riding ponies as they manage to combine good looks and a comfortable action with an agreeable temperament. They are often chosen as a first mount for a child, although they are well able to carry an adult if need be.

Typically a Dartmoor has an intelligent head with small ears. Sloping shoulders contribute to the pony's comfortable ride. Maximum height is 12.2hh (4ft 1in).

FELL

Close neighbor to the Dales pony, the Fell lives on the western side of the Pennines in Cumbria. Like the Dales, the Fell owes its ancestry to the Friesian and the Scottish Galloway. The Friesian influence came about in Roman times, when Friesen people came to England bringing their ponies with them. The Fell was used extensively as a pack pony but did not evolve into such a heavy type as the Dales. When the spread of railways and mechanization put an end to the general use of pack ponies in England, the Fell's usefulness as a trotting pony was instead put to good use as a harness horse. They also took part in trotting races in the 19th century.

These days the breed is in great demand as an all-round ride-and-drive pony. The growing interest in driving has boosted the Fell's popularity in recent years. Sheep herding is another of their uses. It is said that of all of the British mountain and moorland breeds, no other pony breeds to type more truly. The Fell Pony Society was established in 1912.

Although at one time the Dales and Fell were remarkably similar, the two are now very different. The Fell is lighter to look at, and at 14hh (4ft 8in) slightly smaller than the Dales pony. Colors are black, dark brown, dark bay or gray. The head is pony-like, body compact with strong limbs and silky feathering on the legs.

HACKNEY PONY

The Hackney Pony and the Hackney Horse both share the same stud book; they also share a similar ancestry, with their relationship to the Norfolk and Yorkshire Trotters — both of which were breeds of naturally fast trotters and so were used to pull carriages. It is believed that the Hackney Pony first appeared in 1866, when a stallion named Sir George was foaled. The foal could trace its lineage back to the famous racehorse Flying Childers. The breeder responsible for creating the type was Christopher Wilson of Cumbria. Wilson put Sir George to selected Fell mares, and the Hackney Pony evolved: so successful was he that the breed was also known as the Wilson Pony.

Extremely hardy as it had to winter out on the fells, this practice also ensured that the Hackney's height was kept down. The combination of class and the high-stepping action of the Fell pony gave the Hackney Pony an extravagant and fluid action. Spectacular to watch, it soon became popular as a harness horse. Good examples of the breed fetch a very high price. The Hackney's main use is as a harness pony, but some have been occasionally used as show jumpers, making good use of their muscular hocks.

The Hackney Pony should always look like a genuine pony and not just a small horse. The head is small

and intelligent. The neck is long with a high carriage, the body compact. When being driven the knees should lift up high and the hocks should come right under the body. Height stands between 12.2hh and 14hh (4ft 1in–4ft 8in). All solid colors are allowed.

EXMOOR

Great Britain can claim nine indigenous pony breeds, the most ancient of which is the Exmoor pony. A breed of great age, it is a native to Exmoor in south-west Britain, in north Devon and Somerset. It is believed to be the last surviving line of the ancient Celtic ponies – although others like the Connemara have their proponents. Much research shows that the Exmoor relates directly back to Britain's wild horses – strong evidence of the breed's antiquity is its unique jaw formation with a seventh molar. The Exmoor is the only remaining breed to have this feature, linking it to the fossilised remains of ancient ponies found in Alaska.

Exmoor ponies often winter out in hard conditions and over the years have acquired a good deal of stamina and sure-footedness. Because of the isolated position of Exmoor, little crossbreeding has taken place. The ponies are highly intelligent and can be willful if not handled properly. Well trained, they make excellent children's ponies and driving ponies. Although small, such is their strength that they can carry a full-size adult all day.

The Exmoor is quickly recognised by its mealy mouth, and the same colouring around the eyes and underbelly. In configuration they have short ears, wide foreheads and large prominent eyes. The chest is deep and wide, ribs are long, deep and wide apart. Legs are short and clean. Permitted colours are bay, brown or dun. White marking are not allowed. The height limit was 12.2hh (just under 4ft 1in) for mares and 12.3hh (just over 4ft 1in) for stallions but an open height limit was introduced for 1996.

HIGHLAND

Largest and strongest of the British pony breeds, the Highland is a very ancient breed, and was for many years the only form of transport for the Scottish farmers. It is said the Highland was one of a group of ponies who moved westwards from northern Asia after the Ice Age in Europe. Images of horses found in the famous Lascaux caves in France are said to be similar to the Highland.

At one time the Highland was divided into three distinct types. Smallest was the Barra, then a type simply known as a riding pony, while the largest was the Mainland pony, or Garron. Infusions of different blood over the years have made these distinctions largely obsolete. Alien blood has been introduced on several occasions, notably by breeding with the

Arabian, Percheron and Clydesdale. Highland ponies are noted for their great strength and, of course, the Clydesdale influence has much to do with this. It is still not uncommon for the Highland to be used for carrying deer carcasses down from the hills. As with the Shetland, the Highland is a tough and hardy breed; wintering out is helped by having a soft, thick winter coat with another much coarser layer on top. Highland ponies are used as riding ponies, particularly for trekking; they are also crossed with other breeds to produce hunting and eventing horses.

The head of a Highland has an attractive appearance: although broad between the eyes, the neck is strong and arched. The back is very strong and usually has a dorsal stripe. All colors are allowed, but no white markings. Height stands at 14.2hh (4ft 9in).

NEW FOREST

With the exception of the Highland pony, the New Forest is the largest of the British native breeds. Over the years the New Forest pony has had several different breeds of stallion running with the native herds. This is due largely to where the breed originated – in the deciduous forest of Hampshire, southern England, where King William II (1087-1100) met his end. As the county was once the heart of the pre-Norman Kingdom of Wessex, tracks through the Forest were busy and as a result many different types of ponies roamed the New Forest. In later centuries many stallions were turned out deliberately in an effort to improve the breed — for example, Queen Victoria's Arabian stallion Zorah and Marske, the sire of Eclipse.

Feed in the New Forest is generally poor, making for a breed of hardy and economical feeders. Ponies turned out to graze and run in the New Forest are owned by people with commoners' rights. Many are rounded up during the end of the year for sale at the Beaulieu Road New Forest sales. Because of the amount of traffic through the New Forest, the ponies tend to be sensible when ridden on the road. They make an ideal family pony as they can often be ridden by both children and adults, have a friendly temperament and are good in harness.

There is no fixed type of New Forest pony: sizes vary between 12hh and 14.2 hh (4ft–4ft 9in). All colors are permissible, but many of them are bay. The head is always intelligent, but occasionally can be slightly large. Limbs are good, the long sloping shoulder helps makes the breed an exceptional riding pony.

SHETLAND

The diminutive Shetland is the smallest of the British native breeds, standing at no more than 10.2hh (3ft 5in). It is a very hardy breed and may be related to the Tundra horse, although it is also thought that the Shetland was originally from Scandinavia. However, it

ABOVE LEFT: Highland.

BELOW LEFT: Highland.

ABOVE: New Forest.

BELOW: Shetland foal.

ABOVE and BELOW: Welsh Highland ponies.

also shares some of the characteristics of those ponies illustrated in cave paintings in France and Spain. It has lived on the bleak Shetland Isles for centuries and was not exported to the Scottish mainland until the 19th century. During this time it was used for work in the coal mines. Its main activities in Shetland were carrying loads for the crofters, and this could include carrying full-size adults over rough terrain.

A deterioration in the quality of the breed set in when the Shetland began to be exported. Quality was again restored when the Marquis of Londonderry established stud farms to improve the breed. Shetland ponies can claim the distinction of being the first British native pony breed to start its own society. The founding year was 1890 and a stud book was opened at the same time. The Shetland has been exported abroad and there are now many countries with their own stud book.

Shetlands have an intelligent looking head with small ears and large nasal cavities. The latter help to warm up air before it enters the lungs during hard winters. Another unusual winter aid is the coat, which grows two layers in winter months.

WELSH MOUNTAIN PONY

The stud book for Welsh ponies is divided into four sections: Section A is for the Welsh Mountain Pony, Section B the Welsh Pony, Section C Welsh Pony of Cob Type, and Section D the Welsh Cob, which is more truly classified as a horse. For many people the Welsh Mountain is the most attractive of all the Welsh pony breeds. Ponies have roamed the Welsh hills for a long time but it was the influence of Arabian blood, introduced by the Romans, that helped the Welsh Mountain evolve into the elegant little pony that it is today.

The tough environment of the Welsh mountains has made the pony intelligent, brave and very hardy. These days the Welsh Mountain is highly popular as a child's pony. It was often the choice of tradesmen and was at one time widely used in the coal mines. The Welsh Mountain has been used as foundation stock for types such as the Hack and polo pony. It is also claimed that Welsh mares helped to create the English Thoroughbred. It is certainly a fact that the breed formed the foundation stock of the Welsh Pony and Welsh Cob.

The Welsh Mountain Pony's head is always dished like an Arabian's, the body compact with good depth. The limbs should have good bone and rounded hooves. All solid colors are permissible. Height stands at 12hh–12.2hh (4ft–4ft 1in).

WELSH PONY

A favourite in the US, the Welsh Pony is classed as Section B in the Welsh Pony and Cob Society Stud

Book. The description of the Welsh Mountain Pony is also applicable to the Welsh Pony, particularly the quality and constitution, although its action is a little longer than the Welsh Mountain's. A sought-after riding pony, its larger size helps the Welsh Pony excel in competition work. The Welsh Pony stands at 13.2hh (4ft 5in). All solid colors are allowed.

WELSH PONY OF COB TYPE

Small Welsh Cobs are referred to as Welsh Pony of Cob Type and are designated Section C in the stud book. They were originally bred for use on the Welsh hill farms where they were used for all sorts of light agricultural purposes including sheep herding. The breed is a product of the Welsh Mountain Pony and Welsh Cob. Today this breed is particularly useful for pony trekking, being sure-footed and strong. It is also successful in harness.

The head is similar to that of the Welsh Mountain, the neck muscular and curved. The limbs are fine and strong with hard hooves. Height for the Welsh Pony of Cob type should not exceed 13.2hh (4ft 5in), whereas the larger Welsh Cob is classed as a horse.

GREECE

PENEIA

Named for the Peloponnese, the Peneia is the least known of the Greek pony breeds. As with the other Greek ponies, the Peneia is a utility animal used for farm work, and as a riding and pack pony.

The Peneia can grow to a variety of heights ranging between 10hh and 14hh (3ft 4in–4ft 8in). The usual colors are chestnut, gray, brown or bay.

PINDOS PONY

The Pindos pony originates from the mountainous areas of Thessaly and Epirus. The breed is believed to be a descendant of the Thessalanian, one of the traditional horses of Ancient Greece. It is larger than the Skyros, and is used for a variety of work such as in forestry, as a pack pony, for farm work and riding and driving. Living in the mountains has made the Pindos a very hardy breed: their feet are so strong that they are hardly ever shod.

The head is long, as are the limbs but the Pindos has a very light frame and its quarters and neck are poorly muscled. The Pindos Pony is very tough, but does have the reputation of having a stubborn temperament. The usual colours are black, bay and brown. Height stands at 13hh (4ft 4in).

SKYROS PONY

Skyros is situated in the Aegean and is home to the best-known of the Greek ponies: the Skyros pony, also known as the Skyrian Horse. Many of these

ABOVE: Welsh Pony mare and foal.

BELOW: Welsh Pony of the Cob type.

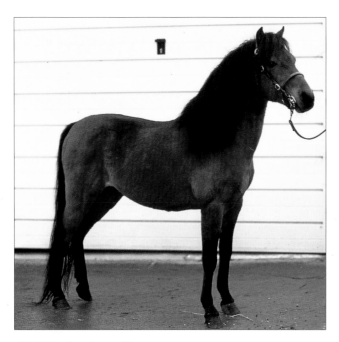

ABOVE: Caspian stallion.

BELOW: Icelandic pony.

ponies are semi-wild and live out in the mountains until they are rounded up and used to assist in threshing the corn at harvest time. However, the breed is domesticated and has many uses in Greece as a pack, harness and also riding pony.

The Skyros is Greece's smallest pony, standing at 11hh (3ft 8in). It has a small head, showing some oriental influence. It has a short neck and narrow body. The quarters carry little muscle. The usual colors are bay, gray, brown or dun.

IRAN

CASPIAN

A horse in miniature, the Caspian is very like the Arabian in appearance, and may well be one of the Arabian's ancestors. The breed was rediscovered after a period of 1,000 years in 1965. Examples of the pony were found living in northern Iran on the shores of the Caspian Sea. It is thought that the Caspian was bred locally and were called Ponseki or Monleki. They were never moved from the area and for this reason remained remarkably purebred since no crossbreeding took place. Pictures showing horses looking like the Caspian were found carved on ruins in Persepolis. The breed's authenticity was verified scientifically. The Caspian has several unusual features different from other horse and pony breeds which have helped research – for example, there are differences in the scapula and the way that the parietal bones of the skull are formed.

After its rediscovery, steps were taken to preserve the Caspian and keep the bloodlines pure. There are now Caspian societies to be found in the US, Australia, Great Britain and New Zealand. The narrow yet strong proportions of the Caspian make it a very athletic pony, a fast and good jumper. Furthermore its conformation makes it ideal as a child's mount.

The Caspian has an Arabian-type head, with large eyes and nostrils. The body is deep but unusually narrow. The shoulders are sloping producing a long comfortable stride, more usually associated with a horse. The feet are very strong. Usual colors are chestnut and bay. Height stands between 10hh and 12hh (3ft 4in–4ft).

ICELAND

ICELAND

An ancient breed, ancestors of the Icelandic horse were known to exist before the Ice Age. It was from the 8th century that settlers to Iceland took their own ponies which merged with the native stock. It was not until 1879 that a selective breeding program was instigated, in the Skagafjorder area.

Many Iceland ponies winter out in the severest of conditions in their native land, where they serve a variety of uses as harness and saddle horses; they are also bred for their meat. In addition to the usual four gaits, two paces are associated with the Icelandic horse: the tolt, a sort of rack, and the skeid, a kind of pace.

All colors are acceptable, one of the most attractive being liver chestnut with a light color mane and tail. The Icelandic horse has a strong compact body with lots of stamina. Limbs are short with short cannon bones. The head is large, yet intelligent. Although only 12.3hh to 13.2hh (4ft 1in–4ft 5in), the Icelandic horse is always known as a horse rather than a pony.

ITALY

BARDIGIANO

A little known breed, the Bardigiano originates in the northern Appenine part of Italy. In looks it is not unlike the British Exmoor pony. Many people think that this breed is related to another Italian breed the Avelignese, which is in turn related to the Haflinger. The Bardigiano is strong and intelligent and often used as a pack pony. Height stands between 12hh and 13hh (4ft–4ft 4in). All solid colors are permissible.

MEXICO

GALICENO

The Galiceno is named for the Galicia area in northwestern Spain where it originated. Famous throughout Europe for its swift running-walke; the Galiceno in turn may have its origins in the Sorraias pony. The founding of the Galiceno breed in Mexico probably happened when Spanish horses were brought to the Americas during the 16th century. The breed was officially recognized in 1958 and the Galiceno is now Mexico's major native breed — its size makes it particularly popular with young riders. Galiceno ponies can now be found throughout the US.

As a breed the Galiceno is hardy and intelligent. It is used as a saddle and a harness pony. The head has a refined look, with large eyes. The body is narrow but compact, the limbs strong. Shoulders are upright rather than sloping. Height stands at 14hh (4ft 8in).

NORWAY

FJORD

No folk museum in Norway would be complete without examples of the Fjord pony living and working on site. A hardy breed, the Fjord has a strong and exuberant temperament. In its native Norway it has a variety of jobs: it is as useful a saddle pony as it is in harness. Parts of Scandinavia can still be difficult to reach by car, and so the Fjord pony makes a useful

TOP: Bardigiano.

ABOVE: Galiceno.

BELOW: Norwegian Fjord pony.

TOP: Norwegian Fjord.

ABOVE: Konik.

BELOW: Sorraia.

RIGHT: Gotland pony.

packhorse. Although mostly bred in Norway, there are other stud farms to be found breeding the Fjord throughout Scandinavia.

The willful Fjord pony is easily recognizable by its light dun coloring and dark dorsal stripe. The body is powerful and stocky with short straight legs. It is traditional to cut the mane so that it stands up with the black central stripe prominent. Height stands between 13hh and 14.2hh (4ft 4in–4ft 9in).

POLAND

HUCUL

This breed has its origins in the Tarpan, which has roamed Poland since before the Ice Age. Indeed, Poland is the only country where examples of ponies resembling the Tarpan can still be seen. Originally found in the Carpathian mountains, the animal is sure-footed, making it ideal for carrying loads over mountain trails and muddy fields; furthermore as a working farm horse, the Hucul can hardly be bettered.

It has a short strong body, with good hind legs. Over the years the Hucul's conformation has been improved by selective breeding, making it stocky and strong. The head is friendly in appearance and medium-sized, but now has a slightly refined look. Height is between 12.2hh and 13.1hh (4ft 1in–4ft 4in). Many examples are piebald in coloring, although dun and bay is also common.

KONIK

The Konik pre-dates the Ice Age, and can claim the primitive Tarpan as an ancestor. Subsequently Arabian blood has been introduced from time to time to improve the breed. The very name Konik translates as "small horse." Its two main occupations are in light farm work and in use as a light harness horse. Latterly it has become popular as a riding pony. Koniks are officially bred at several state stud farms in Poland, the Polish Academy of Science being one of them.

Technically, the Konik is classed because a pony breed as it stands only 13hh (4ft 4in) high; however, in appearance and use the breed is far more horse-like. Similar to the Hucul in appearance, although their limbs are not quite so well developed, like the Hucul the Konik is long-lived and can carry on working well into old age. This may be because they are brought on slowly and not broken in until they reach four years of age. The Konik is usually dun in color, with a black dorsal stripe.

PORTUGAL

SORRAIA

The Sorraia takes its name from the area between the Sor and Raia Rivers. It is very similar in looks to the

Tarpan, from which it may be descended. The Barb is credited with being a later influence on the Sorraia, which is now used for light farm work.

The head is large with black-tipped ears. Another notable feature is the low-set tail. The Sorraia is usually a gray-dun in color, while the height is no more than 13hh (4ft 4in).

SWEDEN

GOTLAND

Gotland ponies are native to Sweden: their original home was the Island of Gotland and it is quite conceivable that they may have lived there since the Stone Age. As with similar breeds, they may also be descended from the ancient Tarpan. Over a period of time, the Gotland has migrated to mainland Sweden and is now bred there also. This integration has allowed a certain amount of selective breeding to take place, with the introduction of Arabian bloodlines. The Gotland has evolved from its original purpose as a farm pony and is now used for riding and harness. Best paces are the walk and trot, and some Gotland ponies have been entered in trotting races. As a breed the Gotland is noted for its stamina.

In conformation the body is light yet strong; the weakest points are the hind legs which lack the strength of the shoulders and front legs. Fairly small, they stand at between 12hh and 12.2hh (4ft–4ft 1in).

UNITED STATES

AMERICAN SHETLAND

Although influenced by the British Shetland Pony, the American Shetland is a totally different breed, which only arrived during this century. Examples of the Shetland were exported to the USA, the first batch being introduced in 1885. America's version of the Shetland was achieved by mating the Shetland with the Hackney Pony. This gave the breed a far more slender appearance — the Hackney blood also gave a much more spectacular trotting action. This in turn has led to the breed's immense popularity in the United States as a harness pony. Later out-crossing took place with Thoroughbreds and Arabians. Not as hardy as the native Shetland, the American Shetland has a good nature and looks very much like a Hackney.

The head is not very pony-like, being long and straight. The body is long and narrow, with long slim limbs. All solid colors are permissible. Height limit stands at 11.2hh (3ft 9in).

CHINCOTEAGUE

These are wild ponies living on the islands of Chincoteague and Assateague, near the coast of Virginia. The herds date back to abandoned stock

TOP: American Shetland.

ABOVE: Assateague pony.

210

ABOVE: Bashkir pony.

from colonial times. Assateague is now a national park that was cut off from the mainland during severe storm weather in 1933. As a result of this the breed is largely degenerative, although Shetland, Welsh and Pinto blood has from time to time been crossbred with the ponies.

ROCKY MOUNTAIN PONY

Latest of pony breeds to be recognised in the US, a register was opened for the Rocky Mountain only in 1986. The breed is believed to originate from Sam Tuttle's riding stallion Old Tobe, a great favorite with riders at the Natural Bridge State Park. He sired a group of horses that took on his appearance, paces and temperament. However, it is not difficult to see the influence of Spanish blood in the breed.

The pony also has an unusual pace — known as an amble — that allows it to carry riders in comfort over the roughest of ground. Overall its conformation is pleasing to look at, and the breed is very hardy, able to winter out in the mountains.

Rocky Mountain Ponies are prized for their beautiful chocolate-colored coat with light mane and tail. Height stands at 14.2hh to 15.2hh (4ft 7in-5ft 1in).

The Former USSR

BASHKIR

Bred by the Bashkiri peoples of the Ural mountains, the Bashkir fulfills that people's every need from packhorse to clothing. An ancient breed, it is able to survive freezing temperatures in the open mostly because of the thick winter coat, which is curly and long. It is so good at insulation that the hair is spun and made into cloth. The Bashkir is reputed to be able to work for 24 hours without being fed.

Another odd feature of the Bashkir is the fact that the mares are actually milked. This milk is turned into cream and butter; it is also possible to drink the milk and concoct an alcoholic beverage from it. These days the pony is bred under Russian state supervision. The breed was also discovered in Nevada in the United States towards the end of the 19th century. It is quite possible that the Russians introduced the breed to the United States. Because of its curly coat, the breed is known as the Bashkir Curly in the US where a register was founded in 1971.

In recent times some cross-breeding has taken place to improve the breed. The head is large with a short thick neck, while the body is wide with a straight back. The legs are short with good bone measurement. The feet are hard enough not to need shoes. Usual colors are chestnut and bay. Height stands at around 13.3hh to 14hh (4ft 5in–4ft 8in).

GLOSSARY OF EQUESTRIAN TERMS

Maureen Sadler, Lynda Springate, Tim Woodcock

AGAINST THE CLOCK A method of judging final positions in a show jumping competition: the horse and rider with the fewest faults in the fastest time wins.

AGED A horse over the age of ten.

AIDS Directions given by the rider to his horse. The hands, voice, legs and body are "natural aids." "Invisible aids" are when these instructions are barely noticeable. Spurs and whips are "artificial aids."

AIRS ABOVE THE GROUND aka "schools above the ground." These are the classical jumps performed by the horse in the air. They are the levade, capriole, courbette and ballotade.

ALBINO Found worldwide in most breeds of horse and pony. They are snowy-white or cream colored, with pink skin around the eyes and muzzle. The eyes can be almost translucent light blue, dark blue or brown. The American Albino Association was formed with the intention of establishing the color as a breed rather than a type.

ALL ON A statement made by the whipper-in to the huntsman when the hounds are altogether as a pack.

AMBLE One of the slower gaits, performed with the horse's hind leg and fore leg moving forward on the same track.

ANKLE Another word for the fetlock joint.

APPRENTICE Young person being trained as a jockey. The usual apprenticeship takes at least five years.

ARENA Fenced off area for equine competition events.

AS HOUNDS RAN Area covered in each particular hunt by hounds.

ALSO-RAN A horseracing term to describe an unplaced horse.

AT BAY Keeping the hounds away from their quarry, once they have run it to ground.

BACK HANDER A backward stroke in polo when the rider is traveling forward.

BACK The time when a horse is introduced to the weight of a rider after becoming accustomed to wearing its tack.

BALLOTADE An air above the ground. A dressage movement in which the horse half rears, then jumps forward kicking the hind legs in below the quarters before landing on all four feet.

BAND Another name for a group of horses.

BARB Originally the name for horses found on the north and northwest coastal regions of Africa. The true barb was a coldblood with a thick neck and large head. Originally used to describe any horse from foreign or barbaric parts of the world.

BAREBACK Riding a horse without a saddle, felt or blanket on its back. A good training exercise for the rider, who needs good balance, a strong grip and a non-slip bottom!

BARRAGE A jump off.

BARREL The horse's body from forearms to loins.

BARRIER a) The point at which a race starts.

b) In a rodeo arena the barrier behind which the roper waits while the steer is allowed into the arena.

BARS OF THE FOOT Part of the foot where the wall turns inward and forward and reinforces the foot.

BARS OF THE MOUTH Diastema. The gap between the incisors and molars are an ingenious evolutionary adaptation where grass is stored temporarily before being passed onto the molars at the back of the mouth for chewing and then swallowing. It is also the part of the mouth where the bit lies.

BAY A horse with dark skin and a brown to red/yellow-brown coat, always sporting a black mane and tail and usually black legs from the knee down.

BEDDING Horse bedding may be of straw, peat, sawdust or shavings; there are also various foamed plastic materials for lining the stable floor which reduce the amount of traditional bedding required.

BIT A metal, plastic or rubber device placed in the horse's mouth which transmits the riders instructions to the horse via the reins. The name for a person who makes bits is a loriner.

BITLESS BRIDLE Any of a number of bridles including the English hackamore and the American bosal that are not fitted with a bit. These work by exerting pressure on the horse's nose and chin curb and not on the mouth. These devices can be very severe in their action and need expert handling to be used properly.

BLACK A completely black horse, but it may have some white markings on the face or legs.

BLACKSMITH Not the same as a farrier. The former is a person skilled in iron work who may also make horseshoes. There are some farrier/blacksmiths who are skilled at both professions.

BLEMISH A mark or scar left by an injury. Sometimes after damage the pigment cells of the hair are killed off and the new hair growth comes back white.

BLINKERS Or winkers. Leather eye shields attached to the bridle to prevent the horse from seeing in any direction other than forward. Primarily used with driving horses.

BLOOD HORSE The English Thoroughbred.

BLOOD The volume of blood in a horse is approximately 5½% of its total body weight. A healthy horse has a body temperature of about 100.5°F.

BLOODSTOCK Racehorses, Thoroughbreds and their breeding stock.

BLOW AWAY A signal blown by the hunt to signal the dogs away after the fox.

BLOW UP a) In the dressage arena or show ring, a term describing a horse that has broken from a given pace or just generally misbehaves.
b) In the US a term meaning to start bucking.

BODY BRUSH A short bristled brush used to draw scurf and dust from a horse's coat.

BOG RIDER A cowboy whose job is to rescue cattle that have been stranded in mud or marshland.

BOIL OVER A US term meaning to start bucking.

BOOKMAKER Bookie. A person who accepts bets placed by others on horses, dogs, etc.

BOUNDARY RIDER A person who is employed by a large cattle or sheep station to ride around the perimeter fencing making repairs.

BOVY TAIL A horse's tail that has been cut off straight with scissors, or confusingly it is also used to describe a horse whose tail is entirely untouched and natural!

BRAN The by-product of the grain milling industry which may be fed to horses as a mild laxative or to aid digestion.

BREAK, BREAKING The training of a young horse to accept tack and to respond to a rider on his back.

BROKEN WIND A chronic and permanent disability of a horse's respiratory system. A persistent cough and shortness of breath are early symptoms. A broken winded animal is of no use for work.

BROWN May vary from a light oak color through to a rich deep brown to almost black.

BRUMBY An Australian wild horse – not a native animal but a feral derived from two herds of 500 horses imported there in 1912 and 1917.

BRUMBY RUNNER An Australian horseman who rounds up and catches wild horses.

BRUSH A fox's tail.

BRUSHING The striking of fore or hind legs against the inside of the opposite hoof. This can lead to injury or lameness but can be cushioned somewhat by the horse wearing special "brushing" boots.

BUCK When a horse jumps straight-legged into the air with its back arched and head held low.

BUCKAROO A cowboy or bronco buster.

BY Reference used in a horse's pedigree or breeding line, eg sired by . . .

BYE-DAY Extra hunt day, usually at Christmas or to compensate for a day lost to bad weather.

CALF HORSE A horse specially trained for calf roping.

CALF ROPING A standard rodeo event where the rider ropes a calf then dismounts to tie it by three legs.

CALKINS The heel on some horseshoes is folded back on itself to provide a better grip on the ground.

CAMERA PATROL Equipment used for filming a horse race in progress.

CAMP DRAFTING An Australian rodeo contest event when a rider separates a bullock from a herd and drives it at a gallop around a course of upright poles.

CANKER A serious foot condition caused by wet and dirty stables. The condition is entirely prevented by proper management.

CANNON BONE The long large bone beneath the horse's "knee" (wrist).

CANTER The comfortable three time gait where the hooves strike the ground in the following order: leading leg off fore, then near hind, near fore and off hind together, or off hind, off fore and near hind together with the leading leg as the near fore.

CANTLE The rear uppermost part of a saddle.

CAP The fee paid by a visitor for a day's hunting.

CAPRIOLE An air above the ground. A difficult but controlled leap upward with the hind legs stretched out behind before landing collected on all four feet.

CASTRATE To surgically remove the testes (male sex organs) of a male animal to render him sterile.

CAVALETTI A series of small wooden jumps used in the training of riding horses to encourage the animal to pick up his feet, to lengthen his stride and improve his balance and muscle tone.

CAVALRY Mounted soldiers divided into the Light Brigade and the Heavy Brigade. Now obsolete.

CAYUSE An Indian horse or pony.

CHAFF Chopped hay or straw used as a feedstuff, often to bulk up other feeds.

CHEF D'ÉQUIPE In the horse world, a team manager who takes care of organization and strategy.

CHESTNUT A horse's color from deep gold to reddish brown, usually with a matching mane and tail, but may also be slightly lighter or darker. In the US this is called sorrel.

CHUKKA In polo a play period of 7½–8 minutes depending on the country being played in.

CINCH US term for the strap of leather webbing or nylon that passes under the horse's body to hold the saddle in place.

CLASSIC The classic races in the UK are the 2,000 Guineas, 1,000 Guineas, Derby, Oaks, and St Leger.

CLEAR ROUND A round in show jumping or cross country where no jumping or time faults are incurred.

CO-FAVORITE Two or more horses in a race equally favored to win and given the same short betting odds.

COB An animal type rather than a breed; one with shortish legs and lots of bone and substance, so able to carry a good weight.

COLIC Abdominal pain usually in the alimentary tract. There are several types affecting the horse including tympanitic, impactive and worms.

COLLECTION To shorten the horse's pace and thereby make it flex its neck, relax its jaw and draw the hocks well under and so improve its balance.

COLT An uncastrated male under the age of four.

COMBINATION An obstacle in show jumping comprising two or more elements, but for the purpose of judging, counted as one.

CONTACT The light pressure on the horse's mouth by the rider's hands through the reins.

CORN A bruising of the sole of the hoof between the hoof wall and the heel.

CORRAL A circular pen or enclosure for animals usually made of timber.

COUPLE Two hounds.

COURBETTE An air above the ground in which the horse rears then makes several small jumps forward on the hind legs.

COURSE a) A racecourse.
b) Cross country circuit.
c) Show jumping.
d) An obstacle course such as cones for driving events.

COURSE BUILDER Someone who actually builds a course and may also be the person who designs it.

COURSE DESIGNER A person who designs courses and may also build it.

CURRY COMB Grooming aid to remove mud and hair from a body brush — not to be used on horse itself.

CUTTING HORSE A horse specially trained for separating cattle from a herd.

DAM A foal's natural mother.

DANDY BRUSH A long bristled brush for removing dirt and mud from a horse's coat.

DARK HORSE In the racing world a horse whose form is unknown outside its own stables.

DEAD HEAT A tie for first, second or third place in racing.

DECLARATION A written statement made by a trainer or owner that a particular horse will take part in an event.

DIASTEMA In a horse's mouth the sensitive whiskers and lips test the forage and manipulate it towards the incisors (cutting teeth) where it is nipped off then passed by the tongue to the diastema – the gap between the incisors and molars – and stored until enough has been grazed to be passed back.

DIRT TRACK A circuit of mixed soil and sand.

DIVIDEND The money paid to a bettor in the UK for a winning bet or series of bets. US — a payout.

DOG FOX A male fox.

DOG HOUND A male dog.

DOPE To administer illegal substances to a horse to either enhance or hamper its performance. Doping is illegal and carries the most severe penalties in all equestrian sports.

DOUBLE a) A combination obstacle comprising two jumps.
b) A bet on two races where the winnings from race one are counted as the stake for the second.

DOUBLE BRIDLE A bridle that has two cheekpieces and two bits – a curb and a snaffle that may be operated independently.

DRAG HOUND A hound trained to follow the scent in drag hunting.

DRAG HUNTING A hunt where the "quarry" is a person who lays a scent trail by dragging a piece of sacking or cloth impregnated with aniseed around a course.

DRESSAGE The art of training a horse to perform all movements in a balanced, supple, obedient and keen manner.

DROVER An Australian horseman who drives cattle or sheep over long distances.

EACH WAY A bet on a horse to come in first, second or third.

EARTH The name given to the lair or burrow of a fox.

ELIMINATION The exclusion of a competitor from taking any further part in a competition.

ENGAGED A term applied to an animal entered in a particular race.

ENTERITIS An inflammation of the lining of the alimentary tract. This may be caused by bacteria, chemical or vegetable based poisons or by mould or fungi from contaminated foodstuffs.

EQUESTRIAN, Equestrienne *(female)* Horsemastership.

EQUINE Anything relating to the horse or the horse itself.

EVENS Betting odds in the UK where the person betting will only win the same amount of money as he stakes. The US term is even money.

EVENT HORSE A horse trained to compete in combined training competitions.

EXACTA A bet on the winner and second placed horse to come in in exact order.

FANCIED The favorite, the horse thought to be the most likely to win a particular race.

FARRIER A highly skilled and highly qualified person who makes horseshoes and shoes horses.

FAULT A scoring method in show jumping where points are awarded against a horse for a knockdown or refusal during his round.

FEI **FEDERATION EQUESTRE INTERNATIONAL**. The governing body of international equestrian sports, it covers all aspects of horse-related competition.

FENCE Any obstacle to be jumped as in a steeplechase, cross-country or show jumping.

FERAL Not fully wild but living and breeding largely without human interference.

FILLY A female horse or pony under four years of age.

FIRST JOCKEY The principal person employed by a trainer or owner to ride for him.

FLAPPER An animal that runs in an unofficial race.

FLAPPING An unofficial race that is not governed by the rules of racing.

FLAT RACE A race where there are no jumps or obstacles.

FOAL A young horse or pony up to the age of 12 months.

FOREHAND The head, neck, shoulders, withers and forelegs; in fact those parts of the horse that are in front of the rider.

FORM The past racing record of a horse's performance.

FOX DOG A foxhound.

FOX HOUND A breed of dog specially bred for hunting. Noted for their good sense of smell and tenacity.

FULL A stallion or uncastrated male horse or pony.

FULL MOUTH A horse's mouth at around six years of age where all the adult teeth have erupted through the gums, and the horse has a complete mouthful!

FURNITURE Any item of saddlery or harness worn by the horse.

FUZZTAIL RUNNING Herding and catching feral horses.

GAD An old English name for a spur.

GAG A gag snaffle bit which has cheek pieces that pass through holes in the top and bottom of the rings and lead right on to the reins. Can be a very severe bit and should only be used by highly skilled riders with good hands.

GAIT Also called pace. Most breeds of horse have four gaits: walk, trot, canter and gallop. However, some special breeds have a further gait, such as the Saddlebred and Paso Fino.

GAITED HORSE One that is trained in both natural and artificial paces.

GALLOWAY In Australia, a pony is an animal under 14hh. A Galloway is a show ring category for animals between 14hh and 15hh.

GALLS Abrasions on the horse's body, particularly around the saddle and girth area. Caused by badly fitting saddlery a sign of very poor horsemanship and stable management.

GARRON A native pony of Scotland or Ireland.

GELDING a) The surgical removal of the testes of a male horse or pony. Castration.

b) An animal that has had this operation.

GESTATION The period of growth in the mother's body of a fetus from the moment of fertilization to the moment of birth. In horses, this takes about 11 months.

GIRTH a) The circumference of a horse taken behind the withers around the deepest part of the body.

b) The strap of leather webbing or nylon that passes under the horse's body to hold the saddle in place. In US called a cinch.

GIVE TONGUE The barking and baying of hounds in full cry when after a quarry.

GO SHORT An animal that is restricted in its action or home for some reason.

GOING The condition of a race course or other ground for horses. Classified as soft, good, firm, etc.

GONE TO GROUND A fox having taken to its earth or some other refuge during a hunt.

GOOD MOUTH An animal with a sensitive and soft mouth that responds to the very lightest of commands from the rider or driver's hands.

GRAY (UK GREY) A dark-skinned horse with a coat comprising a mixture of black and white hairs. Grays usually become lighter with each coat change.

GREEN a) An inexperienced horse.

b) US. Trotter or pacer that has not been raced against the clock.

GROOM a) A person employed for the stable management of horses.

b) An active person who accompanies a driver.

c) To clean the coat and hooves of a horse.

GROUND MONEY The entry fee and purse money that is divided equally amongst contestants in a rodeo when there is no outright winner.

GROUND Or ground tying. US term meaning to allow the reins to touch the ground after dismounting, so that the horse will not move.

GYMKHANA Mounted games, sometimes adapted from party games, for childre.

HABIT The attire of a woman when riding side-saddle, consisting of a matching jacket and skirt or shaped poncho which is worn over breeches and boots.

HACK A riding horse available for hire or a ride for pleasure.

HALTER A rope head collar with leadrope attached. Used for leading a horse not wearing a bridle or other head collar.

HAND A linear measure of a horse's height taken at the withers on flat ground. Hand = 4in (10cm). The fractions are given in inches.

HANDICAP a) Weight allocated to a horse in a race.

b) A race where the weight to be carried by the horses is estimated to give each a fairly equal chance of winning.

HAUNCHES The hips and buttocks of a horse.

HAUTE ÉCOLE "High School." The classical art of equitation.

HAY A mixture of grasses cut and dried and used as fodder. Only the best hay properly made and stored should be given to horses.

HAYLAGE A cross between hay and silage that is mold and dust-free. It is 50 percent moisture compressed.

HEAD COLLAR Headpiece of leather or webbing without a bit, used for leading or tying up a horse.

HIT THE LINE When hounds pick up the scent trail of a fox or other quarry.

HITCH UP US term for harnessing up a horse or horses for driving.

HOG'S BACK A spread obstacle of three sets of poles in show jumping, where the center part is higher than the front or back.

HOLLOU The call made by a hunter when he or she sees the fox during a hunt.

HOLLOW BACK An unnatural exaggerated over-concave back on a horse or pony.

HOOF a) The insensitive outer covering of a horse's foot.

b) A general term for a horse's foot.

HOOF PICK A hooked instrument, usually of metal, used for cleaning a horse's foot or removing stones, grit etc.

HORSE A general term for any equine animal Equus caballus stallion, mare or gelding.

HORSE TAILING Taking charge of the group of horses used by drovers when herding sheep or cattle over long distances.

HORSEMAN a) A rider.

b) A person skilled in stable management or in the training of horses or both.

c) A laborer who works with horses.

HORSESHOE A mild steel or sometimes aluminum band shaped and fitted by a farrier to a horse's hooves to protect them from damage and excessive wear when being ridden or driven. Different designs of shoe may also be used to help correct surgical, medical or other problems.

HOTBLOODS Pure breeds such as Arabian and Thoroughbred.

HULL Another name for a saddle.

HUNT LIVERY The coats worn by the staff of a particular hunt.

HUNT SERVANT A salaried employee of a hunt, eg. huntsman, kennel huntsman, whipper-in.

HUNT TERRIER A small, short-legged terrier used by the hunt to flush foxes from their earths or other places inaccessible to the hounds.

HUNTER A horse type that is specially bred and trained to be ridden for hunting. The best hunters are bred in the UK and Ireland.

HUNTER TRIALS A competitive event in which horses are ridden at a course of obstacles laid out to be as natural and similar to those expected to be encountered when out hunting.

HUNTING CAP A protective riding hat covered with velvet fabric.

HUNTING HORN A short straight horn that is about 10in (25cm) long. Blown by huntsmen to give signals to the hounds and the rest of the field.

HUNTSMAN The person in charge of the hunt on a particular day, this may be the huntmaster or someone appointed by him.

HURDLE An obstacle that horses jump; usually a hurdle is made from wattle fencing but may also be of brush.

HURDLE RACING A race over a course of hurdles.

IN BLOOD A euphemism meaning that the hounds have made a kill.

IN FOAL A pregnant mare.

IN THE BOOK An animal that is accepted for registration in its respective stud book.

IN-HAND CLASS Any number of showing classes where the animal is led in a showing head collar or bridle, but usually without saddlery. Judged chiefly on the animal's manners and conformation.

INBREEDING The mating of genetically related individuals, ie. brother and sister, daughter and sire or dam and son. Something that should be actively avoided as it can exacerbate congenital problems.

INDEPENDENT SEAT A good rider who is able to hold a firm balanced seat on a horse's back without resort to holding the reins or relying on stirrups.

IRONS The correct name for the metal part of the stirrup where the foot is placed.

JOCKEY a) A professional person employed to ride horses in racing.

b) An old term for a disreputable horse dealer — now obsolete.

JOG A short paced trot.

JUMP JOCKEY A jockey who races horses over a steeplechase or hurdle course.

JUMP OFF In show jumping, a final round — usually against the clock — for all competitors who have gained a clear round previously. The winner is the person who completes the course in the fastest time with the fewest penalties.

JUMPER A horse trained to jump either in show jumping or steeplechase.

KEEP A field of grass used as grazing for horses: US pastures.

KENNEL MAN A person who works at a hunt kennels who looks after the hounds' welfare.

KENNELS The buildings and yard where hounds are kept.

LAMINITIS An inflammation of the sensitive laminae or layers that lie between the hoof wall and the pedal bone. A very painful condition.

LENGTH The length of a horse; used as a term to describe the distance by which a horse may be ahead of its nearest rival to win a race.

LEVADE A Haute École movement in which the horse rears, so drawing its forefeet in and with its hind legs strongly bent at the haunches, while carrying the full weight of the rider.

LIGHT HORSE Horses such as hacks and hunters that are suitable for riding, except Thoroughbreds.

LIGHT To dismount.

LINE The course that the fox is travelling while being pursued by the hounds.

LINSEED Seeds of the flax plant. It is fed to horses to improve condition and gloss on the coat when made into a tea or jelly. Also used to stuff the crupper dock of a harness for driving horses.

LIVERY STABLE A stables where privately owned horses are kept, exercised and looked after for an agreed fee: US — livery.

LORINER A skilled metal worker who makes the metal parts of harness and saddlery including bits, stirrup irons, curb chains etc.

LUNGE REIN A nylon or webbing rein, usually about 25ft (7.6m) long attached to the cavesson of the horse being lunged.

LUNGE To work a horse in a circle around the trainer to improve its condition, balance and co-ordination.

MAIDEN A male or female horse which has not won a race of any distance.

MAIDEN MARE a) A mare that has never had a foal
b) a mare that is pregnant with it's first foal.

MAIDEN RACE A race in which all the entrants have never won a race.

MANE AND TAIL COMB Long toothed metal or plastic combs used for pulling the mane and tail.

MANE The long hair growing down the horse's neck.

MARE A female horse or pony aged four years and over.

MARTINGALE Several types of device used to help keep the horse's head in the correct position. Usually comprising a strap or arrangement of straps anchored at the girth at one end, passing between the forelegs and then attached to the reins, noseband or onto the bit.

MASTER Person having overall responsibility for the organization and general running of all aspects of the hunt.

MATCH Competition between two horses under rules set out and agreed by both owners – there is no prize awarded.

MEET a) The agreed meeting place for all members and followers of a hunt.
b) The hunt itself.

MIXED MEETING A race day where both flat racing and steeplechasing are held in the same place.

MIXED STABLES In racing: a stable where both national hunt and flat race horses are kept.

MONTURA Another name for a saddle or a riding horse.

MOUNT a) A riding horse.

b) To get up onto the back of a horse or pony.

MOUNT MONEY A fee paid to a rodeo performer in an exhibition rather than in a competition.

MUCK OUT To clean out a stable or loose box where a horse has been kept, removing any droppings and soiled bedding.

MUD FEVER An inflammation starting on the fetlocks caused by the same bacteria that cause rainscald (*Dermatophilus* sp) and is due to wet muddy conditions.

MUDDER A racehorse that performs well on a muddy course.

MUSTANG A wild horse in the US.

NAP a) In horseracing, a horse that is a good tip.

b) Refusal by a horse to obey instructions from properly applied aids.

NATIONAL FEDERATION The governing body affiliated to the FEI in any country.

NATURAL AIDS The natural aids are the body, the hands, the legs and the voice – used in combination to apply instructions to the horse. In driving the only natural aids are the hands and the voice.

NAVICULAR A serious and insidious condition of the foot or more accurately the navicular bone. Early veterinary examination is needed.

NEAR SIDE a) The left side of the horse as viewed from behind or from the mounted rider's position.

b) The side it is usual to mount from.

NECK In racing one of the terms of measurement of distance by which a horse may win a race.

NOSE The shortest distance by which a horse may be said to win a race. Often decided after a photo finish.

NOSEBAND The part of the bridle that lies around the horse's nose. It hangs 2in (5cm) below the cheek bone above the bit and should be loose by the width of two fingers. In the US, known as a cavesson.

NUMNAH The pad placed under the saddle over the horse's back, in the same shape as the saddle but slightly larger. Made from sheepskin, felt or cloth-covered quilted foam rubber.

OATS A cereal sometimes used as part of the horse's diet. Can be fed whole, bruised or crushed. The latter two are easiest for the horse to digest.

ODDS ON A betting quote of less than even money.

ODDS The betting quote for a horse in a race.

OFF SIDE The right hand side of the horse from behind or from the rider's seat.

ON THE BIT A horse who is going well in his bridle and needs little or no urging from the rider.

ONE-DAY EVENT A combined competition consisting of dressage, show jumping and cross country, completed in one day.

OPENING MEET The first hunt of the season.

OUTFIT a) All a cowboy's personal equipment.

b) A complete ranch with all its equipment and employees.

OUTLAW A horse that is particularly intractable and difficult or impossible to train.

OUTSIDER In racing: an animal that is given long odds by bookmakers because it is not expected to place.

OVERBEND, OVERBENT A horse that carries its neck too sharply arched and consequently tucks its head too close to its chest.

PACE A two-time gait in which the fore and hind legs on the same side are moved forward together.

PACEMAKER In a race, the horse that takes the lead and sets the speed for the race.

PAD The foot of a hound or fox.

PADDOCK a) Grass enclosure usually close to a house or stable where a horse may be turned out.

b) At a racetrack, an enclosure where the horses are paraded before a race.

PALOMINO A horse color, the body being any of a range of shades of gold and sporting a white or silver mane or tail.

PANCAKE An English saddle.

PARABOLA The arc described by a jumping horse from take-off to landing.

PARALLEL BARS A type of spread jump used in cross-country and show jumping comprising two sets of poles and uprights.

PARASITES Creatures which live on or in the horse, feeding from the animal and giving nothing back. eg, worms, botflies, lice, ringworm, ticks and mange. If left untreated they can seriously damage or even kill the horse.

PARI-MUTUEL A mechanised form of betting; in the UK a totalizer.

PASSAGE A classical high school aid, a measured movement comprising a very collected and very elevated trot. The horse makes graceful springy steps with a prolonged moment of suspension between.

PAYOUT The money paid to a bettor for a winning bet or series of bets. In the UK a dividend.

PELHAM BIT A style of bit designed to reproduce the combined effect of a snaffle type and a curb bit.

PHOTO FINISH A race where the winning horses are so close together that the outcome can only be determined by a photograph taken with special equipment at the winning post.

PIAFFE Similar to passage, but the horse does not move forward. A well-schooled dressage animal will be able to transit cleanly between passage and piaffe and vice versa.

PICNIC RACES Race meetings held by amateurs and their mounts on rough bushland racetracks in the Australian outback.

PIEBALD A coat color — large black patches on a white background.

PINTO US name meaning "paint" for a piebald or skewbald horse or pony.

PIROUETTE A dressage movement — a turn within the horse's own length. There are three types: a turn on the forehand; a turn on the center; a turn on the haunches.

PLANKS A show jumping fence made up of painted planks instead of the usual poles.

PLATE A special very light shoe worn by a racehorse for one race only.

POINT TO POINT A UK race under National Hunt Rules over a natural course and only for amateurs with horses that have been regularly and fairly hunted.

POLO A mounted game resembling hockey played by two teams of four.

POLOCROSSE An Australian mounted game — a hybrid between polo and lacrosse, played with lacrosse-type netted sticks.

PONY Breeds of equus that do not exceed 14.2hh at maturity.

PRIX DE NANTES An international team show jumping competition held at an official international horse show.

QUARTER HORSE Small horses bred in the US for cattle roping and racing. An extremely clever and nimble breed able to control cattle much as sheepdogs do in the UK. Also used for racing over a quarter of a mile – hence the name.

QUARTERS Area extending from the back of the flanks to the dock and downward to the top of the leg.

QUIDDING Can be a sign of mouth or teeth problems: the horse tries to chew his food but then sprinkles it out of his mouth.

RACK One of the gaits of the American Saddlebred –

a fast version of the slow gait. The knees and hocks are lifted quickly in a rapid high stepping motion.

RANGE HORSE A horse left to roam semi-wild on the range, until it is herded up to be broken in.

REAR When a horse stands up on its hind legs.

RED FLAG Used to mark a set course, it should be passed on the left hand side. It also marks the right hand side of an obstacle.

REFUSAL The horse stops in front of an obstacle and refuses either to jump or negotiate it.

REIN BACK The horse is asked to step backward when being either ridden or driven.

RENVERS A dressage movement where the horse moves on two tracks — the hind legs on the outer track while the fore legs are on the inner. The horse is bent slightly around the rider's inside leg.

RIDE OFF A movement in polo, when one pony is pushed against another to stop its player from hitting the ball.

ROACH BACK Considered a weakness as the horse's back is convex in shape.

ROMAN NOSE A horse having a face convex in shape – rather than dished like an Arab.

ROPE HORSE A horse specially trained to work with cattle.

RUN MUTE A hunting term used to describe a pack of hounds who are running so fast that they are unable to bark.

RUN OUT Similar to a refusal, a horse will run to one side of an obstacle rather than jump it.

SADDLE BRONC RIDING A rodeo event in which the rider has to stay on a bucking horse for 10 seconds. Only one hand is allowed to guide the horse. The rider is not allowed to touch the saddle, horse or himself during this time.

SADDLE Seat for the rider, designs vary from country to country. There are specific saddles for different areas of work.

SADDLERY Collective name given to the tack of the riding horse, rather than the driven horse.

SCENT Odor of the fox, followed by hounds when hunting.

SCHOOL a) An area for training horses, can be open or enclosed.

b) To teach the young horse routine commands, or give further training for specific jobs to older horses.

SCRUB DASHING Rounding up cattle in wooded areas in Australia.

SERVICE A breeding term to describe the mating of a mare with a stallion.

SHOEING Most breeds need to wear metal shoes in order to work without damaging their hooves. These are put on by a farrier and renewed every few weeks depending on how fast the horse's hooves grow or how much work it has done.

SHOW To take part in a horse show where the animal is judged in classes for conformation, condition and suitability to do its job.

SHY When a horse suddenly veers away from something that has frightened it.

SICKLE HOCKS A point of conformation on the horse. When weak hocks are looked at side-on they are often bent into a shape resembling a sickle.

SIDE SADDLE A woman's saddle designed for coping with the long skirt of a riding habit. The rider keeps both feet on the same side, her right leg over one support and her left leg under and next to a lower one. The left foot goes into the stirrup iron as usual.

SILKS Name given to clothing worn by jockeys in races. Each jockey wears a different color and pattern depending on which owner he is riding for.

SIRE A foal's father.

SKEWBALD A color which has large patches of white in the coat, and any other colour except black.

SLOPING SHOULDER The direction of the slanting line that the shoulders take to the withers.

SLOW GAIT Airy prancing motion of the American Saddlebred. The slow gait is done very slowly with the legs lifted high, especially in front. A faster version is known as the rack.

SNAFFLE One of the simplest and kindest bits for the horse's mouth. The best known has a straight bar running from ring to ring. The bit is married to a bridle known as the Snaffle Bridle.

SNIP A small white mark towards the horse's nostrils.

STALLION Also known as a stud — a male horse which has not been castrated or gelded and is capable of servicing mares.

SORREL A horse's color from deep gold to reddish brown, usually with a matching mane and tail, but may also be slightly lighter or darker. In the UK this is called Chestnut.

SOUND when a horse is sound in "wind and limb" it is free from any illness or imperfection that could stop it from functioning normally.

STANDING SQUARE When a horse is standing in balance with itself.

STAR A white marking on the horse's forehead.

STARTER'S ORDERS In horse racing, the horse may begin when the starter raises his flag, having first assured himself that everything is in order.

STEEPLECHASE A horserace which takes part over rough country or a racetrack, with ditches and hedges to jump. Originally these races were run with the church's steeple as a goal.

STEER WRESTLING One of the five standard events in a rodeo. The idea being to stop a steer by jumping on it from horseback and throwing it to the ground.

STIRRUP IRON A ring suspended from the saddle by a stirrup leather. Its purpose being to support the rider's foot and help him to balance.

STOCK CLASS Event held for working ranch horses.

STOCK SADDLE High-pommelled saddle used by working Australian cowboys.

STRAIGHT SHOULDERS The line that the shoulders take in some breeds is said to be more upright than in others.

STRAWBERRY ROAN Color which gives a pink sheen to the coat. Caused by a mixture of white and chestnut hairs.

STRIPE A white marking extending down the face. Narrower than a star.

STUD a) Name given to a stallion.

b) A place where horses and ponies are kept for breeding.

SWEET ITCH An irritation of the skin suffered by horses that are allergic to a midges. Most likely to happen during the summer.

TACK Another name for saddlery. To tack up means to harness a horse.

TETANUS A usually fatal illness caused by a soil-based micro-organism, which enters the horse's bloodstream through open wounds. An affected animal moves stiffly and its muscles become rigid.

THREE-DAY EVENT Originally a military event, three tests take place over three days; these are dressage, a cross-country course including road work, and a show jumping event.

THRUSH An inflammation of the frog in the horse's foot.

TIME ALLOWED Not only must a competitor in a show jumping event complete a clear round, he must do it within a certain time limit.

TOAD EYE A light colored rim encircling the eye of an Exmoor pony. Sometimes found in other breeds.

TRAIL HORSE A horse which is trained for trail riding. The best are valued for their comfortable gait.

TRAINING TRACKS Found in Australia, these are extra tracks inside the race track used for training horses.

TREBLE A show jumping obstacle made up of three separate jumps.

TRIPLE BAR A spread of three different heights of

poles, starting with the lowest at the front and ending with the highest at the back.

TURF Almost wholly a horse racing term describing where a horse race is held. In America the term is more properly used to describe grass racetracks.

UNSOUND An unsound horse has a problem, either temporary or permanent which stops it performing to its usual standard.

UNWIND Another term for bucking.

VOLTE To execute a full tern on the haunches. Usually seen in dressage.

WALKING HORSE CLASS An event held in shows for the Tennessee Walking Horse.

WALL a) A show jump made up to look like a brick wall. A heavier version is found on cross-country courses.

b) Part of the horse's hoof, known as the hoof wall.

WALL EYE An eye which has no pigment in the iris giving the eye a pink or whitish look.

WARMBLOODS Not so highly bred as the Arab and Thoroughbred, which are hot bloods. Many competition horses are warmbloods — they are generally more robust with a calmer temperament.

WATER JUMP Used as a show jumping obstacle and made up of a small fence fronting a sunken amount of water 15ft (4.8m) long.

WEIGH IN In horseracing – the jockey is weighed before and after a race to make sure that the proper weight was carried while competing. Show jumping is another competition event to make use of this system.

WEIGHT CLOTH To make sure the correct weight is carried during a horserace, a cloth is placed under the horse's saddle, and weights are placed in the cloth to make up the correct weight.

WHIPPER-IN In hunting, the whipper-in acts as assistant to the huntsman, when controlling hounds.

WHITE FLAG Used in competitions to mark a set course. The white flag should be passed on the right. Also used to mark up the left side of an obstacle.

WINDGALL A swelling of fluid which can affect the knee or fetlock joint.

WINDSUCKING The horse sucks in and swallows air, giving itself indigestion. A habit which can be difficult to cure, usually caused by boredom.

WINNER'S CIRCLE (ENCLOSURE) An enclosure set aside for the winners of a horse race — the first three.

WINTER OUT A horse which is left out in the open during the winter. Although not stabled, there should be an adequate supply of shelter.

WITHERS The tallest part of the horse's back, found between the shoulder blades. All horses and ponies are measured from the withers down.

WORMS Most horses have worms, but through regular applications of worm medicine and rotating their pasture, this parasite can be kept under control.

WRANGLE US term referring to the herding and looking after of horses.

YEARLING A young horse over one year old, but not yet two years old.

YOUNG ENTRY The term for young fox hounds, before they start cub hunting. They are usually fully trained before the full hunting season begins.

INDEX

BIBLIOGRAPHY

Ascherson, Neal . . . .   *Black Sea*; 1995.

Braider, Donald . . . .   *The Life and Magic of the Horse*; 1973.

    The Life, History and Magic of the Horse; 1978.

Clutton-Brock, Juliet . . . .   *A Natural History of Domesticated Mammals*; 1987.

    Horse Power; 1992.

Dent, Anthony and Goodall, Daphne Machin . . . . .   *A History of British Native Ponies*; 1988.

Drummond, Marcy . . . .   *Long Distance Riding*; 1987.

Greely, Margaret . . . .   *Arabian Exodus*; 1985.

Hickman, John . . . .   *Farriery*; 1977.

Hyland, Ann . . . .   *The Endurance Horse*; 1988.

Laing, Lloyd . . . .   *Celtic Britain*; 1979.

Loch, Sylvia . . . .   *The Royal Horse of Europe*; 1986.

Parslow, Sue . . . .   *Going the Distance*; 1989.

Podhajsky, Alois . . . .   *The Complete of Horse and Rider*; 1967.

Robichon de la Guérinière, François (translated by Tracy Boucher)

. . . .   *School of Horsemanship*; 1729-31.

Sutcliffe, Antony . . . .   *On the Track of Ice Age Mammals*; 1985.

Tenevix-Trench, Charles . . . .   *A History of Horsemanship*; 1970.

Upton, Peter . . . .   *The Classic Arab Horse*; 1992.

Vogel, Colin J. . . . .   *The Stable Veterinary Handbook;* 1990.

West, Geoffrey (ed) . . . .   *Black's Veterinary Dictionary;* 1992.

Williams, Dorian . . . .   *Great Riding Schools of the World*; 1975.

Xenophon (translated by M. H. Morgan) . . . .   *The Art of Horsemanship.*

PHOTOGRAPHY CREDITS